Everyday Energy Politics in Central Asia and the Caucasus

The perception of Central Asia and its place in the world has come to be shaped by its large oil and gas reserves. Literature on energy in the region has thus largely focused on related geopolitical issues and national policies. However, little is known about citizens' needs within this broader context of commodities that connect the energy networks of China, Russia and the West. This multidisciplinary special issue brings together anthropologists, economists, geographers and political scientists to examine the role of all forms of energy (here: oil, gas, hydropower and solar power) and their products (especially electricity) in people's daily lives throughout Central Asia and the Caucasus. The contributors to this book ask how energy is understood as an everyday resource, as a necessity and a source of opportunity, a challenge or even as an indicator of exclusionary practices. We enquire into the role and views of energy sector workers, rural consumers and urban communities and their experiences of energy companies' and national policies. We further examine the legacy of Soviet and more recent domestic energy policies, the environmental impact of energy use as well as the political impact of citizens' energy grievances.

This book was published as a special issue of *Central Asian Survey*.

David Gullette, PhD, is a social anthropologist and development specialist. His work has focused on 'tribalism' and politics in Kyrgyzstan, and has more recently focused on a range of issues contributing to conflict and poverty in the region. His work includes mining as well as anthropology in international development work.

Jeanne Féaux de la Croix, PhD, is a social anthropologist specializing in resource and development issues. She has conducted studies of ageing, landscape perception and dam development in Kyrgyzstan. Based at the German university of Tübingen, she leads a junior research group on the Cultural History of Water in Central Asia, and co-ordinates a Volkswagen Foundation project on the social and environmental history of the Naryn and Syr Darya river.

Thirdworlds

Edited by Shahid Qadir, *University of London*

THIRDWORLDS will focus on the political economy, development and cultures of those parts of the world that have experienced the most political, social, and economic upheaval, and which have faced the greatest challenges of the postcolonial world under globalisation: poverty, displacement and diaspora, environmental degradation, human and civil rights abuses, war, hunger, and disease.

THIRDWORLDS serves as a signifier of oppositional emerging economies and cultures ranging from Africa, Asia, Latin America, Middle East, and even those 'Souths' within a larger perceived North, such as the U.S. South and Mediterranean Europe. The study of these otherwise disparate and discontinuous areas, known collectively as the Global South, demonstrates that as globalisation pervades the planet, the south, as a synonym for subalterity, also transcends geographical and ideological frontiers.

Everyday Energy Politics in Central Asia and the Caucasus

Citizens' needs, entitlements and struggles for access

Edited by
**David Gullette and
Jeanne Féaux de la Croix**

Routledge
Taylor & Francis Group

LONDON AND NEW YORK

First published 2016
by Routledge

2 Park Square, Milton Park, Abingdon, Oxon OX14 4RN
711 Third Avenue, New York, NY 10017, USA

Routledge is an imprint of the Taylor & Francis Group, an informa business

First issued in paperback 2017

British Library Cataloguing in Publication Data
A catalogue record for this book is available from the British Library

ISBN 13: 978-1-138-12257-4 (hbk)
ISBN 13: 978-1-138-09727-8 (pbk)

Typeset in Times New Roman
by RefineCatch Limited, Bungay, Suffolk

Publisher's Note
The publisher accepts responsibility for any inconsistencies that may have
arisen during the conversion of this book from journal articles to book chapters,
namely the possible inclusion of journal terminology.

Disclaimer
Every effort has been made to contact copyright holders for their permission to
reprint material in this book. The publishers would be grateful to hear from any
copyright holder who is not here acknowledged and will undertake to rectify
any errors or omissions in future editions of this book.

Contents

Citation Information

The chapters in this book were originally published in *Central Asian Survey*, volume 33, issue 4 (December 2014). When citing this material, please use the original page numbering for each article, as follows:

Chapter 1
Mr Light and people's everyday energy struggles in Central Asia and the Caucasus: an introduction
David Gullette and Jeanne Féaux de la Croix
Central Asian Survey, volume 33, issue 4 (December 2014) pp. 435–448

Chapter 2
The illumination of marginality: how ethnic Hazaras in Bamyan, Afghanistan, perceive the lack of electricity as discrimination
Melissa Kerr Chiovenda
Central Asian Survey, volume 33, issue 4 (December 2014) pp. 449–462

Chapter 3
Kyrgyzstan's dark ages: framing and the 2010 hydroelectric revolution
Amanda E. Wooden
Central Asian Survey, volume 33, issue 4 (December 2014) pp. 463–481

Chapter 4
Resource dependence and measurement technology: international and domestic influences on energy sector development in Armenia and Georgia
Jason E. Strakes
Central Asian Survey, volume 33, issue 4 (December 2014) pp. 482–499

Chapter 5
Flows of oil, flows of people: resource-extraction industry, labour market and migration in western Kazakhstan
Philipp Frank Jäger
Central Asian Survey, volume 33, issue 4 (December 2014) pp. 500–516

Chapter 6
Notes on the moral economy of gas in present-day Azerbaijan
Tristam Barrett
Central Asian Survey, volume 33, issue 4 (December 2014) pp. 517–530

Chapter 7

Switching off or switching source: energy consumption and household response to higher energy prices in the Kyrgyz Republic
Franziska Gassmann and Raquel Tsukada
Central Asian Survey, volume 33, issue 4 (December 2014) pp. 531–549

Chapter 8

Bottom-up and top-down dynamics of the energy transformation in the Eastern Pamirs of Tajikistan's Gorno Badakhshan region
Tobias Kraudzun
Central Asian Survey, volume 33, issue 4 (December 2014) pp. 550–565

For any permission-related enquiries please visit:
http://www.tandfonline.com/page/help/permissions

Mr Light and people's everyday energy struggles in Central Asia and the Caucasus: an introduction

David Gullette[a] and Jeanne Féaux de la Croix[b]

[a]University of Central Asia, Bishkek, Kyrgyz Republic; [b]Department of Ethnology, Junior Research Group 'Cultural History of Water in Central Asia', Eberhard Karls Universität Tübingen, Tübingen, Germany

The perception of Central Asia and its place in the world has come to be shaped by its large oil and gas reserves. Literature on energy in the region has thus largely focused on related geopolitical issues and national policies. However, little is known about citizens' needs within this broader context of commodities that connect the energy networks of China, Russia and the West. This multidisciplinary special issue brings together anthropologists, economists, geographers and political scientists to examine the role of all forms of energy (here: oil, gas, hydropower and solar power) and their products (especially electricity) in people's daily lives throughout Central Asia and the Caucasus. The papers in this issue ask how energy is understood as an everyday resource, as a necessity and a source of opportunity, a challenge or even as an indicator of exclusionary practices. We enquire into the role and views of energy sector workers, rural consumers and urban communities, and their experiences of energy companies' and national policies. We further examine the legacy of Soviet and more recent domestic energy policies, the environmental of energy use as well as the political impact of citizens' energy grievances.

Introduction

The 2010 film *Svet-Ake*, directed by Aktan Arym Kubat, poignantly illustrates the challenges people face in accessing electricity. In the small Kyrgyz village of Kok-Moinok, Mr Light connects homes to the electrical grid for those who cannot pay for it. He tinkers with a small wind turbine as an alternative future to their current infrastructure. He is loved by the villagers for his efforts, but is arrested by the police for stealing electricity. However, during the 2005 overthrow of President Askar Akaev's government, his would-be persecutors are replaced and he is freed. At the same time, a young man from the area aspires to become a parliamentary deputy in the new government and is looking for the support of the villagers. He is a populist, giving hope to the community's desire for development and prosperity. He brings in Chinese investors, but hosts them with the same extravagance and disregard for local sensibilities that had led to Akaev's ousting. Mr Light is caught in the middle of this and his vision of accessible electricity remains unrealized. This fictional account highlights the struggles for energy that Central Asian citizens are faced with, the multiple actors involved at different levels in shaping the local energy economy, and how everyday energy needs, national policy-making and political events may influence each other.

The energy sector in Central Asia and the Caucasus presents great contrasts. It has massive oil and gas reserves, as well as large hydroelectric plants generating surplus capacity that can be exported to neighbouring countries. Yet, daily experiences indicate that fuel and electricity supply to citizens is fragile, dependent on a largely decrepit infrastructure and plagued by mismanagement and corruption. While some problems existed during the Soviet Union, the situation has been exacerbated by a number of changes. The Soviet system of integrated energy distribution networks has become more complicated between sovereign states that no longer have common agreements for sharing basic resources. Some countries, such as Uzbekistan, have withdrawn from these networks, which has caused energy deficits and affected neighbouring countries' energy security. Furthermore, market reforms and privatization of strategic infrastructure has led to a change in pricing with a direct impact on businesses and citizens.

The provision of an extensive energy infrastructure and generating capacity in Central Asia was a great achievement of the Soviet Union, but this achievement is no longer matched by the reliability of services or adapted to citizen's ability to pay for energy services. This is particularly the case since the lack of investment in many parts of the region after independence has led to further deterioration of the infrastructure. The decrepit domestic infrastructure contrasts sharply with people's growing expectations, and continuing demands for energy security which are rooted in Soviet habits of subsidized access to utilities and the resulting perception of energy as a basic public good. These views go beyond the promises of benefits from large-scale projects such as big hydropower dams coming online. Policy-makers often do not address immediate concerns or explain changes for the future, and what this will mean for Central Asian citizens.

These bigger political and infrastructural issues have created a mismatch between public demands and policy decisions. The 2008/09 energy crisis in Kyrgyzstan is an example of the situation. Rolling blackouts around the capital Bishkek forced business owners to resort to purchasing generators to keep businesses open, while apartment blocks periodically turned into ghostly concrete and brick shells with wandering, flickering candles. In the following year, the continuing energy crisis and poorly devised government policies drove people to voice their demands in the streets for energy tariffs that met people's ability to pay for them (see Wooden's (2014) contribution in this issue on how this became a factor in the 2010 revolution). Residents in the town of Naryn protested at proposed price hikes, especially as winter in the high valleys of central Kyrgyzstan lasts for six months. Generators have now become part of the Bishkek cityscape as a kind of 'insurance'. Although this cannot be a permanent solution, fundamental issues and how to address them are not a widely discussed topic, in part because this is politically sensitive, but also because the 'stuff' of energy and associated technologies and business models are poorly understood by the wider public. The lessons from the energy crisis have not been learnt and challenges are likely to repeat themselves in the winter of 2014/15 as there is an energy deficit due to a low rain cycle and mismanagement.

Tajikistan provides another example of people's changing energy strategies in response to post-independence energy sector changes. In early 2008, prolonged cold spells increased people's use of electricity for heating. At the time, Tajikistan limited industrial and commercial electricity use, and increased imports. However, in December 2009, Uzbekistan withdrew from the series of high-voltage lines and substations that connect Central Asian republics (United Energy System), severing their lines with Tajikistan, and so creating further energy shortages.[1] In addition, the Tajik Aluminium Company (TALCO) is a huge industrial consumer of electricity and is often seen as a contributor to the lack of electricity, particularly in the winter (International Bank for Reconstruction and Development/The World Bank 2012). The additional cost of electricity usage in some rural areas has forced people to turn to alternative fuel sources. There were reports of higher incidents of tree cutting, putting some communities at greater risk of landslides and mudslides (OCHA 2008). In this issue, Tobias Kraudzun (2014) examines the choices available to Tajikistani citizens in the Eastern Pamir under such conditions, and examines the role of government and development agencies in supporting these choices – not necessarily to the best effect.[2]

The international dimensions of the exploitation of available energy resources, and currency receipts through its export as a basis for government power in Kazakhstan, Turkmenistan and Uzbekistan are well explored (Franke-Schwenk 2012; Kendall-Taylor 2012; Overland, Kjaernet, and Kendall-Taylor 2010; Najman, Pomfret and Raballand 2008). Yet the everyday consequences of these international dimensions and the conflicts over energy distribution have received much less attention. Despite the prominence of these issues, scholars have hardly attempted a closer look at the actions of energy producers and consumers in the region.[3] Work on energy policies and their consequences tends to remain confined to geopolitical visions of a new 'Great Game' (Kleveman 2003; Starr and Cornell 2005), with Central Asian governments seeking profitable economic and political deals with China, the European Union or Russia. The effects of such transnational manoeuvres on the domestic energy market and the region's citizens, or government response to domestic demands hardly feature in this 'game'.

Recently the role of elites and government actors in shaping these policies, and reaping their benefits, has come under scrutiny (Heinrich and Pleines 2012; Overland, Kjaernet, and Kendall-Taylor 2010). Meanwhile ordinary citizens in the region – be they oil workers, government employees, entrepreneurs, school children or pensioners – are all affected by the reliability of access to sources of heating, lighting and motorized transport, and their ability to pay for it. This issue bridges the gap between the discussion of Central Asia and the Caucasus as an energy hub for Eurasia and the paucity of information on citizens' everyday experiences of energy use,[4] and their strategies to overcome challenges; these include the popular contestations mentioned above.[5]

With these serious issues in mind, this multidisciplinary issue – 'Everyday Energy Politics in Central Asia and the Caucasus: Citizens' Needs, Entitlements and Struggles for Access' – explores the role of energy in people's lives throughout Central Asia and beyond. It brings together legacies of the Soviet era with changes since independence that have shaped people's patterns of energy use and their strategies for coping with changes. There are two emerging cross-cutting themes: Soviet legacies and notions of entitlement which underpin people's perceptions of energy provision.

Intertwined historical experiences of energy policies and subsequent expectations and demands have spurred innovations, but also popular unrest. Many citizens continue to have expectations that were fostered during the Soviet era – that access to energy should be universal and cheap.[6] The continued (over-)use of predominantly Soviet-era infrastructure results in people lamenting over unreliable services. The articles in this issue explore how Soviet legacies and perceptions of entitlement continue to shape people's understanding of energy provision and use, and, in some cases, how people are beginning to assert their own expectations in energy sector developments.

Soviet policies and legacies

The Soviet era promoted the largest expansion of energy production and consumption in the region, and helped foster a perception of universal entitlement. Energy sector development in Soviet Central Asia benefitted from the push to electrify all of the Soviet Union and promote industry. Addressing the Moscow *Gubernia* Conference of the Russian Communist Party (Bolsheviks) on 21 November 1920, Vladimir Lenin announced that 'Communism equals Soviet power plus the electrification of the whole country.'[7] Under this slogan, the country set out on an ambitious plan developed by the State Commission for the Electrification of Russia (GOELRO)[8] to base development on electricity and to improve economic output.

In Central Asia before the October Revolution, there were only a few energy-generating facilities which mainly supplied electricity to nearby industrial projects. In Kyrgyzstan, for example, there were five electricity stations built in 1913 and 1914 (Tuleberdiev, Rakhimov, and Belyakov 1997). Hydroelectric technology was also being used at that time in the region; a Tajik border post in Khorog had its first small hydropower station in 1913.[9] As industry grew, small towns began to receive electricity stations together with hydroelectric power stations (Karybekov and Sarybaeva 2004, 46). As part of the second five-year plan in the 1930s, many small-scale hydropower and thermo-electric power stations were installed to provide electricity for the agricultural sector. *Sovkhozes* (state farms) and *kolkhozes* (collective farms) received electricity in the years to come. The Soviet push for electrification also extended to Afghanistan, starting from the 1950s and initiating large-scale hydroelectric projects completed in the 1960s.

The energy revolution was not only intended for industrial and agricultural development to stimulate economic growth, but also to provide the people with the benefits of technological and economic advances, as well as 'modernity' or '*tsivilizatsiya*' (Russian, 'civilisation'). The period of expansion in the 1960s, particularly with thermal power plants located in larger towns, also coincided with Khrushchev's building campaign to bring people to cities and provide affordable, modern apartments with their own kitchens (Reid 2005, 2006). However, for rural communities, particularly in mountainous areas, small-scale hydroelectric stations and generators were still the most economic and feasible way of providing electricity.

While small-scale electricity stations were being installed throughout the region, there were also plans for large-scale hydroelectric power stations. Once these started operating in the 1960s and 1970s, electricity generation capacity rose significantly. In Kyrgyzstan, for example, from 1970 to 1990, electricity generation from hydropower rose over 650% in terms of millions of kilowatt-hours, and again rose over 84% from 1980 to 1990 (Tuleberdiev, Rakhimov, and Belyakov 1997, 134). During this period five hydropower stations collectively known as the 'Naryn cascade' located in southern Kyrgyzstan came online. The largest of these is Toktogul Hydroelectric Power Station with a multi-year storage capacity that generates over 90% of all electricity in the country. In Tajikistan, the Nurek Hydroelectric Power Station forms an important part of the electricity-generating capacity in the country, until larger projects planned in the Soviet era, such as the Rogun Hydroelectric Power Station (currently under review), are completed.

Oil boom and energy (mis)management

The development of the energy sector was supported by the discovery of large oil fields and the export of oil. This allowed for unparalleled economic growth, but came at a cost. Early oil production was centred in the Caucasus and on the Caspian Sea, but from the 1950s onwards more production centres were located in the Volga–Urals region (Dienes and Shabad 1979, 56). With the discovery of large oil and gas fields in western Siberia, the centre of production again shifted to that region, with intensified exploration and development from the 1960s.

The USSR was able to use the benefits of international oil and gas trade. Selling oil on the export market allowed the Soviet Union to enjoy substantial hard-currency revenues. The oil price surges in the mid-1970s enabled the Soviet Union to cover shortfalls in other sectors and help neighbouring countries in Eastern Europe through the additional hard currency revenue. For example,

> [i]n 1976, in response to a disastrous harvest, resulting grain imports and a huge trade deficit of the previous year, the USSR allocated two-thirds of the increment in petroleum output for export, shipping abroad close to 30% of its output. (Dienes and Shabad 1979, 35)

The ability to produce and export so much oil at the time of the price boom helped to provide the Soviet Union with additional economic stability and power.[10]

Throughout the 1970s the Soviet Union profited from the high price of oil. Indeed, the Union increased the volume of net energy exports by 270% from 1970 to 1988 (Gustafson 1989, 55). The energy exports 'accounted for as much as 80% of Soviet hard-currency income' at the beginning of the 1980s (57). Thane Gustafson argues that this boom came at too high a price; it made sense to export more oil throughout the 1970s due to the high price, but there were associated issues that suddenly became apparent once the price fell. For example, the increasing costs of production meant that the rate of return on high prices was less. By the 1980s there was heavy criticism of Brezhnev's management of the foreign-trade policy which was supported by the energy exports. '[Gorbachev] accused [Brezhnev] of masking the worsening economic situation with massive exports of energy and of wasting the hard-currency proceeds mainly on "current tasks" instead of economic modernization. In short Brezhnev had squandered his oil income' (57). Although, as Gustafson notes, Brezhnev's policy may not have necessarily been a bad one at the time – as it sought to buy grain for livestock and provide economic support to Eastern European allies – it was flawed because the system which enabled hard-currency surpluses did not adapt to economic changes or curb high maintenance costs. He continues, 'decision making in foreign energy trade remained opportunistic, changeable, and inconsistent' (57). The policy was focused on supply, 'seemingly oblivious to runaway energy demand, and thus condemned to ever more costly operations in ever more remote wilderness' (41).

The problems extended not just to the type of energy mix and policies, but to the management of the sector. There were 12 Soviet government bodies responsible for various aspects of the energy sector. Furthermore, there were a number of hierarchies between enterprises and their ministries that created distance and inhibited close communication (Dienes and Shabad 1979, 264–265). This created difficulties in coordinating plans and improving efficiency. There was an administrative reform in the 1970s, but this did not apparently improve the sector's overall efficiency, nor significantly change policy decisions. Gustafson argues that conflict had been built into the government structure, which discouraged efficiency and coordination. He notes,

> Stalin exploited conflict to maximize the information flowing to him and hence his control. Multiplication of reporting agencies, proliferation of watchdogs, institutionalization of mutual suspicion, overlapping jurisdictions – these are characteristic feature of the Soviet administration [...], no less under Gorbachev than his predecessors. (Gustafson 1989, 311)

This led to a situation where ministries did not follow economic standards, but fought for their 'fuel' and their 'turf'.

Soviet legacies

The development of the energy sector during the Soviet Union left the independent republics with an extensive energy infrastructure, the technical capacity for its exploitation and further development plans. Yet the republics also inherited policies that were not market driven and complex administrative structures that hindered communication and coordination.[11] Furthermore, the physical infrastructure that connected the various republics was no longer overseen centrally, each country now making independent decisions on how to use the energy network and resources on their territory. Since 1991 the domestic energy infrastructure in many former Soviet republics has been in a state of decline rather than further development (although Azerbaijan, Kazakhstan have made improvements, as well as Armenia and Georgia as explained in Strakes (2014) in this issue). The infrastructure has not been maintained or replaced, and is in some places on the verge of collapse, particularly in Kyrgyzstan and Tajikistan (International Crisis Group 2011). Energy theft and corruption in the sector have also led to significant discontent among citizens, who see energy as an entitlement from the Soviet period that is now being squandered. Kazakhstan has also struggled in this area. Michael Barry notes, 'Kazakhstan suffers from an inefficient domestic delivery system and the failure to utilize natural gas obtained in oil extraction operations' (Barry 2009, 45). Things have improved in the country, but it is likely that improvements in the domestic infrastructure are not necessarily felt in all parts of the country.

However, increasing foreign direct investment in the natural gas and oils sectors of Azerbaijan – which acts as a hub connecting Central Asia to Europe – Kazakhstan, Turkmenistan and Uzbekistan (Paswan 2013) has meant that those countries have improved the infrastructure around those industries to ensure that modes of transportation have improved. China and South Korea have invested significantly in these countries to secure energy exports. The modernization of the export infrastructure is critical. This is a particular issue for Kazakhstan: it has large oil and natural gas reserves, and investment has been strong, but slow due to an insufficient transportation and export infrastructure (Barry 2009, 36; International Crisis Group 2007, 12–13). Kyrgyzstan and Tajikistan have much less foreign investment in their energy infrastructure, as there is less money to be made from hydropower than from oil. The Russian state company RusHydro is supporting Kyrgyzstan to build the US$727 million Upper-Naryn Cascade, a series of four hydropower dams (Kalybekova 2014b). RusHydro is set to receive a majority of the profits until they recoup their investment. Also, Kyrgyzstan sold its bankrupt natural gas company, Kyrgyzgaz, to the Russian state-run gas company, Gazprom, for a token US$1 (Kalybekova 2014a). The country hopes that improved gas service can be restored to Kyrgyzstan, especially for parts of southern Kyrgyzstan which, when the deal took place, had been without natural gas for several weeks, as Uzbekistan had stopped transmission.[12]

One of the main legacies of the Soviet era that is now creating new tensions in Central Asia is the management of energy and water resources. In the Soviet Union, the republics would follow the plans of the United Energy System of Central Asia. This included a water and energy barter deal. Upstream countries such as Kyrgyzstan and Tajikistan – where major rivers originate – would reduce the amount of energy generated through hydroelectric plants in winter and would be supplied with electricity from neighbouring countries. In return, water would be released in spring and summer to provide for cotton crop irrigation. The electricity generated from the spring and summer release of water in Kyrgyzstan and Tajikistan would be sent back to the neighbouring countries. Since all the republics (excluding Turkmenistan) were connected by the United Energy System, this enabled electricity sharing.

Since independence, this arrangement has slowly collapsed and seen the reversal of this trend. Kyrgyzstan and Tajikistan have gradually used more water in the winter months to generate electricity to meet domestic demand and released less water in spring and summer months to replenish their reservoirs. This has created tension with the downstream countries, especially with Uzbekistan, which maintains a large and thirsty agricultural base (Wegerich 2011, 287). Meanwhile poor energy infrastructure in Tajikistan and the heavy energy demands of the TALCO aluminium factory have caused severe drains on the system. As a result, Uzbekistan has largely pulled out of the energy ring, but nonetheless continues to draw some electricity from the ring as its own internal capacity is limited. This has prompted some governments, particularly Kyrgyzstan, to build their own internal rings (such as the Datka–Kemin high voltage line) to ensure energy security and become largely independent of the energy ring. These activities have also sparked discussion of water use and sustainable energy projects, with Uzbekistan objecting to large-scale projects, such as Kambar-Ata dams in Kyrgyzstan and Rogun in Tajikistan, and escalating regional tension by talk of 'water wars' (Lillis 2012).

These projects raise important questions about environmental impact, which was already an issue during the Soviet Union. The use of the Amu-Darya and Syr-Darya Rivers for irrigation in cotton-growing regions of Central Asia has led to the catastrophic drying out of the

Aral Sea. Furthermore, the heavy use of coal is creating pollution and health problems (Chandler 2000). In particular, the use of thermal plants is an environmental concern. In the late 1970s, Dienes and Shabad noted that 'thermal power stations are a major source of environmental deterioration through air pollution, slag disposal and waste heat removal. Soviet electric stations, for example, are responsible for about one-fourth of all air pollutants originating from stationary sources in the country' (Dienes and Shabad 1979, 202). With the slow deterioration of these plants and the lack of technologies to remove carbon dioxide from emissions, the environmental impact of the energy infrastructure continues to play a significant role in the region.

In addition, little revenue can be generated for the maintenance and improvement of the energy infrastructure, as tariffs remain heavily subsidized. Partly out of a sense of entitlement that was fostered during the Soviet era, but also due to populist moves by governments, particularly in Kyrgyzstan, electricity prices have remained heavily subsidized, but are not sufficient to support maintenance or instillation of new equipment. The switch to market-led prices in the energy sector has not been successful, primarily because the provision of energy and the upkeep of infrastructure are seen as responsibilities of the state. This means that provision cannot always be guaranteed because of the old infrastructure.[13] The frequent power failures in parts of the region, as well as well-founded suspicions over corrupt energy sales mean that citizens do not feel that they should pay for a service they are either not receiving or is not properly priced. The reactions of citizens to such felt injustices differ dramatically, as in the case of Kyrgyzstan's 2010 uprisings, described by Wooden (this issue), in contrast to the role of energy poverty as a focus of ethnic grievances among Afghani Hazaras, or the small-scale struggles against individual 'gazoviki' in Azerbaijan described by Barrett (2014) in this issue.

How energy shapes individual and collective life

In light of local and global inequalities in access to energy, predictions of dwindling fossil fuels and dire warnings about the consequences of climate change related to unchecked carbon emissions, social scientists have been increasingly concerned with people's habits and attitudes to energy production and consumption (Nader 2010, cited in Strauss, Rupp, and Love 2013). Energy has been termed a 'master resource' (Strauss, Rupp, and Love 2013, 11), because it is often conceived of as an engine of progress, promising lighter workloads, physical comfort, connectivity and entertainment. The demand for this extremely valuable commodity has surged across the globe over the last 150 years; indeed, this period has been nicknamed the 'age of fossil fuel'. When queues for petrol or frequent blackouts reach citizens, such disrupted public access can quickly turn into full-blown political crises. Such discontents have perhaps joined the call for bread (or other basic foodstuffs) and work as the fundamental economic demands of the global citizenry. At the same time, most forms of energy are distributed through technological systems, a kind of 'magic' little-understood and often opaque to citizens. The consequent 'invisibility' of the stuff of energy, and the evasive concreteness of its substance (what is a 'watt', how big is a barrel of oil?) may thus have limited a highly significant field of social research.

> The staggering significance of energy as the undercurrent and integrating force for all other modes and institutions of modern power has remained remarkably silent, even in this era of so much talk about climate change, energy crisis and energy transition. (Boyer 2011, 5)

Yet 'energy' is not a monolith: there are great and significant differences in modes of production, and consequently in the consumption of electricity and fuel derived from oil, gas, coal and water.[14] Taking our cue from Watts (2008), we regard energy as artefact and artifice: it exists both as material substance and force, as well as creating social, political and economic structures that organize societies (Strauss, Rupp, and Love 2013). For example, Timothy Mitchell has proposed that the contrasting materiality of oil and coal, their varying relations with labour power, and the differing ways of distributing them have shaped state–citizen relations, the emergence of democracy – and its limits (Mitchell 2009). The flow of energy is constructed (also literally, through specific infrastructures and points of delivery) to follow certain avenues. 'The production, delivery and consumption of energy make it the quintessential social good: one having [...] a multi-faceted biography' (Wilhite 2005, 1). The life story of energy, for example in the form of barrels of oil shipped between the littoral states of the Caspian region and newly imagined (politicized) routes through Turkey bypassing Iran and Russia along the proposed Nabucco pipeline,[15] is one shaped by historic struggles and economic and political conventions. These histories and conventions are built into the fundamental concepts of energy. For example, it is a – politically highly freighted – convention that the price of oil is measured in US dollars, or that environmental clean-up costs of oil are not included in this price – though that of cleaning up nuclear fuel waste is (Mitchell 2009, 414, 418). The routes of energy production and distribution shape and are shaped by power relations, for example in the self-identification of certain states as energy superpowers, or the financing of higher education or cultural events by energy companies (cf. Rogers 2011, 2014). In this issue, Strakes provides a striking account of how the choice of energy technologies has been shaped by diplomatic relations with European countries involving the issue of genocide and diaspora connections in Armenia, while Georgia has invited Kazakhstan and Azerbaijan into the arena of energy expertise. Jäger (2014, in this issue) meanwhile focuses on the effect of the oil boom on western Kazakhstan, through the lens of labour, rural–urban relations and migration.

Studies of energy consumption have often been dominated by economists, and thus by rational-actor theories (Wilhite 2005, 2). These have rarely taken into account the choices consumers make, or been able to explain them beyond the principle of greed. Nevertheless, the ways people use energy in the region are shaped by the Soviet system of generation and distribution. Technological developments have increased energy consumption through goods, such as heating, lighting, clean clothes, plasma televisions, smartphones, travel or refrigeration (Wilhite 2005, 2). While heating and industry were the main users of energy, now other electrical goods are increasing demand, as is a fast growing population, still dependent on an energy infrastructure built for the needs of the previous century. In the absence of more qualitative studies of consumption, this issue focuses on the intersections between regional, national and local energy policies and their effects, the kind of demands people make in relation to what they judge to be fair energy tariffs and what they do in their absence.[16] Gassmann and Tsukada (2014) in this issue use data from the Kyrgyz Integrated Household Survey of 2011 to model the impact of electricity tariff increases on how poorer households in particular would cope, likely switching to other forms of heating fuel, as in Tobias Kraudzun's example, also in this issue, of Pamiris partially switching to solar power.

Uncharted waters: people's everyday experience and use of energy

As indicated above, Central Asian citizens might relate to energy as domestic consumers, but also through their work in the energy sector, in ministries, as experts in energy consultancy firms, as opposition leaders, in their businesses, as users of transport or indeed a combination of these roles. It is important to pay attention to the interplay of producer, consumer and citizen interests. What kinds of political considerations are brought to bear on energy policies in the region: international relations, labour power, 'ordinary' citizen demands or other factors (McNeish 2012, 34)? As Strauss, Rupp, and Love have pointed out, 'production, distribution, and consumption of energy almost never follow a simple logic of neoclassical economic efficiency; rather, people tend to switch frames of reference among technical, economic, and cultural logics when considering their uses of energy' (Strauss, Rupp, and Love 2013, 11). This insight helps us focus on how people experience energy in their daily lives – in particular, how they struggle for access to it, what other benefits they may receive or what price they might pay, for example in deteriorating health, for energy production.

Tanja Winther's (Winther 2008) ethnography of the arrival of electricity in rural Zanzibar in the 1990s is an example of how changing relationships to energy can have multiple social and political effects: changing gender relations by keeping men more at home, in front of the television, changing the pattern and mood of night-time socializing, introducing the notion of 'customers' paying punctually, and allowing officials access to their homes to read the meter. In the case of Tanzania, Degani has described how residents manipulate limited access to electricity, laying claims through 'cleverness'. The author argues that this relationship to power grids is symptomatic of post-socialist contexts with tenuous neoliberal reforms that require citizens to improvise and make do, rather than empowering them (Degani 2013, 27ff.).

This issue provides an account of how energy experiences in Central Asia and the Caucasus might articulate conceptions of 'moral economy'. The term 'moral economy' was coined by Thompson (1971) and elaborated by James Scott (Scott 1977) and others to denote a broader conception of economy than one driven by the self-interested individual of neo-classical economics. Moral economies are not 'flat', space-like terrains, but animated with the sense of desires, obligations and entitlements that people feel towards each other in producing and exchanging things. Both the sources of energy in fossil fuels and hydropower, as well as electricity itself move between being seen and handled as a public good, and increasingly, as a marketable commodity. Who owns the wealth and potential resources stored under a nation's 'feet', how and according to what priorities should it be administered? The respondents to the studies by Chiovenda, Barrett and Jäger all articulate very clear, but also varied, ideas about what constitutes fair oil, gas and electricity management practices by the state and companies, and whether they meet these standards.

Proponents of the 'resource curse' theory see oil wealth in particular as hindering, rather than aiding the development of countries. They point to the way oil wealth can create imbalances in the economy by letting other sectors dwindle, the way governments may become less dependent on taxation, thus less accountable and, as 'rentier-states', more able to buy off opposition. A monopoly of oil wealth may thus prop up authoritarian regimes and elites who do not necessarily allow the fabulous profits of the oil trade trickle down (Sakal 2014). A case has been made for Azerbaijan, Kazakhstan and Turkmenistan suffering from the 'resource curse' (Overland, Kjaernet, and Kendall-Taylor 2010; Najman, Pomfret and Raballand 2008). Critics claiming 'oil is not a curse' have pointed to the real issue being the ownership relations and control of resources, rather than the resource per se (Jones-Luong and Weinthal 2010). More generally, critics have pointed to the ahistorical analysis inherent in the 'resource curse' thesis, and the way it is selectively applied to states emerging from colonial relations (similar to the 'failed states' notion) (Jones-Luong and Weinthal 2010; McNeish and Logan 2012, 3–4). They have also highlighted that weak institutions are generally blamed for the resource curse, for which technocratic solutions are sought. This approach ignores the fact that the avoidance of the resource curse in oil-rich countries such as Botswana, Chile, Malaysia or Norway is strongly associated with social struggle, often spear-headed by labour unions (McNeish 2012, 29). The complexities of access to and use of these resources are part of broader issues of relations to the environment and scales of control. For example, despite the pro-indigenous rhetoric of the Bolivian government, the peasants of the oil-rich Tarija region threw up road blocks in 2009, claiming their region should reap more profits from extracting gas in their land, rather than the national, populist government. Or should it in fact be the indigenous people of the region benefitting, rather than the province itself (McNeish 2012, 66)?[17] Such complexities of scale and allocation are clearly described by Jäger in western Kazakhstan and by Barrett in the case of Baku residents.

In Central Asia and the Caucasus, so far most governments seem to have a firm hold on monopolizing and setting the terms of distribution (and often the production) of energy to citizens. Considering the Soviet legacy of a state–citizen social 'contract' over cheap energy, people's access to energy is likely to be linked to their relationship with the government/state. But there are signs in Kyrgyzstan and Kazakhstan, that 'terms of exchange' and conditions of production are increasingly challenged by the people. The riot in the western Kazakhstani town of Zhanaozen started by workers of three foreign oil companies seeking better worker rights is one such example. The police crackdown, in which 16 people were killed, indicates that increased benefits afforded by oil and gas wealth have neither improved the level of poverty experienced by many, nor secured significantly better labour rights. The events in Zhanaozen are an important reminder of the struggles of those who work in the energy sector.

The papers in this collection are grouped into three themes The first theme articulates 'energy dystopias'. Despite the efforts that have been made to improve energy distribution throughout the region, there are many citizens who struggle to secure energy sustainably or who have been constantly excluded from improvements. People's interactions with energy resources, their use, payment and benefits (or lack of them) as part of people's daily lives, their choices, opportunities, limitations and desires are examined closely. These daily practices and desires, in turn, frame their conceptions of and attitudes towards energy. Melissa Chiovenda (2014) presents the case of Hazaras of central Afghanistan, who see their continued energy poverty as a signifier of their oppressed second-class citizenship. The kind of demonstrations focusing on energy grievances in Bamyan have in the Kyrgyzstani case escalated to government overthrow in 2010, as analysed by Wooden.

A second theme centres on 'politics, practices and entitlements', where authors discuss developments in countries' energy sectors and reveal the limitations and opportunities of the Soviet legacies. Foreign direct investment into countries' energy sectors provides new opportunities while building on top of the former model, as described by Strakes in the case of Georgia and Armenia. Despite the very different paths of engagement that the Georgian and Armenian governments have chosen in relation to foreign investment in the energy sector, in both cases this engagement does not seem to have become a widespread grievance among the population. It is not just the legacy of the Soviet era plus new investments that bring change, but also the impact of new systems and lifestyles that are being developed out of the previous structures. These changes spell job prospects, but also challenges for populations, as in the case of the oil industry in western Kazakhstan analysed by Jäger. In his contribution on Azerbaijan, Tristam Barrett argues that privatization has not in fact fundamentally altered the state–citizen relationship in the domain of electricity. What *has* affected consumers however, is the installation of gas meters, and the machinations of meter readers ('*gazoviki*') to maintain a grip on their brokering power.

Finally, two articles explore 'resource consumption and its impacts'. Franziska Gassmann and Raquel Tsukada use statistical modelling to explore the fuel and heating choices people have in Kyrgyzstan, and to provide insight into the effects that higher electricity prices would have on different sections of the Kyrgyzstani population. Such electricity and fuel price hikes have in fact been initiated in summer 2014, the effect will therefore be immediately comparable. Tobias Kraudzun provides an equally detailed analysis of current energy choices, particularly in relation to heating, in Gorno-Badakhshan, suggesting both environmental consequences and discussing potential alternatives.

Conclusions

Mr Light, tapping electricity illegally for his fellow villagers; Hazaras demanding participation in the nation-state through electrification; middle-class residents in Baku debating the merits of electricity meters; or angry Kyrgyzstanis demonstrating against price hikes in the streets of Bishkek: all clearly desire access to energy that meets their ability to pay and view access to energy as something that a citizen should be able to take for granted. Yet all these actors have to juggle frequent blackouts and be resourceful – some every day, some periodically – in meeting their energy needs for cooking, washing, heating or transport through alternative means (Kraudzun, Chiovenda, Gassmann and Tsukada). Both the sense of entitlement and the frequently inadequate ways these demands are met are both legacies of the successful – albeit environmentally costly – call by Lenin to electrify the Soviet Union.

Yet the legacies of Soviet energy policies and new national and international political and economic energy constellations affect citizens in Central Asia and the Caucasus in a broader sense. The intersection of the state, companies and people's political expectations, coupled with their everyday energy needs and strategies are important aspects of people's experiences. The articles collected here indicate limitations and opportunities in people's choices and how these are being incorporated into the moral universes of consumers and producers (Strakes, Jäger, Barrett).

Human rights as well as political issues are clearly integral to these questions at a national and international level. This collection, however, also draws out the distinctiveness and connectedness of Central Asia's network of producers and consumers, their experiences and challenges through analyses that take into account neighbouring regions, including Afghanistan and the Caucasus. Beyond such a regional perspective, further research is needed to understand what people demand energy *for*, what opportunities access to various forms of energy gives or denies them. How do citizens depending, for example on a 'Mr Light', understand or ignore the technologies they rely on – and what difference might such understandings make? How might people make different judgments about the meaning of electricity, or particular energy sources such as oil, hydropower and solar power, beyond simply being a convenient sign of modernity? Can Timothy Mitchell's thesis of oil extraction creating particular social relations and weakening the position of oil workers be confirmed across Central Asia and the Caucasus? In Central Asian 'moral geographies' of energy, where and when might environmental issues fuelled by energy resources become relevant? This issue begins the exploration of such issues and hopes to inspire discussion on a topic that is only marginally understood, yet directly relevant to everyone's daily experiences in the region.

Acknowledgements

The authors thank the anonymous reviewers of the articles as well as the editor of *Central Asian Survey* for their insightful comments and helpful suggestions. We hope that this special issue becomes the platform for a continued discussion and debate on the everyday issues people experience in accessing and using energy.

Notes

1. The United Energy System is also called an 'energy ring', meaning the network of high-voltage transmission wires which allowed for balancing electricity needs, especially during peak hours.
2. We here outline but two examples in the region, for further details on particular histories of energy production and consumption, for example, in the Caucasus, refer to the individual contributions.
3. Donor engagement in Kyrgyzstan's energy companies has produced reports examining the various parts of the sector, e.g. http://www.energo.gov.kg/site/index.php?act=view_cat&id=19 (accessed September 23, 2013) or International Crisis Group (2007, 2011) reports.

4. By the 'everyday' we mean not just the daily use of different forms of energy, but the activities involved in the production, distribution and utilization of energy and how this shapes people's quotidian experiences.

5. We see this special issue as opening up such an enquiry, and there is much more need for research on these issues.

6. Overland and Kutschera (2012) have argued that Putin's government, for example, holds back in its ambitions to raise energy prices to recover costs for fear of popular protest at the disruption of this part of the social contract.

7. For the full speech, see http://www.marxists.org/archive/lenin/works/1920/nov/21.htm (accessed April 1, 2013).

8. GOELRO is the acronym of the Russian title *Gosudarstvennaya kommisya po elektrifikatsii Rossii*.

9. For a brief history of the energy sector in Tajikistan, see http://www.tajhydro.tj/ru/low-energy/history (accessed October 2, 2013).

10. This is an interesting period of economic development and energy sector growth, but little is known about the public response to this.

11. We do not mean to suggest privatization as a panacea here. Indeed, in other parts of the world, versions of privatization have brought about their own negative impact on citizens, and consequent protests (cf. also Barrett in this issue).

12. By November 2014, no sustainable solution had yet been found to provide natural gas to southern Kyrgyzstan.

13. Turkmenistan is an exception to this trend, providing free gas to its citizens. Armenia, also, has privatized the energy sector and energy tariffs have increased to meet market costs for electricity generation and distribution, and maintenance costs, as detailed by Strakes (in this issue).

14. Research tends to be compartmentalized according to energy sectors and type of resource: the literature on oil dominates.

15. Drawing from the operatic imagery from which the name *Nabucco* is derived, it is also a tale of persecution and a descent into madness, which also characterizes the way in which energy policies – official and clandestine – have created global markets based on insecurity, and markets that also fuel armed conflict. This is what is often captured through the tactics of the 'Great Game', where (imperialistic) superpowers are pitted against each other in resource- and merchandise-rich countries.

16. Since much remains to be explored about perceptions of energy and energy consumption in Central Asia, we see this issue as opening up a space of conversation to be continued.

17. Similar contestations are apparent in Alberta, Canada, between indigenous peoples, regions and national governments control of oil.

References

Barrett, T. 2014. "Notes on the Moral Economy of Gas in Present-day Azerbaijan." *Central Asian Survey* 33 (4): 517–530.

Barry, M. P. 2009. "Foreign Direct Investments in Central Asian Energy: A CGE Model." *Eurasian Journal of Business and Economics* 2 (3): 35–54.

Boyer, D. 2011. Energopolitics and the Anthropology of Energy. *Anthropology News,* 5.

Chandler, W. 2000. *Energy and Environment in the Transition Economies*. Boulder, CO: Westview Press.

Chiovenda, M. K. 2014. "The Illumination of Marginality: How Ethnic Hazaras in Bamyan, Afghanistan, Perceive the Lack of Electricity as Discrimination." *Central Asian Survey* 33 (4): 449–462.

Degani, M. 2013. "Ethics and Energy in Postsocialist Tanzania." In *Cultures of Energy: Power, Practices, Technologies*, edited by S. Strauss, S. Rupp, and T. Love, 177–91. Walnut Creek, CA: Left Coast Press.

Dienes, L., and T. Shabad. 1979. *The Soviet Energy System: Resource Use and Policies*. Washington, D.C.: V. H. Winston & Sons.

Franke-Schwenk, A. 2012. "Providing Welfare in post-Soviet Rentier States." In *Challenges of the Caspian Resource Boom: Domestic Elites and Policy-making*, edited by A. Heinrich and H. Pleines, 246–66. Palgrave Macmillan.

Gassmann, F. and R. Tsukada. 2014. "Switching off or Switching Source: Energy Consumption and Household Response to Higher Energy Prices in the Kyrgyz Republic." *Central Asian Survey* 33 (4): 531–549.

Gustafson, T. 1989. *Crisis amid Plenty: The Politics of Soviet Energy under Brezhnev and Gorbachev*. Princeton, NJ: Princeton University Press.

Heinrich, A., and H. Pleines, eds. 2012. *Challenges of the Caspian Resource Boom: Domestic Elites and Policy-making*. Basingstoke: Palgrave Macmillan.

International Bank for Reconstruction and Development / The World Bank. 2012. *Tajikistan's Winter Energy Crisis: Electricity Supply and Demand Alternatives*. Washington DC: International Bank for Reconstruction and Development / The World Bank.

International Crisis Group. 2007. *Central Asia's Energy Risks*. Asia Report No. 133.

International Crisis Group. 2011. *Central Asia: Decay and Decline*. Asia Report No. 201.

Jäger, P. F. 2014. "Flows of Oil, Flows of People: Resource-extraction Industry, Labour Market and Migration in Western Kazakhstan." *Central Asian Survey* 33 (4): 500–516.

Jones Luong, P., and E. Weinthal. 2010. *Oil is not a Curse*. Cambridge: Cambridge University Press.

Kalybekova, A. 2014a. With Americans Taking Off, Kyrgyzstan Mulls Selling Airports to Russia. EurasiaNet.org, 31 March 2014. Accessed August 13, 2014. http://www.eurasianet.org/node/68213

Kalybekova, A. 2014b. Russia Holds Kyrgyzstan's Hydropower Dreams Hostage. *EurasiaNet.org*, 24 June 2014. Accessed August 13, 2014. http://www.eurasianet.org/node/68741

Karybekov, E., and J. Sarybaeva. 2004. *Energeticheskaya bezopasnost' Kyrgyzstana – "kol'tso" integratsii [Kyrgyzstan's Energy Security – The "Ring" of Integration]*. Bishkek: "Kitep kompani" Publisher.

Kendall-Taylor, A. 2012. "Purchasing Power: Oil, Elections and Regime Durability in Azerbaijan and Kazakhstan." *Europe-Asia Studies* 64 (4): 737–760.

Kleveman, L. 2003. *The New Great Game: Blood and Oil in Central Asia*. London: Atlantic Books.

Kraudzun, T. 2014. "Bottom-up and Top-down Dynamics of the Energy Transformation in the Eastern Pamirs of Tajikistan's Gorno Badakhshan Region." *Central Asian Survey* 33 (4): 550–565.

Lillis, J. 2012. Uzbekistan Leader Warns of Water Wars in Central Asia. EurasiaNet.org. 7 September 2012. Accessed April 25, 2013. http://www.eurasianet.org/node/65877

McNeish, J.-A. 2012. "On Curses and Devils: On Resource Wealth and Sovereignty in an Autonomous Tarija, Bolivia." In *Flammable Societies: Studies on the Socio-economics of Oil and Gas*, edited by J.-A. McNeish and O. Logan, 47–69. London: Pluto Press.

McNeish, J.-A., and O. Logan, eds. 2012. *Flammable Societies: Studies on the Socio-economics of Oil and Gas*. London: Pluto Press.

Mitchell, T. 2009. "Carbon Democracy." *Economy and Society* 38 (3): 399–432.

Najman, B., R. Pomfret, and G. Raballand, eds. 2008. *The Economics and Politics of Oil in the Caspian Basin: The Redistribution of Oil Revenues in Azerbaijan and Central Asia*. London: Routledge.

OCHA. 2008. Tajikistan: Compound Crises Flash Appeal (Revision).

Overland, I., and H. Kutschera. 2012. "Subsidized Energy and Hesitant Elites in Russia." In *Flammable Societies: Studies on the Socio-economics of Oil and Gas*, edited by J.-A McNeish, and O. Logan, 201–18. London: Pluto Press.

Overland, I., H. Kjaernet, and A. Kendall-Taylor, eds. 2010. *Caspian Energy Politics: Azerbaijan, Kazakhstan and Turkmenistan*. London: Routledge.

Paswan, N. 2013. "Investment Cooperation in Central Asia: Prospects and Challenges." *India Quarterly* 69 (1): 13–33.

Reid, S. 2005. "The Khrushchev Kitchen: Domesticating the Scientific–Technological Revolution." *Journal of Contemporary History* 40 (2): 289–316.

Reid, S. 2006. "Khrushchev Modern: Agency and Modernization in the Soviet Home." *Cahiers du Monde russe* 47 (1/2): 227–268.

Rogers, D. 2011. "Oil into Culture: Energopolitics in the Russian Urals." *Anthropology News* 6.

Rogers, D. 2014. "Energopolitical Russia: Corporation, State and the Rise of Social and Cultural Projects." *Anthropological Quarterly* 87 (2): 431–451.

Sakal, H. B., 2014. "Natural Resource Policies and Standard of Living in Kazakhstan." *Central Asian Survey*. doi:10.1080/02634937.2014.987970

Scott, J. C. 1977. *The Moral Economy of the Peasant: Rebellion and Subsistence in Southeast Asia*. Ithaca, NY: Yale University Press.

Starr, F. S., and S. E. Cornell, eds. 2005. *The Baku–Tbilisi–Ceyhan Pipeline: Oil Window to the West*. Washington and Uppsala: CACI and SRSP.

Strakes, J. E. 2014. "Resource Dependence and Measurement Technology: International and Domestic Influences on Energy Sector Development in Armenia and Georgia." *Central Asian Survey* 33 (4): 482–499.

Strauss, S., S. Rupp, and T. Love, eds. 2013. *Cultures of Energy: Power, Practices, Technologies*. Walnut Creek, CA: Left Coast Press.

Thompson, E. P. 1971. "The Moral Economy of the English Crowd in the Eighteenth Century." *Past and Present* 50 (1): 76–136.

Tuleberdiev, Zh. T., K. R. Rakhimov, and Yu. P. Belyakov. 1997. *Razvitie energetiki Kyrgyzstan [Development of the Energy Sector in Kyrgyzstan]*. Bishkek: Sham.

Watts, M., ed. 2008. *Curse of the Black Gold: 50 Years of Oil in the Niger Delta*. Brooklyn, NY: PowerHouse Books.

Wegerich, Kai. 2011. "Water Resources in Central Asia: Regional Stability or Patchy Make-up?" *Central Asian Survey*, 30 (2): 275–290.

Wilhite, H. 2005. "Why Energy needs Anthropology." *Anthropology Today* 21 (3): 1–2.

Winther, T. 2008. *The Impact of Electricity: Development, Desires and Dilemmas*. Oxford and New York: Berghahn.

Wooden, A. E. 2014. "Kyrgyzstan's Dark Ages: Framing and the 2010 Hydroelectric Revolution." *Central Asian Survey* 33 (4): 463–481.

The illumination of marginality: how ethnic Hazaras in Bamyan, Afghanistan, perceive the lack of electricity as discrimination

Melissa Kerr Chiovenda

Department of Anthropology, University of Connecticut, Storrs, CT, USA

In Afghanistan ethnic Hazaras are a group with a long history of marginalization, and even outright persecution, mainly because of their Shi'a Muslim faith. Only after the international intervention in 2001 have socio-economic opportunities started to open up for Hazaras. Hazaras, however, maintain a strong perception of still being considered second-class citizens, claiming to be overlooked by the Afghan government and allotted fewer funds by the international development community. This paper examines Hazara perceptions of marginality with reference to one issue: the lack of state-provided electricity in Bamyan province, which many consider the Hazara homeland. Anti-government protests in Bamyan often revolve around this particular issue, and the demand for electricity has become part of the permanent landscape, through a lantern sculpture in Bamyan's main square, as well as through the experience of living one's everyday life with a lack of easily available electric light. The lack of electricity becomes an embodied, daily reminder of perceived subordination to other religio-ethnic groups and the feeling of being left behind by the international community.

Karzai, shame on you and your corrupt government!
In the center of Bamyan people are still suffering from lack of electricity!
Tonight is very cold, and it is the first night of the hunger strike![1]

The quote above was posted on Facebook in March 2013 by a friend and informant I had interviewed and accompanied to many protests by civil society organizations and events in Bamyan, Afghanistan. I was nearing the end of 18 months in Bamyan, where I conducted research with civil society activists who are involved in a struggle for improved rights for Hazaras, an ethnic group in central Afghanistan. These activists employ a number of methods, such as marches, which they base on United States' civil rights-era protests, and handing out pamphlets and posters. Memorialization events are held to remember one of many massacres or incidents which targeted Hazaras, such as during the civil war period, the Taliban period, or today in Afghanistan and Pakistan. On-going efforts are being made to reclaim a history that many Hazaras believe has been lost or manipulated by those in power, and to advance Hazaras' position in the Afghan state. The issues of infrastructure, in general, and electricity, in particular, have been given considerable attention by activists since the US invasion, and have become symbolic of Hazaras' perceived underdevelopment, as was illustrated in the opening quote, referring to the chronic lack of electricity. When I first arrived in Bamyan, I found that protests often started, or finished, at Alakain (Lantern) Square, where a giant lantern sculpture was on display.[2] 'Why a lantern, as opposed to some other symbol, to serve as your main gathering point? Was there any particular significance?' I asked activists. The answer was almost always the same: 'Our biggest problem is lack of electricity, so this was the focus of one of our first protests.'

At night in Bamyan, the darkness serves as a physical reminder to the inhabitants which leads many to believe they are kept in an underdeveloped state, illustrating Madeleine Reeves' (2011, 307) assertion that 'places are lived', and in Bamyan, that living is experienced as one finds oneself inhabiting a place of darkness as soon as the sun sets. During the day, the reminder is not so obvious, but Bamyan University cannot operate as many computers as are needed (and sometimes none), while only those offices with enough funds (in practice generally those with foreign or foreign-funded organizations) have regular electricity. Additionally, few industries are able to operate. No electricity being provided by the state in Bamyan means that no type of heavier industry which relies on electricity, for example, any sort of factory work, is possible. Construction work, wood working and blacksmithing using flame and bellows all exist. But nothing more industrial is possible, so that Bamyan appears as a relic of the past, with most residents relying on simple agricultural techniques for subsistence, with few options to move towards a more promising economic future based on industry. The people are very aware of this and believe that without state and international community cooperation there is little they can do to help themselves. Jeanne Féaux de la Croix (2011, 487) wrote of a hydroelectric dam in Kyrgyzstan: 'This is not a credible place; this is truly a miracle of technology.' For Hazaras, the only such miracle, that is, the only such large-scale infrastructure visible are the glaring lights of the Provincial Reconstruction Team (PRT) run by New Zealand, a military base whose technology they are excluded from. Such miracles are, from their point of view, for others to experience, even as Hazaras fight for inclusion. What Hazaras seem to be seeking is not simply access to electricity, but also access to modernity, and a feeling that they have achieved parity with the rest of Afghanistan. The type of electric supply they dream of is something large-scale that will bring industry, and which will allow them to advance in order to help them contribute, as full members of the Afghan state, to the development of the country as a whole. The type of electric supply they dream of, it seems, is something that would alter the landscape, the world in which they live, bringing it from a life of subsistence farming to something modern, developed.

Stephen Feld and Keith Basso posit that 'places become sites of power struggles' and that 'ethnography's stories of place and places are increasingly about power struggles' (Feld and Basso 1996, 115). For the Hazaras in Bamyan, this manifests itself in issues of historical memory and ethnic identity. For example, they assert that they are the descendants of an ancient Buddhist civilization of Afghanistan and by extension can claim what are essentially indigenous rights in Afghanistan, in particular in the central highlands region of the country. Infrastructural landscape, most obviously the distribution of electricity, is symbolic of such power struggles, as it is emblematic of development or lack thereof. This is particularly painful in the case of Bamyan, a landscape whose place name – according to some interlocutors – means 'shining light'. Staying in the dark at night, and maintaining the belief that other ethnic groups in similar regions are not experiencing such darkness, reaffirms Hazara beliefs that they remain the most disadvantaged, the most oppressed, group in Afghanistan. Being kept in the dark[3] comes to be a sort of prison one cannot break out of. For the Hazaras, the lack of electricity is a visible reminder of a playing field that, politically and economically, is not level. To be sure Hazaras are not the only ones who experience a lack of electricity or other infrastructure. The point I am making is that Hazaras choose to see this as an intentional and instrumental act of the state apparatuses in order to further disenfranchise and marginalize them as an ethnic group.

This article is based on ethnographic fieldwork conducted in Markaz Bamyan and surrounding districts during the summers of 2010 and 2011, and a 12-month period in 2012–13 for the completion of my dissertation in the field of anthropology. During this time, while researching Hazara ethnic identity, I also carried out numerous interviews with inhabitants concerning the developmental and infrastructural problems in Bamyan. Protests addressing electricity problems directly, they reported, were common when they first started such actions until about 2010, when they came to believe that the issue was simply not getting attention. However, it remains a constant theme woven throughout their activist work. Activists were usually young men and sometimes women who had at least a high-school education, although this was not always the case. Many worked in various non-governmental organizations (NGOs) in Markaz Bamyan (Bamyan Centre), many were university students, and some worked for local government apparatuses, although I did meet others of all ages and from all walks of life. I also carried out numerous interviews with inhabitants concerning the developmental and infrastructural problems in Bamyan.

In this article, I will next briefly discuss the historical origins, experiences and perceptions of marginality as experienced by Hazaras. This is necessary to understand in order to perceive the ways in which collective trauma has led to a suspicion against the state and other groups within Afghanistan that many Hazaras view as antagonistic. I will then explore the ways in which my informants came to see their lack of electricity as a symbol of social exclusion, and the ways that electricity as a symbol of exclusion is perceived through landscape features in Bamyan. I will continue with an overview of aid delivered to Bamyan in general, and the electricity situation in Bamyan as it stood during the time of my research. Finally, I will discuss Hazara perceptions of the most well-known electricity projects in Bamyan until the time of my research, and whether they are viewed as successes or failures by the population in Bamyan. To conclude, I will return to the issue of marginality, landscape and electricity and put forth the idea that residents of Bamyan are seeking not simply electric light but entry into modernity by way of more advanced industry and hence an end to marginality.

The Hazaras and marginality

Before addressing the issue of energy, electricity and infrastructure in Bamyan, the historical context of the Hazara people within Afghanistan must be briefly addressed. Many sources claim that Hazaras make up 9–10% of Afghanistan's population, making them the third largest ethnic group in the country, after Tajiks (roughly 27% of the population) and Pashtuns (42% of the population),[4] while others claim Hazaras constitute at least 20% of the population.[5] The Hazara homeland, known as Hazarajat or Hazarestan, is located in the central highlands of the country and adjoining areas. The dominant narrative concerning the origin of Hazaras posited by most scholarly historical books on Afghanistan and written by non-Hazaras has long been that they are descended from Mongols, who in the 13th century invaded what is now Afghanistan (Bacon 1951). There is some linguistic support, provided by Bacon (1951) and others, and referenced by Hazaras I met in Bamyan as well, for this possibility. Hazara Asiatic physical features also seem to support this possibility. Yet many Hazaras today, particularly in Markaz Bamyan, are at least partially rejecting this theory as their main identity marker. Rather they maintain that they are a mix of Mongol and earlier inhabitants of the region, or that they have very little Mongol blood at all (Poladi 1989; Mousavi 1997). My own research showed that many Hazaras are trying to establish themselves as the indigenous people of not only Hazarajat but also much of Afghanistan, in order to strengthen a vulnerable position within the Afghan state. Many of my informants claim descent from the Gandharan civilization that built the giant Buddha statues in Bamyan in the sixth and seventh centuries CE. Through a relationship to this historical landscape they highlight a direct connection to this region which they believe will strengthen their legitimate claim to the territory. In the late 1800s, after a series of wars and rebellions, much Hazara land was redistributed to other Afghan groups by the state. Disagreements over the ownership of these areas still exist and contribute to an on-going anxiety that Hazaras might, in the future, suffer further loss of land or displacement. Non-Hazaras who feel they have a right to the land may invoke the idea that as 'Mongols' Hazaras do not belong on that land anyway. Hazaras hence try to counter by laying an ancient, pre-Mongol claim to the land.

This understanding of Hazara autochthony is useful to look at through the lens of 'ethnoscapes', as used by Conrad Schetter (2005) rather than with the original usage introduced by Arjun Appadurai (1996).[6] Schetter follows the ideas of Anthony Smith (1996), defining ethnoscapes as 'the belief shared by ethnic groups in a common spatial frame of origin' (52). Hazaras remember a homeland from which they were driven out, mainly by the encroachment of Pashtun and possibly Tajik migrations, or through political struggles that resulted in the loss of land. The imagined homeland of the Hazaras is hence much greater than the current land occupied by Hazaras. This vision of their ethnoscape plays two roles. First, Hazaras have a difficult time reconciling with groups such as Pashtuns, who have defined imagined homelands that overlap. And second, this vision reinforces Hazara perceptions of past and on-going marginalization and social exclusion.

There is more clear documentation of Hazara history after they were forcefully incorporated into a centralized Afghan state by Amir Abdur Rahman in the late 1800s. Until this point, Hazaras, although their land was nominally within the Afghan state, generally had a high degree of autonomy.[7] Any group such as Ghilzai Pashtuns, Nuristanis and Uzbeks that had operated with some autonomy were considered a threat to Abdur Rahman's power and affected by this campaign (Barfield 2010, 160). At the time, Hazaras were living in a very homogenous region in a defendable, contiguous mountainous area in the centre of the country, which would have made them seem particularly threatening to centralization. Hazara social structure had been agriculture-based, with a feudal and tribal social system, governed by local *mirs*, *khans* and *begs*.[8] All these actors lost their power and were replaced by Pashtun and Tajik rulers, or in some cases Hazara arbitrators, after Abdur Rahman's campaigns, thus effectively dismantling the entire social system (Mousavi 1997, 91–92). As the majority of Hazaras are Shi'a Muslims, the operations carried out against them were particularly harsh, as they were conducted with the help of a sectarian religious division to mobilize the Sunni soldiers and others acting against Hazaras in the name of *jihad*.

Between 1888 and 1894, Hazaras carried out three unsuccessful uprisings against the state, followed by severe reprisals. Hazaras were sold into slavery – between 1892 and 1894 alone 9000 Hazara men are reported to have been sold into slavery in Kabul. They could be killed with next to no pretext, particularly as some Sunni mullahs are said to have issued *fatwas* stating that killing a Hazaras would guarantee one's entry to paradise (Mousavi 1997). Large tracts of Hazara lands were confiscated, and Pashtun Kuchi nomads were invited to use Hazara lands as summer grazing pastures (Ibrahimi 2009). Taxes levied against Hazaras were prohibitive, sending many into irrevocable debt. Pashtun and Kuchi traders offered Hazaras goods at such a premium that each year debts grew higher, which resulted in further acquisition of Hazara land to pay off the debts (Ferdinand 1962). Mousavi maintains that half of population was displaced or killed (Mousavi 1997, 136). Hazara activists currently estimate that at least 60% of the population was killed or forced out of its homeland during Abdur Rahman's campaigns. There is the possibility that some of these numbers are inflated, but enough credible sources (e.g. Mousavi 1997; Poladi 1989; Karimi 2011; Ibrahimi 2012, to name but a few) exist to indicate that the effects on the population, whether through exposure to violence, later economic policies that favoured other groups over Hazaras, or forced migration, were considerable. The effects of what seems to many to be a repetition of historical Hazara oppression today is not without consequence. An activist at a protest I attended against killing of Hazaras in Pakistan told me, 'This is a genocide. It started with Abdur Rahman, it continued with the other kings, the mujahedin, the Taliban, also in Pakistan ... it is always Hazaras who are targeted' (January 23, 2013).

In the years following this conflict, Hazaras became part of an established lower class among Afghans. Very few had opportunities to attend school or university. Those in Hazarajat for the most part scraped by as subsistence farmers. Markaz Bamyan, the commercial and administrative centre of Bamyan, was controlled, economically and politically, largely by Tajiks with close state relations (Canfield 1973). The many Hazaras who fled to large cities, especially Kabul, Mazar-e-Sharif and Herat, found themselves restricted to a servant/manual labourer class (Mousavi 1997; Karimi 2011; Barfield 2010). Politically, Hazaras were excluded, and in fact the borders of Hazarajat were drawn so that only one province, Bamyan, was Hazara majority.[9]

During the Soviet invasion (1979–89) and civil war period in Afghanistan (1992–96), Hazara political groups underwent a period of conflict followed by consolidation under the party Hizb-e-Wahdat, which was headed by cleric and political figure Abdul Ali Mazari (Harpviken 1998). Hazara political and ethnic consciousness grew and became more unified, both under Wahdat and among the diaspora, particularly in Quetta, Pakistan, a city that has long received Hazara migrants (Ibrahimi 2012). After the United States-led intervention began in 2001 and 2002, with the removal of the Taliban and installation of a new government, Hazaras took advantage of the chance to improve their situation, particularly through education. Numbers of Hazara boys and girls attending school are thought to be higher in comparison with other ethnic groups,[10] while at the same time Hazara political and community leaders are very vocal in demanding equal rights.

Assessing Hazaras' status today is difficult because whereas in the past discrimination has been generalized, in the last 12 years opportunities provided by the occupation and post-Taliban period have given more advantages to *some* Hazaras, although the idea of Hazaras as second-class citizens is maintained. Social exclusion is now more difficult to detect and measure, since even if some Hazaras are successful in fields of education, government and business, this does not mean that all Hazaras are able to take advantage of these opportunities. When Hazaras in a particular location such as Bamyan latch on to an issue such as electricity as symbolic of greater problems, it can be used to understand one part of a group's reaction to something so ambiguous as the concept of social exclusion. Social exclusion does not affect group members in the same way or to the same degree, as it is not necessarily institutionalized. Therefore, examining the symbolic meanings acquired by electricity in Hazaras' understanding of social exclusion thus illuminates their exclusion more generally. The relation between current lack of electricity, exclusion and past suffering was recently highlighted by a friend in Bamyan, who was also an activist and a university student, as we discussed the 2013 Afghan football team win of the South Asian Football Federation Cup. This was heralded as an important moment of unity for Afghanistan, a moment that could be celebrated by an Afghan nation. When I mentioned this, Hassan said:

> What Afghan nation? We Hazaras know a dark history of deprivation and genocide. There is no justice and equality! People all over Afghanistan are celebrating, but we Hazaras are forced to celebrate by the light of our cell phones. The building of a nation for all groups is what the government keeps talking about, but there can be no nation until the government distributes assets equally and stops ignoring smaller ethnicities and tribes. Until then, there will be no nation! (September 14, 2013)[11]

Hassan was not explicitly speaking of electricity, but he clearly referenced the lack of infrastructure, particularly electric infrastructure, as he moved from the topic of celebrating by the light provided by a cell phone to the topic of unequal distribution of resources to be used for electricity. The event that brought on this declaration, the celebration in Afghanistan for its football team's victory, was for him meaningless because of the darkness, and this meaninglessness was underlined by the meagre light produced by cell phones. Hassan made clear that darkness to him was both metaphorical in referring to Hazaras' situation in general and literal in that they had no electric light. Hassan also alluded to the general social exclusion of Hazaras through the feelings that moment created. He felt excluded from the national celebration as a Hazara, yet what reminded him of this exclusion was the lack of electricity. This reminder caused him to recall the historical roots of Hazara social problems, topics one might not normally put together. But for Hassan, electricity had become the trigger that raised these issues. It was, for him, both a continuation of the oppression suffered by Hazaras in the past and a symbol evidenced in the landscape, as he tried to celebrate in the streets in the dark and found himself frustrated.

Landscape in the place of shining light

In Bamyan, people are attuned to the land around them, as are people everywhere, and they read a history in that landscape. Yet because of the specific historical contingencies in the region, Hazaras both remember events that happened during the years of conflict and recall a more ancient past. An attachment to certain features of the landscape serves to root them in a history that established them as legitimate, and even original, inhabitants of the area, rather than interlopers who do not belong, a claim which non-Hazara informants put forward when questioning Hazaras' right to live on the land they inhabit today. Electric light is a feature of the landscape, and hence plays a role along with other landscape features as people seek to establish themselves in a particular piece of land, or a particular ethnoscape. Empty holes where Buddha statues once stood, the ruins of the old bazaar, sites of massacres and battles, all hold meaning. As Hazara activists and the general population of Markaz Bamyan read the landscape, they also read the full darkness that comes after sunset, broken only by the bright islands of non-Afghan outsiders, the lights of the PRT and of the United Nations Assistance Mission in Afghanistan (UNAMA) headquarters, for example.

For Hazaras in Bamyan, these features of the landscape remind them not only of their past, but also of the tenuous position they perceive themselves to occupy in the Afghan state. Referring to those living in the hills of West Virginia, Kathleen Stewart (Stewart 1996, 137) writes:

> The detritus of history piled high on the local landscape has become central to a sense of place emergent in re-remembered ruins and pieced together fragments. [...] Far from being a timeless or out of the way place, the local finds itself reeling in the wake of every move and manoeuver of the centre of things.

The same description could be applied to the mountains and high plateaus of Bamyan. For the Hazaras living there, the historical landscape through which they move becomes a physical reminder of identity. In the niches where ancient giant Buddhist statues, destroyed by the Taliban, emerged from a cliff face, they see their heritage, a heritage they believe to have been assaulted along with the statues. In the ruins of Shahr-e-Gholghola, or the city of screams, they see more destruction of their heritage – paradoxically at the hands of those same Mongols that many see as their ancestors.[12] Various sites mark massacres where Hazaras have been killed, either by Taliban or other political entities that have opposed the Hazaras. The place in which they live not only contains reminders of the past, but also evidence of the current situation, in which Hazaras believe that they remain a persecuted minority and that the state ignores them intentionally, focusing valuable resources on peoples it favours because, as I was told repeatedly, they are not Hazaras and hence more valuable. Other times, they remember that the centre, that is the state apparatus, lashed out and destroyed people, landscape and livelihoods – Amir Abdur Rahman, the *mujahedin* government of Rabbani, the Taliban, all targeted Hazaras. Sitting with several informants and discussing Hazara history, they switched easily between tales of over a century ago, to the civil war in Afghanistan, to the problems experienced under the current government, and back. Haliq told me, 'Abdur Rahman killed us and took our land, Massoud killed us in

Afshar, the current government watches as the Taliban kills us, and does not provide protection for our roads, does not help us!' (February 10, 2013). They were teaching me about their history as they spoke, but the history was tied to the land of Afghanistan and to their suffering. They wanted me to know that their people had experienced a chain of events designed to shut them out from any real power, any control over their destiny. Physical reminders became important – both the ruins of giant Buddha statues and the darkness that surrounded them at night, as they told this story.

The lack of light at night, as well as permanent monuments such as the lantern sculpture in Alakain Square and power lines that stretch along streets but do not bring electricity – some international development organization's good intention that was abandoned – also serve to reinforce perceptions of marginalization and victimization. Sometimes the link between landscape, electricity and history was brought into relief. One friend and informant, Farid, who worked with the PRT on development issues, came to my house for dinner with me and my husband in April 2013. As we relaxed on pillows after dinner, talk turned to a project planned by the state-owned Chinese Metallurgical Company (MCC) project. Farid began by discussing how this project would give only 10% of its output to Bamyan, an amount he viewed as unfair. Furthermore, this is the company that will excavate the Mes Aynak mine, where a treasure trove of Buddhist statues and artefacts have been uncovered and which will be destroyed as copper excavation continues (Dalrymple 2013). As discussed above, the identity many Hazaras favour relates directly to a past tied to the Buddhist period in Afghanistan. To informants such as Farid, China thus seemed to be offering them very little – electricity that would not meet their most important needs – in exchange for the destruction of their heritage, and what they see as one of their links to the land. Mes Aynak is located in Logar, not a Hazara-inhabited area but a region that the staunchest proponents of Hazara indigeneity claims was stolen from them. Receiving what they believe to be a basic need not from the state but from a Chinese company that would destroy their heritage is further evidence to them that they are intentionally forgotten by the Afghan state.

Overview: aid and electricity in Bamyan

The electricity situation in Markaz Bamyan was nearly untenable while I conducted my research. Almost everyone had at least a weak solar panel or battery, but few had any power source more effective than this, which provides only several hours of weak electricity a day, perhaps enough to run one television and charge a couple of cell phones. Many of the most impoverished still relied on oil lanterns, although this was seen as a last resort as it is considered dangerous and old-fashioned. Some paid into a local generator project, in which one neighbourhood member buys a generator and maintains it, and others pay a fee. This was not a popular solution because – should there be a problem with the generator – the owner may simply not attend to the repairs; something that happens fairly often. Outside of Markaz Bamyan, the National Solidarity Project (NSP), an Afghan government programme created to foster development, promoted micro-hydroelectric power in the many rivers that flow from the mountains. A report carried out by CDA Collaborative Learning Projects, which included a research project in Bamyan, indicated that rural Afghans are generally happy with the NSP ("Listening Project Field Visit Report Afghanistan" 2009). My own informants indicated that they found the NSP favourable, particularly in Fulladi Valley, as well as the village Saidabad, both a short distance from the centre. 'Here in Fulladi, we have strong electricity, we have strong light in several rooms,' said one young man, a friend who worked as a journalist (November 19, 2012). A grandfather from Saidabad I visited to discuss the recent history of Markaz Bamyan stated: 'We have enough electricity for lights and to power a television' (December 2, 2012). A common theme when discussing development and in particular projects to provide electricity was that although some people might have electricity, the fact that Markaz Bamyan, where real political, educational and infrastructural development should be taking place, seemed to remain underdeveloped, pointed to politically motivated exclusion.[13] Many inhabitants expected underdevelopment in remote, rural areas, but believed that the seat of government should be more modernized, as it was from this place that development, economic and educational opportunities for the entire region should stem.

In Afghanistan less stable conflict-ridden regions receive more aid, and stable, calm regions such as Bamyan often receive less aid, because of the importance placed on winning 'hearts and minds' of people away from the insurgency. Aid delivered through PRTs can often be delivered with military, as well as development, goals in mind – with military often taking precedence. In Bamyan, stories (whether accurate or not) abound about other regions that have secure access to electricity – Herat, Parwan, Nangarhar.[14] A 2008 report carried out by the Agency Coordinating Body for Afghan Relief and Development (ACBAR) indicated that there is some truth to these perceptions. This study points out that if Helmand, a hotspot of Taliban insurgency, had been a state, it would have been the fifth largest recipient of aid. Volatile Nimroz, Helmand, Kandahar, Zabul and Uruzgan receive an amount of aid two to three times greater than other, more stable provinces (Waldman 2008, 5).[15] The same report points out that as aid distributed through the government is disbursed outwards from central government, it tends to remain in urban rather than in rural areas – Kabul, for example, accounts for 70% of the national operational budget (12). It is clear that smaller, rural areas with relatively good security such as Bamyan often receive less. How does Bamyan compare with similar rural regions, however? In 2007–08, Bamyan ranked 11th out of 34 provinces in per-capita donor spending. Nimroz was awarded about US$450 per capita, Bamyan about US$200 per capita, and at the low end Wardak at around US$50 per capita (15).[16] These figures, taken at face value, indicate that it is not discrimination against Hazaras per se that decides which areas receive more or less money. After all, while Wardak does have a considerable Hazara population, the majority are Pashtuns.[17] How these funds affected overall development in each region is not clear. It is possible that a province such a Bamyan, described by the United Nations Development Programme (UNDP) as 'one of the poorest, most mountainous, and agriculturally least productive areas' in Afghanistan ("Regional Profile for Bamyan" n.d., 1) might make improvements with reasonable aid amounts when compared with the rest of the country, and yet starting with such a disadvantage, residents comparing themselves with others might perceive discrimination. And if discrimination is known to exist anyway, residents might be more likely to blame problems on this rather than on other factors.

The point is, for Hazaras in Bamyan underdevelopment was *perceived* to be the result of a systematic discrimination, and lack of electricity was a glaring reminder of this. Again and again my informants' narratives in Markaz Bamyan on these issues overlapped when I would sit with them and interview, have group discussions or just chat. As I sat with activists protesting the targeted killing of Hazaras in Quetta during a hunger strike outside the UNAMA Bamyan headquarters, frustration mounted and activists spoke over each other. 'We are the people who built the Buddhas, but today, a genocide takes place against us. The state would give all our land to nomadic *kuchis* if we do not fight. Look at the conditions in which we live!' said Jawad, referencing lack of electricity, lack of school facilities and poor roads in the region (January 13, 2013).

However, in the numerous protests I took part in, very few addressed the issue of electricity directly, contrasting with the themes of earlier protests described by civil society activists that focused more exclusively on such development issues. Civil society activists seem to have moved on at first glance, to newer issues, such as the safety of the roads to Kabul which have over the past several years deteriorated considerably, because their protests concerning electricity did not seem to be making progress. As other problems are discussed, electricity invariably comes up. When activists address problems relating to the quality of Bamyan University, they focus on books, teacher training and the subjects available to students. And yet the activists, many who are themselves students, almost always then move on to the problems of electricity, a problem which proves too great to overlook. 'How can we connect to the outside world?' one student, Arifa, not a member of the core group of activists but someone who did take part in protests from time to time, asked. She went on, while we relaxed in her rented room after eating lunch together:

> The university does not have enough electricity access to supply computers for us, but those of us with laptops cannot charge them. We cannot study more than a couple hours after it grows dark. If it is a cloudy day, our solar panels do not charge at all, and then we have nothing. (May 3, 2013)

Parents also expressed these concerns. A neighbour, and a highly involved activist, who is also a mother, Tahra, said, 'My children want to read at night. They need television so they have some idea about the outside world, to help them in their education, but we do not have a strong enough solar panel to allow them to do these things' (April 15, 2013). Through these narratives, people were telling of trying to recover from the discrimination they faced, but with the belief that this discrimination is on-going.[18]

For others, the electricity problem was expressed as a safety issue. Mothers were afraid of children falling into stoves because of poor lighting. People fear using oil lamps because of the risk of fire. Most do not go out after dark because the rugged terrain is dangerous when it is difficult to see, and criminality has been on the rise as the security situation slowly declines. For still others, industry is the biggest concern. An informant, and activist, who, when not working during normal business hours at a small local radio station, sought to become an entrepreneur, was frustrated because he lost several business opportunities. 'Bamyan is well known for its potatoes, and a foreigner had visited to see if investment in a potato chip factory might be a possibility. The lack of electricity led him to decide to abandon the project. At the same time,' sighed the entrepreneur, 'Herat makes ice-cream, cola, all sorts of goods, because of its reliable power supply' (February 12, 2013). The same individual also hoped to become involved in the mining of marble, but again, lack of electricity for processing put a halt to his plans.

Attempts and failures to solve the electricity crisis in Bamyan[19]

During my time in Bamyan, I relied almost exclusively on solar power for electricity, which provided about three hours of power each evening, just enough to type field notes. Some foreign offices use generators, particularly for their guest houses at night. But these are all individual initiatives. Local Hazara concerns focus on the lack of state-provided electricity to Bamyan. The state, as well as several international development organizations, has made attempts to provide electricity, but all have yet to deliver to the Markaz at the time of writing.[20]

During a meeting in his small office, the local representative from the Ministry of Energy and Water discussed his misgivings about a project (briefly mentioned in my conversation with one of my informants, Farid, above) in Kahmard district, to the north of Markaz Bamyan, being implemented by a state-owned Chinese company (Chinese Metallurgical Company – MCC). MCC plans to begin with coal extraction, which will later be expanded to other types of mineral extraction. The coal will be used to create power plants which will run the Chinese mining efforts and provide electricity to Bamyan. Each district of Bamyan would get a substation. But when I asked whether the representative thought this to be a beneficial project, he said, 'Absolutely not. The Chinese are only thinking of themselves.' The actual amount of electricity that goes to the residents of Bamyan will be quite small, the main point being to operate the Chinese extraction industries (which, he added, will likely employ Chinese, and not local, workers). Plus, he worried that coal would create too much pollution. 'Why should we rely on coal,' he asked, 'when we have so much water?'

And yet, solar panels and generators are considered by many organizations to be a good alternative to large-scale projects, such as dam building, which in other regions of the world have had mixed results – pushed through by the centre, they can result in environmental problems and cause people to lose land in flooded areas, although for some in Bamyan, such as the Ministry of Water and Electricity official I spoke to, they represent a real solution to the problem. Several civil society activists told me of projects that intended to use these alternative types of technology, rather than larger scale projects, with the worry that such smaller projects would not bring major development to Bamyan. The Aga Khan Foundation wanted to bring electricity to the nearby Fulladi Valley area using generators (Ghafari 2011). The project was destined to fail, activists said, because the inhabitants of the villages of Fulladi Valley could not afford to pay for the fuel needed for generators. Likewise, during one of my first visits to Bamyan, a USAID representative was very excited to discuss a proposed plan to bring electricity to Markaz Bamyan using underground generators.[21] This project fell apart in the planning stages, I later found out, when discussing it with government officials in Bamyan. 'That project never would have worked, it was a waste of time,' stated Akbar, affiliated with the local Provincial Council. 'Petrol is too expensive for our people' (March 27, 2013). A New Zealand-funded project was working to bring large numbers of solar panels to Bamyan (*Bakhtar News* 2012). They were, however, not intended to serve Markaz Bamyan, but rather the villages of Saidabad, Hyderabad and Saroa-e-Syob. While these villages are very close to the centre, people again felt that it was catering to individual households and not designed to foster real economic development, for example, by targeting areas where businesses are located. In Bamyan, it is very clear where businesses are located in the bazaar and where private households are located. They generally do not overlap. Another informant, Daoud, who had worked with development projects at the PRT doubted the efficacy of either of these types of electricity sources. 'Generators cost too much,' he said. 'Solar panels, however, are almost always not of the best quality, and break after a few years' (April 13, 2013). He had serious doubts as to whether the international community would have any interest in replacing broken solar panels – as the panels were for household use, they would not promote economic growth, in his opinion, and many people would, several years from now, still not be in a position to buy their own.[22]

The official with the Ministry of Energy and Water in Afghanistan who I interviewed made it clear he did not have much hope for the development of electricity in Bamyan. He said that the NSP is in fact building a generator for Markaz Bamyan, which will be used by local businesses. Would this foster the development those in Bamyan told me they sought? No, was his straight answer. The businesses would have to have enough capital to use electricity from the generator, which, being paid by the kilowatt, would be quite expensive. But it would only be strong enough to power lights, and maybe computers and copy machines. It would by no means sustain any sort of industry. The expense also meant that students at Bamyan University, almost all Hazara, would also not benefit. Female students not from Bamyan live in dorms or rent private rooms, and usually have to supply their own solar panels. The quality of the panels is very poor, as they are able to scrape together little money for their purchase. Male students do not have dorms and are not able to rent rooms, as culturally it is not appropriate for a non-family male to live in one's household. They rent tiny rooms behind bazaar shops, with little heat and little access to electricity. Some use solar panels, but with as many as 12–15 people packed into a tiny room, they have no more than a few hours of light and maybe the chance to charge their cell phones.

What most informants, like the ministry official, said they would like is a large-scale infrastructural project that will deliver electricity without the problems of generators and small-scale solar power: in other words, a dam. All who knew about the long-planned Tupchi dam project stated unequivocally that it should be completed. Plans to build a dam in Tupchi, just outside of Markaz Bamyan, have been considered since before the wars in Afghanistan began, during the government of Daoud Khan. To the people of Bamyan, building a dam and creating a strong source of electricity is the obvious answer. It would be proof that the state is, in fact, working for them. From their standpoint, it would be solid, it would become part of the landscape, and it would make use of a part of the landscape that so many are familiar with – the rapidly flowing streams that run from the melting mountain snow. I felt that this sort of solidity, of a project that would be born from the landscape and become part of the landscape, seemed to dispel the anxiety created by the problems experienced by the unreliability of other electricity sources. The poetic aspect of this, a new, solid part of the landscape that would drive away the ephemeral, and yet harmful, darkness, was appealing. Among those I spoke with, there seemed to be hope that if this was done, something so solid and unbreakable built, one of Féaux de la Croix in-credible places, miracles, that this might be a true indication from the government that years of exclusion might be ending. Rumours of a plan to continue with the Tupchi dam project abound. One informant said they went to a talk in which a US Embassy representative discussed the project. The representative for the Ministry of Energy and Water said that a German NGO, Integration, was conducting surveys to look into the feasibility of the dam project. He had little hope, however. It seemed as if Hazaras in Bamyan, who had been waiting possibly 30 years for the project, did not believe it would actually materialize.[23]

Conclusions: meaning of the lantern in Alakain Square

To conclude, I will return to the lantern statue displayed in Alakain Square. The lantern holds a very important place in the minds and imaginations of Hazara activists and residents living in Bamyan. It represents an early attempt on their part to demand social justice, in the form of electricity. And yet, it has also come to represent a closing of opportunities, and the further marginalization of Hazaras on the part of the Afghan state and, perhaps, those international organizations that work with the state. It has also become an important feature of the landscape of Bamyan and as such is a constant reminder of what is lacking and what they hope for, as individuals 'read' the landscape they traverse each day.

Several of the most prominent civil society activists installed the lantern in Alakain Square in 2009, after walking with it through the length of the bazaar in a protest march.[24] The lantern itself is large – about the height of a man, almost 2 metres, and sits upon a dais. The initial point was only to bring attention to the issue of not having electricity. A smaller version of the lantern was given to Farouk Wardak, the Education Minister, when he visited Bamyan, and asked that it be delivered to Ismail Khan, Minister of Water and Energy, as a sarcastic 'thank you' for his services. Giving small lanterns to officials who visit Bamyan has since become a repeated action for civil society members. The activists then decided they would seek a larger audience. They created another large lantern statue and delivered it to the US Embassy in Kabul, with a letter asking that it be sent to President Barack Obama. The activists told me they wanted to send the lantern so that they could 'light the way' for Obama to improve his policies in Afghanistan. It would, they said, 'illuminate' better policies for Afghanistan, policies that would treat minorities more fairly, as much of what the United States was doing was seen as well-intentioned, but misguided.[25] The lantern was, of course, never given to Obama. The activists who sent the lantern believe that Karzai blocked the movement, and he is responsible for hiding the truth about the situation of the Hazaras from the United States, one more way of taking part in a continuation of centuries of social exclusion, they say. Today, this second lantern is on display at a restaurant in Kabul. The owner of the restaurant, a woman, donates proceeds to programmes for drug addicts.

Activists say that the lantern for them became a symbol of democracy, in a land where democracy does not work. The lantern was not delivered, they say, the light was extinguished, and they have not been given their full voice in the corrupted democratic process. The original lantern still stands in Bamyan, a now permanent-seeming aspect of the landscape, and Hazaras still congregate around it in protest. For some, it continues to stand mainly for electricity. For others, it takes on different meaning. Some see it as a reminder that through illumination of the mind through education Hazaras can succeed. Some see in it the danger that oil lamps cause, and a reason to continue to fight for electricity. For those who installed it, it stands for hope and broken promises. When international intervention in Afghanistan began, Hazaras believed they might have a chance to live equally with other Afghans. They then saw the funnelling of development projects to areas gripped by insurgency. They tried to gain attention with the lantern, but in the end these attempts did not lead to significant improvements. In some ways, the hopes for the lantern were extinguished, as Markaz Bamyan struggles with development. In other ways, however, the lantern, and the lack of electricity it represents, remains a rallying point around which Bamyan activists gather and continue to try to fight against all sorts of perceived injustices. In fact, the lantern, a permanent part of the landscape, serves all these purposes. Initially it symbolized Bamyan's lack of electricity, and it has never lost that meaning. But other layers of multiple meanings are laid upon it as it serves as both a possibility for hope for the future and a reminder of a history of social exclusion.

Notes

1. A Facebook post of an ethnic Hazara civil society activist announcing the start of a hunger strike by civil society members to protest Hazara inequality in Afghanistan.
2. The lantern, according to local civil society activists, was installed in 2010 in a protest led by several lead civil society activists in Bamyan. It was intended to bring attention to problems of electricity specifically and, more generally, to the underdevelopment experienced in Hazara areas.
3. In Dari, the phrase *dar tariki negoh kardan* has a similar connotation to the meaning of the phrase in English.
4. Currently, there are no reliable state-provided figures that can be used to determine percentages based on ethnicity in Afghanistan. A census was carried out in 1979, before 30 years of war and upheaval changed the face of society, with millions both externally and internally displaced, as well as millions killed. A census was carried out in 2013 that intentionally avoided questions relating to ethnicity and mother tongue, so as not to upset the balance of power currently in the government. For Hazaras, who believe they are undercounted, this decision reinforces the belief they are intentionally marginalized by the government. For this reason, scholars must rely on other sources, which are not always in accordance. For instance, see *The CIA World Factbook* (https://www.cia.gov/library/publications/the-world-factbook/geos/af.html; accessed on September 4, 2013); IndexMundi (http://www.indexmundi.com/afghanistan/demographics_profile.html; accessed on September 4, 2013); and Civil Military Fusion Centre (https://www.cimicweb.org/Documents/CFC%20AFG%20Social%20Well-being%20Archive/CFC_Afg_Monthly_Ethnic_Groups_Aug2011%20v1.pdf; accessed on September 4, 2013). After having spent extensive time in some of the largest Hazara enclaves in Afghanistan, Bamyan and West Kabul, the low figures of 9–10% seem unlikely.
5. See Library of Congress Country Studies (http://lcweb2.loc.gov/cgi-bin/query/r?frd/cstdy:@field (DOCID+af0037; accessed on September 4, 2013).
6. Appadurai defines ethnoscapes as people who migrate, move and travel for extended or short periods of time, so that which was once local becomes global in nature. Media, technology, commerce and other global forces connect those thus scattered, making them into a truly global force (Appadurai 1996, 306). Appadurai's concept is useful to understand the connections of Hazaras in Afghanistan, Pakistan, Iran, as well as asylum-seekers, refugees, students and others in Europe, Australia, India and the United States, individuals and micro-groups that make use of technology to interact with and influence each other. In fact, the wide use of social media, such as Facebook referenced in the opening quote above, is made use of by these widely dispersed individuals so that they still maintain a feeling of being part of the same group, of taking part in politics and ethnic and cultural developments. Hazaras nearby in Afghanistan and far away in Europe or elsewhere made certain their voices were heard upon any important event: elections, protests, and so on.

7. This autonomy was actually dependent upon locality. Areas closer to Kabul, including Bamyan, did offer some sort of tribute to Kabul, but involvement in day-to-day affairs seems to have been minimal.
8. These terms are used somewhat interchangeably to refer to tribal leadership positions.
9. Since the formation of the most recent government under Karzai, a second Hazara majority province, Daikundi, was established from part of Uruzgan province. Hazaras also hope that the Hazara majority areas of Ghazni might be established as a separate province, but this has yet to materialize.
10. With no reliable census or statistics concerning ethnicity available in Afghanistan, it is difficult to provide hard data to support these claims. However, it is clear, when spending time in Afghanistan, that Hazaras do value education as a way to improve their situation, and that there are fewer restrictions against children going to school because of insurgency, the necessity to seclude girls, and so on (e.g. Oppel 2010).
11. While many Hazaras in more rural areas, and many students, might not be able to watch such a game, enough people did have solar or generator electricity to power a television for several hours in the evening. Watching would often be done in a group setting. Hassan was, hence, not excluded from the experience of watching the game, but was reminded that he did not, in fact, feel a part of the Afghan nation when outside celebrating on a darkened street due to the lack of electrical development in Bamyan. Hassan imagined other Afghans in other regions celebrating with electricity.
12. Some Hazaras, especially those from the city of Quetta in Pakistan, take pride in a belief in Mongol ancestry. Many in Bamyan, particularly in rural areas, do not have a problem with the idea that they are descended from Mongols. In Markaz Bamyan, however, it is becoming more coming for people to reject this facet of their identity and to link themselves to civilizations that were in the region before than Mongols.
13. While in other parts of the world development may be focused on rural areas, as they have been determined to be the most vulnerable areas, this is not the case in Bamyan, nor in much of Afghanistan. Projects are often implemented in more secure areas, and rural areas are often more prone to insurgent activities. Additionally, Markaz Bamyan actually seems quite rural from the point of view of planners in Kabul. It is not a town, but simply a bazaar surrounded by several villages. As there are few good roads, travel to more remote areas that might also be deemed needy is difficult. Working in Bamyan, it is very clear most development activities are centred around Markaz and nearby villages.
14. The veracity of these claims is not verified and surely not consistent. I know from experience in Nangarhar, and in Jalalabad, the provincial capital, that there is some access to state-powered electricity provided by a Russian-built dam. The dam is in need of repairs, however, and electricity for most citizens is just a few hours a day. Those with more money can pay for what is termed '24 hour electricity', but this is also likely to go out for long periods of time, despite its name.
15. This phenomenon has also been discussed via private correspondence with Thomas Barfield.
16. These figures do not take into account the aid activities of PRTs, or provincial reconstruction teams, which further complicate the situation. Most provinces or grouping of several provinces were home to a PRT which was run by whichever country from among the coalition forces that had been put in charge militarily of that geographical location. Each PRT could choose to spend on resources on development projects as it saw fit, with no unifying guidelines. For an understanding of PRT spending on development, see Waldman (2008, 14).
17. This, of course, does not take into account possible intra-provincial discrepancies, which might lead to fewer funds for Hazara districts within provinces. Such questions were out of the scope of this paper to answer.
18. While many provincial centres do have better access to electricity than Bamyan, many also suffer similar problems, although perhaps at different scales.
19. This section does not intend to document every project planned, attempted or failed in Bamyan. Rather, it highlights those projects that my informants were the most aware of.
20. A New Zealand-based NGO was planning a large solar energy project when I left the field. Reports from my informants after my departure stated that the project was working, but that the electricity provided was extremely weak.
21. Personal correspondence with a USAID representative, July 2011.
22. See Kraudzun (2014, in this issue) for problems of solar-panel use in Tajikistan.
23. A Wikileaks document indicates that the Tupchi dam project was discussed by PRT officials with locals in 2007; however, there is no evidence that these discussions ever lead to action: http://wikileaks.org/afg/event/2007/07/AFG20070709n859.html (accessed on September 10, 2013).
24. Interestingly, according to a plaque on the lantern, the improvements to the square were funded in part by the Agha Khan Foundation. Informants all related the establishment of the lantern to civil society activists though, and not to the foundation.

25. Hazara activists often maintain that many of the advisers to the US Embassy and other US development workers in Afghanistan are Pashtuns, and that these Pashtuns mislead the Americans into carrying out projects that discriminate against Hazaras.

References

Appadurai, A. 1996. *Modernity at Large: Cultural Dimensions of Globalization*. Minneapolis: University of Minnesota Press.

Bacon, E. 1951. "The Inquiry into the History of the Hazara Mongols of Afghanistan." *Southwestern Journal of Anthropology* 7 (3): 230–247.

'Bamyan Electricity to be Met by Solar Energy'. October 14, 2012. *Bakhtar News*. Accessed September 20, 2013. http://www.bakhtarnews.com.af/eng/business/item/4472-bamyan-electricity-to-be-met-from-solar-energy.html.

Barfield, T. 2010. *Afghanistan: A Cultural and Political History*. Princeton: Princeton University Press.

Canfield, R. 1973. "The Ecology of Rural Ethnic Groups and the Spatial Dimensions of Power." *American Anthropologist* 75 (5): 1511–1528.

Dalrymple, W. 2013. "Mes Aynak: Afghanistan's Buddhist Buried Treasure Faces Destruction." *The Guardian*. Accessed September 20, 2013. http://www.theguardian.com/books/2013/may/31/mes-aynak-afghanistan-buddhist-treasure

Féaux de la Croix, J. 2011. "Moving Metaphors We Live By: Water and Flow in the Social Sciences and Around Hydroelectric Dams in Kyrgyzstan." *Central Asian Survey* 30 (3–4): 487–502.

Feld, S., and K. Basso, eds. 1996. *Senses of Place*. Santa Fe: School of American Research Press.

Ferdinand, K. 1962. "Nomad Expansion and Commerce in Central Afghanistan." *Folk* 4: 123–159.

Ghafari, H. July 14, 2011. "Electric Project Launched in Bamyan." *The Afghanistan Express Daily*. Accessed September 20, 2013. http://www.pajhwok.com/en/2011/07/14/electric-project-launched-bamyan

Harpviken, K. B. 1998. "The Hazara of Afghanistan: The Thorny Path Towards Political Unity, 1978–1992." In *Post Soviet Central Asia*, edited by T. Atabaki and J. O'Kane, 177–292. London: Taurus Academic Studies.

Ibrahimi, N. 2012. "Shift and Drift in Hazara Ethnic Consciousness: The Impact of Conflict and Migration." *Crossroads Asia Working Paper 5*.

Ibrahimi, N. 2009. "Divide and Rule: State Penetration in Hazarajat (Afghanistan) From the Monarchy to the Taliban." *Working Paper 42: Development as State Making*. London: Crisis States Research Centre.

Karimi, M. A. 2011. "'The West Side Story': Urban Communication and the Social Exclusion of the Hazara People in West Kabul." University of Ottawa, unpublished MA thesis.

Kraudzun, T. 2014. "Bottom-up and Top-down Dynamics of the Energy Transformation in the Eastern Pamirs of Tajikistan's Gorno Badakhshan Region." *Central Asian Survey*. doi:10.1080/02634937.2014.987516

"Listening Project Field Visit Report Afghanistan". April–May 2009. *CDA Collaborative Learning Projects*. Accessed June 15, 2014. http://reliefweb.int/report/afghanistan/listening-project-field-visit-report-afghanistan

Mousavi, S. A. 1997. *The Hazaras of Afghanistan: An Historical, Cultural, and Political Study*. New York: St. Martin's Press.

Oppel, R. 2010. "Hazaras Hustle to Head of Class in Afghanistan." *New York Times*. http://www.nytimes.com/2010/01/04/world/asia/04hazaras.html?pagewanted=all&_r=0

Poladi, H. 1989. *The Hazaras*. Stockton: Mughal.

Reeves, M. 2011. "Introduction: Contested Trajectories and a Dynamic Approach to Place." *Central Asian Survey* 30 (3–4): 307–330.

"Regional Profile for Bamyan." n.d. UNDP Regional Rural Economic Regeneration Strategies (RR ERS). Accessed June 15, 2014. http://www.undp.org.af/publications/RRERS/Bamyan%20Provincial%20Profile.pdf.

Schetter, C. 2005. "Ethnoscapes, National Territorialisation, and the Afghan War." *Geopolitics* 10 (1): 50–75.

Smith, A. 1996. "Culture, Community, and Territory: The Politics of Ethnicity and Nationalism." *International Affairs* 72 (3): 445–458.

Stewart, K. C. 1996. "An Occupied Place." In *Senses of Place*, edited by Stephan Feld and Keith Basso, 137–65. Santa Fe: School of American Research Press.

Waldman, M. 2008. "Falling Short: Aid Effectiveness in Afghanistan." ACBAR Advocacy Series.

Kyrgyzstan's dark ages: framing and the 2010 hydroelectric revolution

Amanda E. Wooden

Environmental Studies Program, Bucknell University, Lewisburg, PA, USA

Prior to the 2010 overthrow of Kyrgyzstan's government, there were tangible signs of popular dissatisfaction with the ruling Bakiev regime. Beginning in spring 2008, electricity shortages and forced restrictions became a daily reminder of the government's ineptitude, corruption and regional vulnerability. This article reports the results of a survey and interviews conducted in 2009–10. The results reveal how popular perceptions of energy and water supply shaped the average Kyrgyzstani's frustration with the ruling regime in the year before the revolution. The paper explores how the Bakiev administration attempted to frame the electricity crisis in nationalistic and naturalized ways, and how this framing only partly resonated and created mismatch with daily lived experiences and widespread suspicions of corruption in the hydroenergy sector. Ultimately, this mismatched framing generated collective emotions of shame and blame, creating the context for revolution.

Context for revolution

When people are dissatisfied with public service provision – water, electricity, public transport – price increases or privatization, this can spark outright contestation. Contemporary examples include Bangladesh in 2008, Brazil in 2013, Ecuador in 2003, Haiti in 2008, Madagascar in 2008, Peru in 2000 and Tunisia in 2011. Recent research identifies food prices as the most important trigger of mass protests and revolution (Barrett and Bellemare 2011; Bellemare 2011; Lagi, Bertrand, and Bar-Yam 2011; Maystadt, Tan, and Breisinger 2014). In Kyrgyzstan, much of the population associated their everyday hardships with President Bakiev's corrupt and 'unpatriotic' practices in the hydroenergy sector. Approximately 90% of energy produced in Kyrgyzstan is hydroelectric – 10.9 billion kilowatt-hours (kWh) in 2009, which is equivalent to the combined production of the Niagara Power Plant, Hoover and Glen Canyon dams – and 97% of hydroelectric capacity is from Toktogul dam and the Naryn River cascade.[1] Despite the country's status as – on average – water wealthy, there were water deficits in the Toktogul Reservoir leading to an electricity shortage and daily blackouts during winter 2008–09, and in early 2010 the government raised electricity and water tariffs as well as privatized key state hydroenergy distribution companies. 'What role did the energy situation play in the April events?' I asked Felix Kulov, opposition politician and former high-ranking member of the Bakiev government, in July 2010. He answered:

> Tariff politics – without an increase in tariffs, it was not possible. Lenin had a saying: 'Communism is Soviet power plus the electrification of the entire country. […] When the light was turned off […] people became angry. […] People believe it [electricity] is their property, and it must not be sold.'

The ouster of President Bakiev was a hydroelectric revolution.

Several themes emerged from my research that revealed the texture of this revolutionary moment: water conceived of as power, official crisis framing, relative deprivation, geographies of energy, poverty and blame attribution. There are two main findings: first, the Bakiev administration failed to frame the energy crisis in a way that was popularly credible and therefore it backfired and the government was blamed by a large enough portion of the population to instigate political action. Second, the nationalistic and environmental framing of the crisis which the Bakiev administration ineffectively used produced a lasting echo in Kyrgyzstan's politics. Since the 2010 revolution, subsequent administrations have baulked at raising tariffs while committing to attracting investments in the sector and developing the power grid and hydroelectricity capacity. In 2014, President Atambayev's government faces another water deficit year in the midst of gas cut-offs from Uzbekistan. The likely outcome will again be electricity shortage and possible power cuts during fall and winter 2014–15.

The main purpose of this article is to present some average Kyrgyzstan citizens' perspectives about hydroelectricity resources before 2010, specifically how a sense of nationalism with environmental content, sometimes referred to as resource or eco-nationalism (Dawson 1996; Schwartz 2006) – in contest with Bakiev's naturalistic nationalist (Hamilton 2002) discourse – led people into the streets and ultimately forced Bakiev out of the White House. In order to explore the role of contestations and blame over hydropower management in the 2010 events, I build on my previous work (Wooden 2013) to argue that mass discontent has a clear influence on political outcomes and elite behaviours. It is not enough to understand policy choices, organization of discontent and elite defection. We also must dig into public discourse, beliefs and expectations in order to understand revolutionary political change. I draw upon the work of three authors: Heathershaw (2007) who calls for a more complicated social–political view of revolution in the post-Soviet space; Laruelle (2012) who explores the central role of nationalistic discourses in Kyrgyzstan post-2005; and Mehta (2010, esp. p. 373) who applies a political ecology approach to examine contested meanings of water scarcity and how scarcity is politically created through competing claims.[2] An imperilled sovereignty theme and ethnonationalist 'differing legitimacy' became key components of public discourse in the Bakiev era (Laruelle 2012; Megoran 2012). Bakiev's 'more affirmed Kyrgyz nationalism' (Matveeva 2009, 2010; Laruelle 2012, 42) created a new mobilizing politics at a time of economic upheaval and uncertainty. Bakiev's political legitimacy was also 'borne of the streets' which 'left a non-negligible influence on the idea that popular mobilization is a driver of political change' (Laruelle 2012, 42).

Part of this nationalistic discourse was applied to nature – particularly water resources and the Naryn River – in discussions of how to solve the hydropower crisis. A national environmental ideology (Short 1991) captures environmental 'myths mobilized in the course of state formation and nation-building' (xvi). Nature is instrumentalized symbolically or practically to support an idea of the nation-state. This can be expressed in multiple ways, such as a nation's or a group's 'closeness to nature' or alternatively as a reaction to nature, often considered an 'enemy' of the nation to be controlled. The Bakiev regime promoted environmental myths about the Naryn River, Toktogul Dam and Kambar-Ata Dam projects, in particular by using the language of an enemy creating problems – parallel to and in cahoots with neighbouring countries – in need of taming and control.

Nationalist politics should be seen as at least a bidirectional relationship – and quite often a multinational, multiscalar process – developed between elites and popular imaginings and identities. It is not only top-down, elite constructed as often represented in nationalism scholarship (Smith 2009). We should explore

> how popular beliefs, memories and cultures have influenced the views and actions of the elites as they first propose and then promote the idea of the nation; and conversely, how far the various ideas and

proposals of nationalist elites have struck a chord among the different strata of the designated populations whom they seek to mobilize and empower. (Smith 2009, p. 19)

Thus, I dissect the 'naturalistic nationalism' (Hamilton 2002) discourse used by the Bakiev administration about regional waterways, power generation and the control of nature – such as dam construction – as symbols of state power. This nationalistic discourse about nature raised emotive popular expectations about government solutions to everyday problems.

Research methods

A gap between the lived experiences of average people and the understanding of those experiences by the wealthy elite and the country's leadership became clear to me as a resident in Osh, Kyrgyzstan, in 2006. I set out to evaluate systematically how nature, and water more specifically, was understood by talking to a cross-section of the general population, elites and experts. By the time I was preparing to conduct this study in spring 2009, the energy crisis became a daily concern and frustration. It became the central political topic and part of my study.

In March–April 2009, I oversaw the implementation of a nationwide, random-sample survey of 1500 people in Kyrgyzstan.[3] From 2009 to 2010, I also conducted approximately 80 interviews with key informants across six stakeholder groups in all seven *oblast*s.[4] In addition to the survey and interview data, I conducted a content analysis of environmental protest coverage in 13 news sources.[5] In this article, I interpret the survey, interviews and news coverage using a mixed-methods, discursive approach. This is not a deductive research project, because generating and testing hypotheses after the revolution would be inappropriate, post-hoc analysis. Rather, the data collected before the revolution revealed patterns of anger and blame, and I investigated these patterns more deeply in interviews conducted afterwards. Therefore, this is an inductive study, focusing on presenting and interpreting public sentiments about the Bakiev regime and hydroelectricity.

I will first outline public policy choices in the months preceding President Bakiev's ouster, what happened on the day Bakiev was run out of office, and social science insights into causation. I then discuss how people experienced the 'dark ages' and the ways the Bakiev administration sought to frame this period. Finally, I turn to evaluate how people responded to official framing of the crisis (attempts to shape public opinion), which frames resonated and which did not, and how the mismatch between official representations of nature and the direction of blame led to revolution.

The final months – selling electricity and privatization policies

Three policy choices combined with the blackouts to create serious public backlash about hydro-energy, especially when put into the context of public expectations. First, survey participants suspected that the Bakiev administration quietly produced excess electricity in 2007 and sold it to neighbouring countries, thus releasing extra water leading to low reservoirs levels the following year. Some identify Kazakhstan as the purchaser of the electricity, some say Uzbekistan, but it is clear that Kyrgyzstan's government did sell 1 billion kWh in 2007 above the typical annual amount (AKIpress 2010a; ICG 2010). As it turns out, that year the market price of electricity rose considerably, ostensibly making this sale profitable. However, officials recorded these unannounced electricity sales at below-market prices, and rumours persist that they pocketed the difference between the recorded and actual prices. An extremely cold winter in 2007 which taxed the energy grid and low precipitation during spring and summer 2008 combined with the extra water release for electricity sales led to drastically low Toktogul Reservoir levels, sparking the crisis in 2008–09. In other words, this was not just a 'natural' drought or an event to be blamed on neighbouring countries' irrigation needs.

Secondly, on 1 January 2010, the government more than doubled tariffs for electricity, water and district heating for domestic users and increased prices by about 30% for businesses.[6] Analysts had for years commented on the need to increase tariffs to address infrastructural vulnerabilities and improve maintenance, and prices had been increased once. In early 2010 the Bakiev administration decided to pursue cost recovery more rapidly. However, pensions and subsidies for vulnerable populations, which were increased at the same time, were improperly distributed and did not compensate for the simultaneous suspension of other subsidies (Slay 2010). The discount for electricity in mountainous places – such as for Naryn *oblast* – was ended at the same time the doubled tariffs went into effect. There was a resounding public outcry about the net effect of the electricity payments changes, in light of perceptions that members of the regime had benefitted from selling electricity and recent nationwide energy deprivation (Osmonalieva 2009).

Third, in February 2010, the administration privatized two key state regional distribution companies – Severelektro JSC and Vostokelektro – which were sold to Chakan GES, headed by an associate of Maxim Bakiev. Severelektro was sold for US\$3 million, despite being valued for 45 times that amount (Osmonalieva 2009). Purportedly consulting in this privatization process was the company MGN Asset Management, run by Eugene Gourevitch who was also a close associate of Maxim Bakiev. The '"gut-level belief" that the President's son had advantageously sold these companies to himself had an explosive effect. […] People finally emerged from apathy and passive criticism' (International Crisis Group (ICG) 2010, 9). Protests in Naryn and Talas over the energy crisis, corruption and tariffs resulted after the government engaged in electricity privatization (RFERL 2010).

The April uprising: 'They turned off the lights'

On 6 April 2010 Kyrgyzstan's security[7] services arrested most opposition leaders and held them in prison overnight in the capital, Bishkek. Protesters captured the Talas *oblast* (province) administrative building, held the governor and purportedly beat the Minister of the Interior, Moldomusa Kongantiev. As the demonstrations grew and moved to Bishkek on the morning of 7 April, riot police and snipers mobilized to protect the main government building.[8] After lunch, approximately 1300 people moved from Almatinskaya Street to Ala-Too Square across from the White House. When troops used live ammunition against the protestors, some of whom were armed, news spread by cell phone, mobilizing more to join – totalling around 5000 – and fight the police. Approximately 85 people were killed. Facing enraged crowds and failing military support, President Kurmanbek Bakiev fled to his hometown of Teiit in Jalalabad province. He remained in southern Kyrgyzstan threatening civil war, but on 15 April fled to Belarus. Seemingly overnight, Kyrgyzstan had its second revolution in five years.

In 2005 the so-called 'Tulip Revolution' took place when President Askar Akaev fled from protesting crowds. Scholars have convincingly argued that this was not a popular revolt, but rather a putsch orchestrated by regional elites, some of whom lost seats in parliament in fraudulent elections (Cummings and Ryabkov 2008; Hale 2006; McGlinchey 2011; Radnitz 2006, 2010; Tudoroiu 2007). It may also have been influenced by the example of other revolutions in the post-Soviet space (Beissinger 2007).

However in April 2010, although opposition politicians quickly scrambled to create an interim government and stabilize the situation – following rioting and looting when the president left Bishkek – opposition leaders appeared not to have been in control of the protests. In March 2009, the year before the uprising, opposition leaders organized small-scale protests, corralled by

Bakiev-era crowd-control laws, with speeches demanding the removal of energy sector officials and using 'Energy Barons to Answer!' and 'For Kyrgyzstan: Peace, Order, and Light!' slogans. Roza Otunbaeva – who became the post-revolution interim president – gave an early 2010 speech about the energy crisis in the Jogorku Kenesh. Other opposition politicians made statements critical of the tariff increases, notably Bakyt Beshimov and Omurbek Tekebaev (Osmonov 2009). Opposition leaders were speaking to popular concerns about the energy crisis. Kyrgyzstanis did not need their everyday hardships to be translated by elites to know they existed; instead, opposition politicians smartly reacted to those concerns. There was no opposition politician powerful enough to mobilize people and Bakiev's regime had become repressive enough to silence public dissent; Baisalov was in exile, Kulov withdrew from politics and was working on hydroelectricity issues, Atambayev roundly lost the July 2009 presidential election which was not a triggering event as is often the case (Baev 2011; Beissinger 2007; Kulov 2008; Kuntz and Thompson 2009). Savvy opposition leaders went to places like Naryn where public attitudes were 'heating up' after tariff increases (Ferghana.ru 2010).[9]

The uprising had the hallmarks of a mass or loosely coordinated popular mobilization, not a controlled coup. The alternative explanation of Russian government manipulation – which the International Crisis Group (ICG) (2010, 11) called only a belief 'among the country's elite' – is not supported by evidence. The Russian media pressure and imposition of excise tax on fuel came after protests began, although the absence of promised Russian Kambar-Ata-1 Dam construction funds did further delegitimize Bakiev regarding hydroenergy solutions. The triggering event was not a falsified election or other political opportunity. Protesters used no coordinated symbol or slogan to emblemize what drove this political discontent. Four years hence this political event remains unnamed and under-analysed by political scientists. This is intriguing in contrast to how the 2005 revolution has been a central focus of this literature.

Theories of organized, elite-led overthrow do not fit the 2010 events well. Kubicek (2011, 120) argues that the 'central lesson from events in Kyrgyzstan is preventing a breakdown in the ruling political machine', but goes on to say, '[d]isaffection with Bakieyev boiled over in April 2010 when the government announced an increase in fuel prices' (116). Arguments about the causes of revolutionary political change based on political scrambling afterwards require more evidence about causation and the political change process. A disorganized, divided and imprisoned opposition would not have the support of thousands to rally against a government violently suppressing protests if those people did not have a grievance or feel grieved ('moral shock'; Jasper 1998). They needed to be aggrieved to mobilize; it was a necessary condition. Felix Kulov flatly rejected any planning of the April turnover: 'if there were leaders they would have suspected snipers to be at the White House and would not have gone there'.[10]

Several commentators identified the 2010 revolution, in contrast to 2005, as a popular uprising (Collins 2011; ICG 2010; Temirkulov 2010). 'The events of 2010 represent an organic and successful attempt by Kyrgyzstan's political and civil society to overthrow a dictatorship […]' (Collins 2011, 151). Temirkulov (2010, 597–598) notes that although the causes of the 2005 and 2010 revolutions are similar, 2010 was a mass, not elite, mobilization and 'the mechanisms of mass mobilization however, differed considerably'. Gullette (2010a, 90) contrasts the two turnovers, saying that during April 2010, 'public anger quickly resulted in a desperate attempt to overthrow the government […]' The ICG (2010, 9) refers to the 6–7 April protests as 'largely self-led, or at best under the improvised control of junior opposition leaders. […] Many people were motivated by pent-up anger'.

Insights from sociologists and anthropologists help explain why anger mattered so much. Reeves (2010, 4) argues that both absolute poverty – worsened by the electricity rate hikes – and inequality reaching 'colossal proportions […] brought people out to demonstrate'. Relative deprivation is the idea that individuals perceive a gap between their expectations and what they or others have (Davies 1962; Gurr 1970, 13); those deprived are more likely to take political action (Brush 1996). Katz (2007) uses political relative deprivation theory to explain the 2005 revolutionary sentiment, finding that Kyrgyzstanis were the most likely in the region to perceive temporal disparity because of the country's initial improvements in political freedom. In 2007, Junisbai (2010, 1697) conducted an Inequality Survey in Kazakhstan and Kyrgyzstan and found that 'In Kyrgyzstan, due to government's failure to achieve sustained economic growth, a perceived lack of opportunity and hopelessness regarding the country's economic prospects are widespread'. From a group psychology perspective, de la Sablonnière et al. (2010) use collective relative deprivation theory to analyse a perception of change in conditions among ethnic Kyrgyz students in Bishkek prior to the 2010 'uprising' and find evidence of temporal relative deprivation perceptions, particularly frustration with weakening political influence.

Observers highlight three key structural factors as the most important proximate causes of the 2010 uprising: economic upheaval, mass deprivation and the hydroenergy crisis (Gullette 2010a, 2010b; Reeves 2010; Temirkulov 2010). As a likely determinative cause most analysts mentioned the Bakiev regime's mishandling of hydroenergy (e.g. Trautman 2010; Wood 2010). 'That this revolt was triggered in part by utility shortages is not incidental. The shortages are extreme, and a constant source of irritation to all but the wealthiest citizens' (Trautman 2010). Kyrgyzstan experienced a period of water shortage and subsequent electricity cuts in 2008–09, popularly referred to as 'the dark ages'.[11] Since 2007, Bakiev had become increasingly authoritarian: privatization and increased prices in telecommunications, silencing critical press, corralling the opposition (literally, by limiting the public spaces available for protest), and a crackdown on southern Uzbek leaders (Judah 2009; Toktonaliev 2009). A compound economic crisis affected the country in 2007–10: combined with the water–energy crisis were the 2008–09 Russian financial crisis, global food price spikes and global financial crisis (Dhur 2009). Public anger with the Bakiev administration grew with suspicions of extensive corruption and nepotism, most evident in the energy sector.[12] In the first few months of 2010, protests primarily about electricity outages and price hikes began in February outside the capital. It is most notable that protests began in northern energy-insecure cities Naryn and Talas and primarily about power outages the previous year and the price hikes that followed.

The energy sector and water in Kyrgyzstan: dark age experiences, 2008–09

In order to understand better why people in Naryn, Talas, and elsewhere were frustrated enough to protest about electricity, it is important to step back and look at survey evidence and interview narratives about what the 'dark age' experience was like the year prior to the revolution. The first question I asked survey participants (open-ended) in spring 2009 was: 'What is the single most serious problem that Kyrgyzstan faces right now?' Economic concerns came first for 31% of survey participants, followed closely by the electricity crisis for 28%. A large majority of people in every one of the seven provinces surveyed and interviewed in 2009 identified water issues – both water supply and quality issues – as the 'most important environmental problem[s]' they faced (Wooden 2013). Several interview participants said directly that energy – as experienced everyday – is equated with water in Kyrgyzstan. In talking about nature, environmental problems, environmental awareness and the 'resource wealth' of Kyrgyzstan, water and hydroenergy were most often discussed.

The hydroelectricity crisis was a central concern in public discussions as well, as evidenced by the types of news stories that research participants reported reading, hearing or seeing in 2008–09; 89% read, heard or saw news about Kyrgyzstan's energy situation, and 81.3% read, heard or saw news about Kyrgyzstan's water resource issues (Table 1).

Table 1. Comparing energy, water and environmental news consumption

	Specifically about Kyrgyzstan's energy issues	Specifically about Kyrgyzstan's water issues	General environmental issues
Have you read, heard, or seen news about __ in the last year? ($n = 1500$)	89	81.3	55.6

Note: n = number of participants responding to that question.

This compares with 55.6% who were exposed to general environmental stories. From my content analysis of news stories about 'environmental protest' in 13 news sources about Kyrgyzstan from 1 December 2003 to 1 December 2007, water resource issues are a dominant theme. The two most common issues covered for all sources were water and gold, with stories about hydropower and Issyk-Kul figuring prominently (Wooden 2013).

Together with this broad linkage of key 'resource problems', my study participants talked about water in romantic, historical, territorial and Kyrgyz identity terms. Water for energy is conceived differently in terms of water reservoirs and water politics than it is in terms of celebrated places connected to moving water, such as *mazârs* (holy pilgrimage sites) and *jailoos* (summer pastures) (Féaux de la Croix 2011). Water is valued not just as a resource to be used, but is also expressed by some in romanticized historical ways, where water was purportedly properly and respectfully used in a nomadic lifestyle and central to spiritual practices.

Around the country, daily 8–12-hour cuts in power began in earnest during the winter of 2008–09. One year prior to the revolution that would unseat President Bakiev, 71.4% of the people I surveyed – an overwhelming majority – answered that electricity shortages had a serious impact in the places where they lived over the previous year (Table 2).

People across different wage brackets expressed these experiences, but proportionally more poor people noted these problems than wealthier individuals. This was higher than the still sizeable 56.4% who reported suffering from water shortages and the 14.7% affected by natural gas shortages (concentrated in urban areas). A local official in Sumsar, Jalalabad province told me: 'All winter we sat here without power, you know about this. There were rolling blackouts. They were forced.'[13]

Respondents linked the blackouts to water mismanagement. Gulmira Temirbekova, a nongovernmental organization (NGO) leader in Talas town, spoke to me about power outage implications for water availability.

Table 2. 2008–09 Reporting electricity, water, and natural gas shortages and shutoffs

	Electricity shortages or shutoffs have had a serious impact over the last year in the place where I live	Water shortages or shutoffs have had a serious impact over the last year in the place where I live	Natural gas shortages or shutoffs have had a serious impact over the last year in the place where I live
Percentage who answered 'yes' (total $n = 1500$)	71.4	56.4	14.7

Note: n = number of participants responding.

> Around the city there is also sometimes no water. […] There are these transformers [pumps], run by the water utility. […] When they are turned off, the water drains out automatically. When the power is turned on, it takes an hour and a half to fill. Sometimes it is just starting to fill up and the power is turned off again. It doesn't have enough time to collect the water.

A number of my research participants complained about the international development project, *Taza Suu* (Clean Water) funded by the Asian Development Bank, Department for International Development (DFID UK) and the World Bank, which in some rural locales utilized electric pumps to deliver well water. During an electricity crisis, electric pumps clearly cannot function. In the winter, cutting off electricity to pumps can lead to frozen and burst pipes, elongating water cut-offs during repairs and risking sewage overflow.

Relative impacts and the distribution of anger

While the majority of people in every province experienced electricity blackouts, the relative impacts were diverse and help explain where animosity was higher. Rural residents often experience and are accustomed to service disruption in non-crisis years and also are more likely to have alternative sources of energy – coal fire or dung stoves – to heat their homes. Urban dwellers in apartment buildings do not have the option to switch to these sources of fuel.

Even in urban places where natural gas for cooking and heating became an alternative, gas prices skyrocketed and shutoffs occurred during this time period, making this source unaffordable and unavailable. Nurmamat Saparbaev, a forestry specialist advising on local governance and collaborative forest management for the KIRFOR programme[14] in Jalalabad, discussed how the interaction between gas and electricity shutoffs created no alternative for heating apartments:

> You know, last year was so cold. My one-year-old granddaughter lives in our house. […] How could they turn off the electricity in homes, where it is also minus 25 [Celsius degrees below zero] and there are small children? […] This year, too, there were [serious power outages]. I went to the RES, the district power station. […] I said, we live in a three-storey building. About 120 families live there. If you disconnect [us], there are small children from one month to three years who will freeze. How can you do this? But still they cut [the electricity] off. And then I went and said, soon I will come with all these kids, your office is warm, you are going to feed them here, until we have electricity on. Since that time, they have not cut off the electricity. So was there a problem or not?[15]

Despite these obvious difficulties, in the warmer parts of the south such as Osh, wintertime loss of electricity did not have the same impact as it did for those living in colder, highland areas. Electricity distribution problems and the fiscal vulnerability of the extremely poor is concentrated in the south while arguably there is a greater need for social protection in the form of heat in northern Kyrgyzstan where the bulk of the energy-insecure live. The bulk of electricity need – both domestic and commercial – is in the north; 70% of the demand arises here (Zozulinsky 2010), however, government energy subsidies (e.g., for the purchase of coal and electricity payments for pensioners, state workers and the poor) and other offsetting primary costs subsidies were both inadequate and not concentrated in the north.

> Apparently only 16% of poor family monthly benefit recipients in April 2010 were in Kyrgyzstan's northern regions. […] Small wonder then, that the April 2010 protests over higher energy tariffs that unseated the Bakiyev government were centered in northern regions like Talas and Naryn. (Slay 2010, 29)

Edil Baisalov – a former Social Democratic Party of Kyrgyzstan (SDPK) party member in exile during the revolution, who returned to serve as President Otunbaeva's interim chief of staff – talked about his parents' and friends' frustration in Naryn city. 'It's a heroic act of living in Naryn. […] But without electricity? [T]hat makes no sense.'[16] In all parts of the country, the poorest in both urban and rural areas had inadequate access to alternatives. For example, in rural areas people without property and livestock, the least expensive alternative – dung – was not an option (USAID 2008).

In my survey 60% reported using less water than usual in the last year and 66% reported using less electricity, most in addition to the forced reductions. Participants increased their use of firewood and dung (see the Gassmann and Tsukada article on Kyrgyzstan, and Kraudzun on Tajikistan in this volume), or used solar panels and generators purchased in China, while others installed coal stoves, leading to unfortunate instances of carbon monoxide poisoning and a few deaths (UNOCHA 2009).[17] Along Lake Issyk-Kul, people worried about significant deforestation that resulted from the electricity crisis. Yuri Nagorniy, a businessman in the tourism sector in Issyk-Kul province:

> Today the very first problem [for the average citizen] is energy supply […] it affects everyone very hard, it is a problem for the whole republic […] for small businesses it was completely bad. For example, you cook *pelmeni* [small dumplings], the refrigerator doesn't work, and that's it, you lose your product. The next time [you] will be afraid, and so the business dies.[18]

Resonant frames and blame

Both sociologists and political scientists problematized the assumed automatic relationship between grievances and political outcomes, as clearly not all grievances equally mobilize the discontented. It matters how a government responds to grievances (Gizelis and Wooden 2010). One indicator of this response is the discursive construction of scarcity and shortage, otherwise known as 'framing' (Iyengar 1987; Snow and Benford 1988; Snow et al. 1986). Shmueli (2008) discusses the importance for environmental studies of understanding how stakeholders' frames are elicited, the way frames simplify complexity, provide particular interpretations of events, and thus create realities. Buijs et al. (2011) combine Snow and Benford's (1988) focus on cultural resonance ('does the framing strike a responsive chord with those individuals for whom it is intended?') with ideas about the social representation of nature. At the time the survey was conducted in spring of 2009, the Kyrgyzstani government was engaged in a public relations campaign to frame the drought and neighbouring country demands as the key limitations on electricity generation. So first I examine the framing and representations of nature used in official discourse and then evaluate how these frames resonated with everyday experiences.

Blaming neighbouring countries for the crisis

One of the key discourses about hydropower in Kyrgyzstan is that the country is politically and economically dependent on its downstream neighbours. This situation is due to the breakdown of the Central Asia Power System (CAPS) bartering and regional water sharing agreements. This system collapse resulted in monetarization of energy but not water. Kyrgyzstan maintains the upstream storage reservoirs and delivery infrastructure on its territory – an exception is the Chui-Talas basin to which Kazakhstan contributes maintenance funds – and releases water downstream for irrigation in summertime, limiting its capability to produce hydroelectricity when most needed in the winter. Kyrgyzstan must purchase alternative sources of power – coal, oil, and natural gas – from its energy-wealthy neighbours when electricity shortages occur, negotiate an exchange of electricity in winter for water storage and release in the spring and summer. Otherwise, Kyrgyzstan must release more water for hydroelectricity production, which is what the government has done increasingly since the breakdown of CAPS over the last half decade. This puts Kyrgyzstan, a poorer country, generally at an economic disadvantage. The perceptions of dependency contribute to tensions over this poorly managed energy and water trade relationship.

In 2005, Adakhan Madumarov, a nationalist politician (Laruelle 2012) and leader of the political party Butun Kyrgyzstan (United Kyrgyzstan) joined other members of parliament in opposing ratification of a friendship treaty with neighbouring Kazakhstan over the issue of joint waterways use, including the Toktogul and Orto Tokoy Reservoirs (in the Naryn and Chui-Talas River basins, respectively). Madumarov stated, 'Water resources are an integral part of our natural wealth, just like our land, but the agreement states that we must coordinate our policies with Astana in the use of water resources. Why should we? Our water resources have no relation to Kazakhstan' (Saralaeva 2005). In May 2008, when Madumarov was Speaker of Parliament, he stated that Kyrgyzstan can provide water to neighbouring countries for irrigation if they provide gas and fuel oil at reasonable prices. This perspective became a central part of media and political discourse about the regional water–energy network.

On 28 April 2009, Bakiev gave a speech at the Meeting of Heads of the States-Founders of the International Fund for Saving the Aral Sea (IFAS) in Almaty, Kazakhstan, and voiced concern about an imbalanced regional water–energy relationship. He stated that Kyrgyzstani citizens suffered because of this imbalance and 'the difficulties to overcome low-water problems', asking downstream neighbours for financial assistance to address water delivery and electricity production problems (Bakiev 2009a). On 6 October 2009, the Minister of Foreign Affairs of the Kyrgyz Republic, Kadyrbek Sarbaev, gave a speech at the Carnegie Center in Washington, DC, reiterating this blame of neighbouring countries for the energy crisis.

As you know, the lack of long-term cooperation has resulted in 2008 electricity crisis in our country due to insufficient water supplies in the region's biggest reservoir, Toktogul, due to low precipitation and accumulation of sharply reduced inflows. We had to impose restrictions on electricity consumption for the population (Sarbaev 2009).

In these speeches, officials used the terms 'energy security', 'environmental security', 'drought' and 'low-water year' repeatedly. These phrases frame the issue as both natural and national, using defensive, foreign policy language and identifying the key elements as purely 'natural' and therefore beyond government control.

Nature's fault

A common national 'modernizing' response to flooding, water storage concerns and electricity production shortage is to build large hydroelectric dams and channel rivers, which symbolizes the nation-state's power over a wild, unpredictable river harnessed for citizens' benefit (Kaika 2006; Molle, Mollinga, and Wester 2009; Steinberg 1987; Swyngedouw 2009). The Bakiev regime sought to make the Kambar-Ata projects – 'Kambar-Ata the Saviour' – serve this nation-building purpose to overcome droughts and regional dependency (Kruglov 2007). To tackle energy insecurity and regional dependency, in 2009 President Bakiev signed an agreement with Russian leaders to relieve Kyrgyzstan's debt and fund the Kambar-Ata-1 and Naryn River cascade hydropower dam construction, seemingly in exchange for closing the US-led NATO airbase 'Manas' outside of Bishkek.

In many interviews and speeches, officials talked about the situation as a natural event – drought – in passive terms ('it happened to us'). President Bakiev explained the rationale for accepting Russian funding for the Kambar-Ata-1 hydropower station as follows: 'Last year was the peak of the low-water cycle in all of Central Asia, there arose a threat of reaching the "dead level" of the Toktogul reservoir […] a threat to the country's energy supply and energy security' (Bakiev 2009b).[19] However, there was public debate about expected and reported figures for Toktogul reservoir levels and to what extent this 'drought' was actually wholly 'natural' or also the consequence of extra water releases. '[C]ritics say it is not good enough to blame unusual natural conditions and thriftless consumers. […] There are persistent rumors that water has been released and sold on the quiet to neighboring states' (Mambetalieva 2008; also see PR.kg 2008).

The national security-regional dependency argument came into stark contradiction with the 'nature's fault' argument. During the energy crisis, Duishon Mamatkanov, Director of the Institute of Water and Irrigation at the National Academy of Sciences of the Kyrgyz Republic, said drought conditions in the Naryn River (which flows into the Toktogul reservoir) did not exist, highlighting the problems of water sector mismanagement creating the electricity crisis and contradicting reports by the Ministry of Industry, Energy and Fuel Resources that there was a drought (Esenalieva 2012; Gorbachev 2008; Yuldasheva 2008). However, Mamatkanov identified regional relationships as root cause of reduced power production, not the drought, and a belief that Kyrgyzstan should tax its neighbours.

Accommodations to, acceptance and rejection of frames

In order to understand the reception of the framing the Bakiev administration was using, I asked the question: 'If water shortages/shutoffs are a problem, do you think these are caused mostly by human behaviour/mismanagement (or) caused mostly by natural changes in the environment?' A small percentage – 6% of those who experienced water shutoffs – accepted that natural changes drove the shortages.[20] The largest percentage of survey participants, 34.4%, identified human behaviour or mismanagement as the primary cause, while 15.1% identified both natural changes and human behaviour/mismanagement.

Accepting nationalist framing

Another consideration is how people 'consumed' and articulated the nationalist frames that were used by the Bakiev regime about the regional water–energy relationship. I first asked 'Do you believe that hydroelectricity generation decisions in Kyrgyzstan depend on neighbouring countries' needs and interests?' to examine people's acceptance of the Kyrgyzstan watershed dependency idea. In response, 52.8% of my survey participants responded yes or yes, to some extent; 41.8% think they do not depend on neighbouring countries (Table 3).

Among the 53% who believe Kyrgyzstan is dependent on neighbouring countries for hydroelectricity decisions, 85.5% of them are concerned about this dependency to varying degrees.[21]

In response to the follow up question 'What do you think the Kyrgyz government should do about this situation?' approximately 19% of my survey participants (of the 687 people answering this question)[22] answered in ways that reflect some of the nationalist discourse used by Bakiev administration officials. These responses included expressions about: (1) pursuing the national interest first and foremost, regardless of regional commitments or regional ramifications, (2) the idea that the Kyrgyz government should not sell water or electricity to neighbouring countries, and generally (3) a wish for Kyrgyzstan not to be dependent on or make concessions to other countries. These comments fit into a nationalistic discourse about nature one year prior to the

Table 3. Hydroelectricity dependency framing acceptance and concern intensity

	Yes and yes, to some extent	No, do not depend
Do you believe that hydroelectricity generation decisions in Kyrgyzstan depend on neighbouring countries' needs and interests?		
Percentage (*n* = 1500)	71.4	56.4
If you believe that decisions in Kyrgyzstan depend on neighbouring countries' needs and interests, how concerned are you about this dependency?	Very concerned, concerned and fairly concerned	Not too concerned, not at all concerned
Percentage (*n* = 777)	85.5	11.4

Note: n = number of participants responding to that question.

revolution. Approximately one-fifth of my participants answering this question accepted the nationalist framing that the Bakiev administration used.

Among my key informants, several similarly expressed the same variety of nationalism. Even some people who were otherwise critical of the Bakiev administration were positive about Bakiev's April 2009 IFAS speech (as interviews were conducted in the months immediately following that event). One academic I spoke with in Jalalabad expressed his perspective on Kyrgyzstan's dependence on neighbouring countries for hydroelectricity development as follows:

> I'm not that concerned, just that it is not nice. We have, for example, with Uzbekistan, a lot of misunderstandings. [...] Because they accuse Kyrgyzstan, they say that we are to blame, that the Aral Sea has dried up due to the fact that we have constructed the Naryn [River] hydropower stations. We believe that they are guilty that all the water has gone to the cotton fields. This is a misunderstanding, I think, and of course I am concerned about that. It is soon becoming not just a concern, but [specific] anger toward people. Why do they shift their blame onto Kyrgyzstan when it is Uzbekistan that is 100% to blame?[23]

One NGO representative in Jalabad city said that international conflict had already began at the April 2009 Almaty meeting of presidents, and specifically referred to Bakiev's speech.

> At that time Bakiyev said, look, for the storage of water you have to pay. Karimov and Nazarbayev, they said no, we will not. [...] Why does Kyrgyzstan have to suffer all the time? For example, for this water reservoir [Andijan] we lost so many acres. [...] Since the water level has dropped, you can see how many hectares were cleared. And in Toktogul too. [...] Why do our people have to suffer? Because of the neighbors? Why do they not pay for it, do not compensate us?[24]

One NGO leader from Issyk-Kul province, otherwise critical of the ruling regime, referenced Bakiev's speech at the 2009 IFAS summit in response to what she described as demands by Kazakstani President Nursultan Nazarbaev for summertime and constant water delivery.

> Well then Bakiyev said, 'You do not think about the warming [...] our glaciers are melting [...] deforestation is happening. [...] You must in some way invest money or help us, to keep the water normal and flowing.' [...] They have to get used to us selling them water. [...] They sell us gas and we can't sell water? Then we should not give them water. How dearly does Uzbekistan charge us for gas? They sometimes even shut it off in the winter.[25]

She seemed to accept Bakiev's blame attribution to neighbouring countries for demanding to the impoverished, vulnerable Kyrgyzstan, 'Let us have water.'

Blame and revolution

In this context of concern about dependency and acceptance that international/neighbouring countries are to blame, we would expect that subsequent survey questions asking who is to blame might identify those international actors. However, the results reveal the ire was mostly directed at the Kyrgyzstani government. Among those concerned about this regional hydroelectricity dependency, my research participants blamed first the government of Kyrgyzstan (52%) and then specifically President Bakiev (21%) – rather than neighbouring countries' leaders – followed distantly by parliament, the Jogorku Kenesh (8.6%) and the economic situation (8.4%).[26] What is most interesting about this result is that a very low percentage of respondents who are concerned about dependency on neighbouring countries actually blame those neighbours for the situation; the majority of concerned survey participants blamed the Bakiev regime for the problem and dependency. So although half of the attribution of responsibility to the regional level was accepted by some people with whom I spoke, they still did not redirect blame away from the Kyrgyzstani government. With government officials 'passing the buck', frustration about the energy crisis fed into the larger discourse of the president's unpopularity.

A large part of the public relations campaign was to ask people to use less electricity and water, especially during hot periods and in the months before winter. In March 2010 during an address at the Congress of Harmony (*Yntymak kurultaiy*), Bakiev blamed people for not economizing (Reeves 2012, 113). In stark contrast to how he asked people to live and how most Kyrgyzstanis were forced to cope with the crisis, the government and Bakiev relatives publicly used energy frivolously. During the height of this electricity crisis a particularly ironic electrified portrait of President Kurmanbek Bakiev was installed at a central bus stop on Kurmanjan Datka Street in Osh, business in Bishkek were told to put up holiday street lights, and Maxim Bakiev's 'Soho Night Club' in the capital had a searchlight waving late into the night. The sounds of generators in urban areas constantly reminded those who could not afford an alternative source of power that they were relatively deprived.

In response to the survey question, 'What do you think the Kyrgyz government should do about this situation?' participants blamed the government for corruption in the energy sector, putting personal interests over national interests, supposedly selling water to Kazakhstan and Uzbekistan, and not listening to people's concerns about this issue. Those most concerned about regional dependency and critical of the government argued that the government should resign or be removed because of their mismanagement of hydroelectricity.

Gulmira Temirbekova (an NGO activist in Talas) voiced a typical reaction expressed when I asked people what they thought about the electricity situation.

> For so many years [...] – more than 50 years – we have had normal electricity [...] when we asked why [there were shortages and cut offs], they said, there was less intake of water in the Toktogul plant. But we have heard a lot of people say that they sold the water. [...] They leaked water for Uzbekistan, and so there is decreased water level and lower generation of electricity. Such a scandal we had last year![27]

Gulmira's view about the government's surreptitious sales of electricity to neighbouring countries was echoed by survey participants, who commonly expressed frustration that officials did not consider livelihood impacts of the electricity crisis and did not work for the Kyrgyz people. Some interviewees who did not blame Bakiev for this situation blamed Akaev instead for not defending the national interests earlier. One of the most common views expressed by survey participants who were concerned about the energy situation and dependency was that the Bakiev administration should *listen to public concerns* to prevent such mistakes. Some of these expressions about what the government should do are similar to the concept of *uiat* (shame) which Beyer (2009) investigated in her research about *salt* (customary law), in Talas, Kyrgyzstan. Beyer suggests *uiat* as related to 'awareness of other's expectations'. It is 'tied to interactions such as listening, behaving, being heard or seen. [...] Thus, *uiat* has a preventive dimension: it enforces conformist behavior to prevent bonds from breaking [...]' (Beyer 2009, 194). However, after 2009, the Bakiev administration demonstrated quite the opposite of this expectation, and took steps that contradicted the regime's own framing, which was discordant with daily lived experiences, and ignored vocal contestation of these policies. The Bakiev government stood publicly accused as shameful for ignoring the peoples' everyday needs, lying about the shortages and trying to redirect public anger, then not recognizing this shame when discovered. The power of this accusation may derive from the collectivity and commonality of these experiences, as Guenther (2011) elaborates, and the expectation of government responsibility to address collective concerns. Jasper (1998) identifies shame as a potential protest motivator which can lead to anger and aggression. In 2010, a collective specification of blame and the shared emotion of shame operated as 'a site of resistance, a feeling for justice' (Guenther 2011, 6). Together with the specification of blame of the Bakiev government, shame was a powerful and widely shared motivating emotion, which catapulted dissent into anger and indignation with the 'moral shock' (Jasper 1998) of government forces killing protesters on 7 April.

Conclusions

The interim government that came to power after Bakiev's ouster in April 2010 recognized the role public frustration about hydroenergy played in the revolution. Officials immediately made cosmetic changes to energy policies, restructured regulatory bodies for improved transparency, cancelled electricity and water tariff hikes. However, the interim government made mistakes that reinforced the nationalistic tone about water resources. For example, on 19 May 2010, seemingly in response to the prolonged border closure that Kazakhstan maintained post-revolution, Kyrgyzstan shut off irrigation water deliveries from the Talas River to two irrigation districts in southern Kazakhstan (Rogers 2010; Trilling 2010). This prompted a diplomatic outcry and an opened border. This regionally tricky move at a politically difficult time seemed intended to bolster popular belief in Kyrgyzstan's negotiating strength, the power of wielding water upstream. Heathershaw (2010) suggested that regional leaders desist from non-transparent purchases of electricity from the country. 'Now is not the time to have the tit-for-tat struggles over water, hydropower and (in the opposite direction) gas that have characterized Kyrgyzstan's energy relations with its neighbors since independence.' This approach was reinforced by nationalistic rhetoric administration officials used. In 2010, then interim government member and now President Almazbek Atambayev remarked, 'Water is the main wealth and weapons that we can use' (AkiPress 2010b). In 2012, Economy Minister Temir Sariev talked about Kyrgyzstan becoming 'masters of Central Asia' once the Datka-Kemin transmission line and Kambar-Ata-1 are completed. There is currently much discussion about possibly repeating the mistakes of the Bakiev regime regarding privatization and tariff increases, and dependency on Russia for completion of infrastructure development (Kostenko 2014; Kalybekova 2014).

The misjudgement of popular sentiment about hydroenergy management by Bakiev administration officials proved politically fateful. Their tone-deaf framing of the crisis created more intense popular opposition, while the nationalistic narrative resonated widely. What upset many of the people with whom I spoke was Bakiev officials' illicit sale of electricity to neighbouring countries, which they see as taking advantage of Kyrgyzstan.

People do not simply consume media and government messages; they do not always accept the framing provided for them. In this instance, it was easy for people to see the mismatch between official explanations and likely causes for the serious problems they faced daily. It took blatant corruption and short-sighted policies, on top of several years of hardship, to mobilize people in the hardest hit areas. Anger that was just under the surface boiled over when the government used force to suppress picketers. The combination of mass perceptions of relative deprivation (which had both a physical and political basis) and the government's appeals to nature in fashioning a nationalistic argument may be a more complete explanation for the 2010 April revolution in Kyrgyzstan than mono-causal arguments such as outside forces or elite manipulation. The ramifications of this framing for future national energy and environmental policies in Kyrgyzstan are significant. Kyrgyzstanis will remain vulnerable as long as systemic problems in the water and energy sectors remain and government attempts to increase tariffs or privatize will be met with distrust. The challenge is figuring out how to resolve these vulnerabilities in response to popular concerns without contributing to the development of dangerous nationalist discourses that bolster antagonistic regional and ethnic politics.

Acknowledgements

The author is grateful to all the people in Kyrgyzstan who participated in this research. Thanks to Bermet Zhumakadyr kyzy, Morgane Treanton, and Nurshat Ababakirov for research assistance, and Elena Perminova for interview transcriptions.

Funding

This work was supported by funding from the American Councils for International Education ACTR/ACCELS Special Initiatives Fellowship, International Research & Exchanges Board (IREX) and Bucknell University.

Notes

1. For energy sector background, see Zozulinsky (2010) and Peyrouse (2007). Toktogul is the largest reservoir in Kyrgyzstan and the third largest in Central Asia, in water storage capacity terms (Economic Commission for Europe 2007, Annex I).
2. For discussion of political ecology, see Blaikie and Brookfield (1987), Blaikie (2008), Peet and Watts (2004), Robbins (2004), and Zimmerer and Bassett (2003).
3. SIAR-Bishkek implemented the survey using cluster sampling and Kish grids to achieve proportional representation by *oblast*, gender, age and ethnicity: 857 females, 643 males; participants' language: 876 Russian, 542 Kyrgyz and 82 Uzbek.
4. Six interview groups consisted of academics, journalists, environmental NGO leaders, government officials, businesspeople and international development representatives.
5. Newspaper content analysis of five Russian, one Kyrgyz, seven English language newspapers; they were chosen by accessibility online for two periods: 1 December 2003–23 March 2005 (pre-'Tulip Revolution'); and 24 March 2005–1 December 2007 (post-'Tulip Revolution').
6. For a detailed discussion of tariff politics in Kyrgyzstan, see Gullette (2010b).
7. Author interview with Felix Kulov, Bishkek, 19 July 2010.
8. For a timeline, see Azzatyk.kg (2010).
9. Author interview with Edil Baisalov, Bishkek, 16 July 2010.
10. Author interview with Felix Kulov, Bishkek, 19 July 2010.
11. 'The dark ages' phrase was used by Edil Baisalov; author interview with Bishkek, 16 July 2010.
12. Many international news analyses summarized this growing discontent and political implications: Juraev (2009), IRIN Asia (2008), Dzyubenko (2008), and Abdurasulov (2008).
13. Confidential interview by the author with a local official in Sumsar, Kyrgyzstan, 14 May 2009.
14. For KIRFOR documents and an explanation about the project, see http://msri-hub.ucentralasia.org/project-resources/.
15. Author interview with Nurmamat Saparbaev, Collaborative Forest Management (CFM) Project Advisor, Kyrgyz–Swiss Forestry Support Programme 'KIRFOR', Jalalabad city, 6 May 2009.
16. Author interview with Edil Baisalov, Bishkek, 16 July 2010.
17. Author interview with Nurkul Mamatkulovich Stamov, Director of the NGO 'Pravo i Ljudi' ('Rights and People'), Kerben, Jalalabad province, 13 May 2009; author interview with Edil Baisalov, Bishkek, 16 July 2010; visit with a former housemate in Osh, a Kara-Suu market trader, who installed a solar panel purchased in Xinjiang, China, in 2009.
18. Author interview with Yuri Dimitrievich Nagorniy, Sary-Oi village, 25 July 2009.
19. The Toktogul reservoir has a maximum capacity of 19.5 km^3, and the average late spring level was approximately 12 km^3 (2002–07). The dead level of the Toktogul reservoir is 5.5 billion m^3, and the water reached a low of 6.8 km^3 in May 2008.
20. This figure is of the 56.4% who answered 'yes' to the question 'Water shortages or shutoffs have had a serious impact over the last year in the place where I live.'
21. Of these 777 people who believe that decisions in Kyrgyzstan depend on neighbouring countries' needs and interests, 688 of them are concerned to some degree: 237 participants are very concerned, 312 are concerned and 139 are fairly concerned. In other words, 46% of the total of 1500 survey participants are concerned to some degree about hydroelectricity dependency.
22. This number, 687, is 9% of the total of 1500 surveyed. Those asked the question 'What should the government do about this problem?' were only those who expressed a belief that Kyrgyzstan is dependent on its neighbours for hydroelectricity decisions, and also – among those who expressed this belief – those who were concerned at all about this dependency.
23. Author interview, Jalalabad city, 6 May 2009.
24. Ibid.
25. Author interview, Bishkek, 28 July 2009.
26. This is in response to 'Whom do you blame for this situation?', an open-ended question. 'Whom do you blame … ' was only asked of participants who (1) believed that hydroelectricity generation decisions in

Kyrgyzstan depend (or depend to some extent) on neighbouring countries' needs and interests and (2) were 'very concerned', 'concerned' or 'fairly concerned' 'about this dependency.'

27. Author interview with Gulmira Temirbekova, Talas city, 18 April 2009.

References

Abdurasulov, A. "The Dark Days Return" Transitions Online, September 16, 2008.

AkiPress. 2010a. "Veernoe otklyuchenie elektroenergii v 2008 godu proizvodilis' iz-za plokhogo upravle-niya energosektrom – nezavisimyi ekspert" ("Electricity blackouts in 2008 happened because of poor management of the energy sector – independent expert"), October 4, 2010. Accessed November 11, 2014. http://business.akipress.org/news:119111

AkiPress. May 20, 2010b. "VP sozdalo Goskomitet po vodnomu hozjajstvu i melioracii i naznachili ego glavu." "IG (the Interim Government) has established the State Committee for Water Resources and Irrigation, and appointed its head." Accessed November 11, 2014. http://kg.akipress.org/print:209781/

Azzatyk.kg. 2010. "Kyrgyzskaja revoljucija: Hronologija tragicheskih sobytij 6–7 aprelja 2010 goda v Kyrgyzstane." May 6, 2010. http://www.azattyk.org/content/article/2033316.html (accessed October 2, 2013).

Baev, P. 2011. "A Matrix for Post-Soviet 'Color Revolutions': Exorcising the Devil from the Details." *International Area Studies Review* 14 (2): 3–22.

Bakiev, K. 2009a. "Vystuplenie Prezidenta Kyrgyzskoj Respubliki Kurmanbek Bakieva v hode vstrechi Glav gosudarstv- uchreditelej MFSA v rasshirennom sostave Uvazhaemyj Prezident Mezhdunarodnogo Fonda Spasenija Arala" ("Statement by H.E. Mr. Kurmanbek Bakiev, President of the Kyrgyz Republic at the Meeting of Heads of the States-Founders of the International Fund for Saving the Aral Sea (IFAS))." April 28, 2009, Almaty, Kazakhstan.

Bakiev, K. 2009b. "Prezident Kyrgyzstana Kurmanbek Bakiev: 'Glavnyj resurs razvitija – soglasie i dialog'" (President of Kyrgyzstan Kurmanbek Bakiev: "The most important development resource – agreement and dialogue"), *Izvestia*, July 10, 2009. Accessed November 11, 2014. http://izvestia.ru/news/350587

Barrett, C. B., and M. F. Bellemare. 2011. "Why Food Price Volatility doesn't Matter." *Foreign Affairs* 12.

Beissinger, M. R. 2007. "Structure and Example in Modular Political Phenomena: The Diffusion of Bulldozer/Rose/Orange/Tulip Revolutions." *Perspectives on Politics* 5 (2): 259–276.

Bellemare, M. F. 2011. "Rising Food Prices, Food Price Volatility, and Political Unrest." Accessed November 11, 2014. http://mpra.ub.uni-muenchen.de/31888/

Beyer, J. 2009. *According to Salt. An Ethnography of Customary Law in Talas, Kyrgyzstan.* Dissertation. Martin-Luther University, Halle-Wittenberg.

Blaikie, P. 2008. "Epilogue: Towards a Future for Political Ecology that Works." *Geoforum* 39 (2): 765–772.

Blaikie, P. M., and H. C. Brookfield. 1987. "Land Degradation and Society. USA: Methuen & Co in Association with Methuen."

Brush, S. G. 1996. "Dynamics of Theory Change in the Social Sciences: Relative Deprivation and Collective Violence." *The Journal of Conflict Resolution* 40 (4): 523–545.

Buijs, A. E., B. J. M. Arts, B. H. M. Elands, J. Lengkeek. 2011. "Beyond Environmental Frames: The Social Representation and Cultural Resonance of Nature in Conflicts Over a Dutch Woodland." *Geoforum* 42: 329–341.

Collins, K. 2011. "Kyrgyzstan's Latest Revolution." *Journal of Democracy* 22 (3): 150–164.

Cummings, S. N., and M. Ryabkov. 2008. "Situating the 'Tulip Revolution'." *Central Asian Survey* 27 (3–4): 241–252.

Davies, J. C. 1962. "Toward a Theory of Revolution." *American Sociological Review* 27: 5–19.

Dawson, J. I. 1996. *Eco-nationalism: Anti-nuclear Activism and National Identity in Russia, Lithuania, and Ukraine.* Durham, NC: Duke University Press.

Dhur, A. "Secondary Data Review On The Food Security Situation In The Kyrgyz Republic." Food Security Analysis Service, World Food Programme. Accessed November 11, 2014. https://www.ids.ac.uk/files/dmfile/SecondaryDataReviewKyrgyzstan161008.pdf

Dzyubenko, O. 2008. "Kyrgyz energy crisis a political risk: think tank." *Reuters.* Fri, Aug 15 2008. http://uk.reuters.com/article/2008/08/15/businessproind-kyrgyzstan-risks-dc-idUKLF2159520080815

Economic Commission for Europe (ECE). 2007. "Dam Safety in Central Asia: Capacity-Building and Cooperation" *Water Series No. 5,* New York and Geneva: United Nations.

Esenalieva, D. 2012. Dujshon Mamatkanov, direktor instituta vodnyh problem i gidrojenergetiki NAN KR: Summa godovyh postuplenij v bjudzhet Kyrgyzstana v sluchae vvedenija naloga na vodu mozhet sostavit' $9 mln. ("Duishon Mamatkanov, Director of the Institute of Water Problems and Hydropower of NAS KR: Total annual revenue of Kyrgyzstan in case a tax on water is introduced could reach $9 million") *KyrTAG*. September 28, 2012. Accessed November 11, 2014. http://www.kyrtag.kg/interview/detail.php?ID=118051

Feaux de la Croix, J. 2011. "Moving Metaphors we Live by: Water and Flow in the Social Sciences and Around Hydroelectric Dams in Kyrgyzstan." *Central Asian Survey* 30 (3–4): 487–502.

Ferghana.ru News Information Agency. 2010. "Kyrgyzstan: V Naryne prohodit massovyj miting protiv povyshenija tarifov na jelektrichestvo i teplo." ("Kyrgyzstan: In Naryn a mass rally was held against the increase in tariffs for electricity and heat.") March 10, 2010. Accessed November 11, 2014. http://www.fergananews.com/news.php?id=14178

Gizelis, T.-I., and A. E. Wooden. 2010. "Water Resources, Institutions, & Intrastate Conflict." *Political Geography* 29 (8): 444–453.

Gorbachev, I. 2008. "Dujshon Mamatkanov, direktor instituta vodnyh problem i gidrojenergetiki NAN KR" (Duishon Mamatkanov: In the Naryn River in Kyrgyzstan there is no shortage of water"), «24.kg», Oct. 15, 2008

Guenther, L. 2011. "Resisting Agamben: The Biopolitics of Shame and Humiliation." *Philosophy and Social Criticism* 38 (1): 1–21.

Gullette, D. 2010a. "Institutionalized Instability: Factors Leading to the April 2010 Uprising in Kyrgyzstan." *Eurasian Review* 3

Gullette, D. 2010b. "Resurrecting an Energy Tariff Policy in Kyrgyzstan." Central Asia Security Policy Brief No. 1. OSCE Academy and Geneva Center for Security Policy. Accessed November 11, 2014. http://www.osce-academy.net/en/research/policy-briefs/. November 29, 2010b.

Gurr, T. R. 1970. *Why Men Rebel*. Princeton: Princeton University Press.

Hale, H. E. 2006. "Democracy or Autocracy on the March? The Colored Revolutions as Normal Dynamics of Patronal Presidentialism." *Communist and Post-Communist Studies* 39 (3): 305–329.

Hamilton, P. 2002. "The Greening of Nationalism: Nationalising Nature in Europe." *Environmental Politics* 11 (2): 27–48.

Heathershaw, J. 2007. "The Tulip Fades: 'Revolution' and Repercussions in Kyrgyzstan." *Perspective* 17 (2): 1–8.

Heathershaw, J. 2010. "Beware of Meddling in Kyrgyzstan!" *Open Democracy*. Aug. 25, 2010. Accessed September 6, 2013. http://www.opendemocracy.net/od-russia/john-heathershaw/beware-of-meddling-in-kyrgyzstan)

International Crisis Group. 2010. "Kyrgyzstan: A Hollow Regime Collapses." Asia Briefing No 102, Bishkek/Brussels, April 27, 2010

IRIN Asia – Kyrgyzstan. 2008. "Poor hit hardest by rising food prices and energy crisis", UN Office for the Coordination of Humanitarian Affairs, Osh/Bishkek, December 8, 2008

Iyengar, S. 1987. "Television News and Citizens' Explanations of National Affairs." *The American Political Science Review* 81: 815–831.

Jasper, J. 1998. "The Emotions of Protest: Affective and Reactive Emotions in and around Social Movements." *Sociological Forum* 13 (3): 397–424.

Judah, Ben. 2009. "A Sinking 'Island of Democracy.'" *Transitions Online* (TOL). August 26, 2009. Accessed November 11, 2014. http://www.tol.org/client/article/20800-a-sinking-island-of-democracy.html

Junisbai, A. K. 2010. "Understanding Economic Justice Attitudes in Two Countries: Kazakhstan and Kyrgyzstan." *Social Forces* 88 (4): 1677–1702.

Kaika, M. 2006. "Dams as Symbols of Modernization: The Urbanization of Nature between Geographical Imagination and Materiality." *Annals of the Association of American Geographers* 96 (2): 276–301.

Kalybekova, A. 2014. "Russia Holds Kyrgyzstan's Hydropower Dreams Hostage," June 24, 2014. Accessed November 11, 2014. http://www.eurasianet.org/node/68741

Katz, M. 2007. "Will There be Revolution in Central Asia?" *Communist and Post-Communist Studies* 40 (2): 129–141.

Kostenko, Y. 2014. "Tarifnaja politika.kg. 'Opyt' Bakieva?" (Tariff politics: Bakiev's "experience"?) *24.kg*. April 29, 2014, Bishkek. http://www.24 kg.org/economics/177991-tarifnaya-politikakg-laquoop ytraquo-bakieva.html

Kruglov, E. 2007. "Spasitel'naja Kambarata. Jenergeticheskie nadezhdy i riski Kirgizii" (Saviour Kambar-Ata: Energy hopes and risks of Kyrgyzia") *CentralAsia*.ru, July 9th, 2007. Accessed November 11, 2014. http://www.centrasia.ru/newsA.php?st=1183965060

Kubicek, P. 2011. "Are Central Asian Leaders Learning from Upheavals in Kyrgyzstan?" *Journal of Eurasian Studies* 2 (2): 115–124.

Kulov, E. 2008. "March 2005: Parliamentary Elections as a Catalyst of Protests." *Central Asian Survey* 27 (3–4): 337–347.

Kuntz, P., and M. R. Thompson. 2009. "More than Just the Final Straw: Stolen Elections as Revolutionary Triggers." *Comparative Politics* 41 (3): 253–272.

Lagi, M., K. Z. Bertrand, and Y. Bar-Yam. 2011. "The Food Crises and Political Instability in North Africa and the Middle East." Available at SSRN. Accessed November 11, 2014. http://ssrn.com/abstract= 1910031 or http://dx.doi.org/10.2139/ssrn.1910031

Laruelle, M. 2012. "The Paradigm of Nationalism in Kyrgyzstan. Evolving Narrative, the Sovereignty issue, and Political Agenda." *Communist and Post-Communist Studies* 45 (1): 39–49.

Mambetalieva, G. 2008. "Energy Fears as Kyrgyz Winter Approaches: Threat of more blackouts despite efforts to hoard water for hydropower ahead of cold season." IWPR Special Report, RCA Issue 557, Dec. 3, 2008. Accessed November 11, 2014. http://iwpr.net/report-news/energy-fears-kyrgyz-winter-approaches

Matveeva, A. 2009. "Legitimising Authoritarian States in Central Asia: Political Manipulation and Symbolic Power." *Europe-Asia Studies* 61 (7): 1095–1121.

Matveeva, A. 2010. *Kyrgyzstan in Crisis: Permanent Revolution and the Curse of Nationalism*. Crisis States Research Centre.

Maystadt, J.-F., J.-F. Trinh Tan, and C. Breisinger. 2014. "Does Food Security Matter for Transition in Arab Countries?" *Food Policy* 46: 106–115.

McGlinchey, E. M. 2011. *Chaos, Violence, Dynasty: Politics and Islam in Central Asia*. Pittsburgh: University of Pittsburgh Press.

Megoran, N. 2012. "Averting Violence in Kyrgyzstan: Understanding and Responding to Nationalism." Russia and Eurasia Programme Paper, Chatham House.

Mehta, L. 2010. "The Social Construction of Scarcity: The Case of Western India." chapter 17 In *Global Political Ecology*, edited by Peet, Richard, Paul Robbins, and Michael Watts, 371–386. USA and Canada: Routledge.

Molle, F., P. P. Mollinga, and P. Wester. 2009. "Hydraulic Bureaucracies and the Hydraulic Mission: Flows of Water, Flows of Power." *Water Alternatives* 2 (3): 328–349.

Osmonalieva, A. 2009. "Electricity Price Shock for Kyrgyz Consumers." Institute for War and Peace Reporting (IWPR). December 5, 2009.

Osmonov, J. 2009. "Sharp Rise In Electricity And Heating Rates Cause Public Discontent In Kyrgyzstan." *CACI Analyst*. December 10, 2009. Accessed November 11, 2014. http://cacianalyst.org/publications/ field-reports/item/11965-field-reports-caci-analyst-2009–12–10-art-11965.html

Peet, R., and M. Watts, eds. 2004. *Liberation Ecologies: Environment, Development, Social Movements*. London: Routledge.

Peyrouse, S. 2007. "The Hydroelectric Sector in Central Asia and the Growing Role of China." *China and Eurasia Forum Quarterly* 5 (2): 131–148.

PR.kg. 2008. "Minpromjenergo KR: V reke Naryn nabljudaetsja malovodnyj cikl" ("Ministry of Industry and Energy of the Kyrgyz Republic: In the river Naryn a low water cycle is observed") Oct. 16, 2008. Accessed November 11, 2014. http://www.pr.kg/news/kg/2008/10/16/8203/

Radio Free Europe/Radio Liberty. 2010. "Kyrgyz Protest Electricity Price Hike" Feb. 25, 2010. Accessed November 11, 2014. http://www.rferl.org/content/Kyrgyz_Protest_Electricity_Price_Hike_/1968192.html

Radnitz, S. 2006. "What Really Happened in Kyrgyzstan?" *Journal of Democracy* 17 (2): 132–146.

Radnitz, S. 2010. *Weapons of the Wealthy: Predatory Regimes and Elite-led Protests in Central Asia*. Cornell University Press.

Reeves, M. 2010. "Breaking Point: Why the Kyrgyz Lost Their Patience." *Open Democracy*. Accessed September 6, 2013. http://www.opendemocracy.net/od-russia/madeleine-reeves/breaking-point-why-kyrgyz-lost-their-patience

Reeves, M. 2012. "Black Work, Green Money: Remittances, Ritual, and Domestic Economies in Southern Kyrgyzstan." *Slavic Review* 71 (1): 108–134.

Robbins, P. 2004. *Political Ecology: A Critical Introduction*. Vol. 20. Oxford: Blackwell.

Rogers, Stan. 2010. "Kyrgyzstan Reportedly Shuts Off Irrigation Water to 2 Kazakhstani Districts," *Central Asia Online*. May 19, 2010. http://centralasiaonline.com/en_GB/articles/caii/newsbriefs/2010/05/19/ newsbrief-06

de la Sablonnière, R., É. Auger, N. Sadykova, and D. M. Taylor. 2010. "When the 'We' Impacts How 'I' Feel About Myself: Effect of Temporal Collective Relative Deprivation on Personal Well-being in the Context of Dramatic Social Change in Kyrgyzstan." *European Psychologist* 15 (4): 271–282.

Saralaeva, L. 2005. "Water War Threatens Treaty," *International War and Peace Reporting*. RCA Issue 337, Feb. 21, 2005. http://iwpr.net/report-news/water-war-threatens-treaty

Sarbaev, K. 2009. Centre Karnegi na temu «Kyrgyzstan i nekotorye voprosy bezopasnosti» (Speech by the Minister of Foreign Affairs of the Kyrgyz Republic at the Carnegie Center roundtable on "Kyrgyzstan and Some Security Issues"). Washington, October 6, 2009.

Schwartz, K. ZS. 2006. *Nature and National Identity after Communism: Globalizing the Ethnoscape.* Pittsburgh: University of Pittsburgh Press.

Shmueli, D. F. 2008. "Framing in Geographical Analysis of Environmental Conflicts: Theory, Methodology and Three Case Studies." *Geoforum* 39: 2048–2061.

Short, J. R. S. 1991. *Imagined Country: Society, Culture, & Environment.* Syracuse, NY: Syracuse University Press.

Slay, B. 2010. "Recent developments in the Poverty/Energy/Vulnerability nexus in Kyrgyzstan and Tajikistan," Unofficial UNDP Report. Accessed November 11, 2014. http://europeandcis.undp.org/uploads/public1/files/vulnerability/Senior%20Economist%20Web%20site/Slay_PEV_paper_May_2011.pdf

Smith, A. D. 2009. *Ethno-symbolism and Nationalism: A Cultural Approach.* Abingdon: Routledge.

Snow, D. A. and R. D. Benford. 1988. "Ideology, Frame Resonance and Participant Mobilization." *International Social Movement Research* 1 (1): 197–219.

Snow, D. A., E. B. Rochford, S. K. Worden, and R. D. Benford. 1986. "Frame Alignment Processes, Micromobilization and Movement Participation." *American Sociological Review* 51: 464–481.

Steinberg, G. M. 1987. "Large-scale National Projects as Political Symbols: The Case of Israel." *Comparative Politics* 19: 331–346.

Swyngedouw, E. 2009. "The Political Economy and Political Ecology of the Hydro-Social Cycle." *Journal of Contemporary Water Research & Education* 142 (1): 56–60.

Temirkulov, A. 2010. "Kyrgyz 'Revolutions' in 2005 and 2010: Comparative Analysis of Mass Mobilization." *Nationalities Papers: The Journal of Nationalism and Ethnicity* 38 (5): 589–600.

Toktonaliev, T. 2009. "Kyrgyz Leader Edges Toward Reform." *Institute for War and Peace Reporting* Oct. 26, 2009. (IWPR) RCA Issue 591. http://iwpr.net/report-news/kyrgyz-leader-edges-towards-reform

Trautman, T. 2010. "In Kyrgyzstan, The Utility of Revolution – Again." *World Politics Review*, April 13, 2010. Accessed December 2, 2014. http://www.worldpoliticsreview.com/articles/5404/in-kyrgyzstan-the-utility-of-revolution-again

Trilling, D. 2010. "Under [Water] Pressure, 'Fraternal' Kazakhstan Reopens Kyrgyzstan Border." *Eurasianet.* May 20, 2010. Accessed November 11, 2014. http://www.eurasianet.org/node/61105

Tudoroiu, T. 2007. "Rose, Orange, and Tulip: The Failed Post-Soviet Revolutions." *Communist and Post-Communist Studies* 40 (3): 315–342.

UN Office for the Coordination of Humanitarian Affairs. 2009. "Kyrgyzstan: Winter Energy Crisis" OCHA Situation Report. Jan. 12, 2009.

USAID. 2008. *Kyrgyzstan Household Energy Analysis and Proposed Social Protection Measures.* Bishkek, November 2008, 4.

Wood, D. 2010. "Electricity Plays Key Role in Kyrgyzstan Uprising." *World Resources Institute*, April 19, 2010. Accessed September 6, 2013. http://www.wri.org/stories/2010/04/electricity-plays-key-role-kyrgyzstan-uprising

Wooden, A. E. 2013. "Another Way of Saying Enough: Environmental Concern and Popular Mobilization in Kyrgyzstan." *Post-Soviet Affairs* 29 (4): 314–353.

Yuldasheva, N. 2008. "Problemy V Jenergetike Kyrgyzstana Svjazany S Otsutstviem Nauchno Obosnovannogo Podhoda I Nejeffektivnogo Upravlenija, A Takzhe Neracional'nogo Puska Vody V Interesah Sosednih Gosudarstv." ("Problems in the energy sector of Kyrgyzstan related to the lack of scientifically proven approaches and mismanagement and unsustainable water release for neighboring states.") *24.kg,* Nov. 5, 2008. Accessed November 11, 2014. https://ca-news.info/2008/11/05/61

Zimmerer, K. S., and T. J. Bassett, eds. 2003. *Political Ecology: An Integrative Approach to Geography and Environment-Development Studies.* New York: Guilford Press.

Zozulinsky, A. 2010. "Kyrgyzstan: Power Generation & Transmission." *US Embassy Bishkek.*

Resource dependence and measurement technology: international and domestic influences on energy sector development in Armenia and Georgia

Jason E. Strakes

International School for Caucasus Studies (ISCS), Ilia State University, Tbilisi, Georgia

The effective measurement of natural gas consumption has become a central component of energy sector development in resource-dependent post-Soviet states such as Armenia and Georgia. Yet, while policy assessments have often emphasized the significance of technology upgrades in increasing the efficiency of gas distribution in Central Eurasia, it is necessary to consider other types of exogenous political and economic influences upon sourcing and adoption of measuring devices by national industries and their resultant impact upon energy sector performance. This study presents empirical data collected in northern Armenia and Tbilisi, Georgia, as well as from secondary sources, in order to examine the effect of both domestic and international factors upon the technology–performance relationship in the natural gas industries, and compares their relative implications for energy sector development in both countries since independence.

Introduction

Within the expansive field of post-Soviet or Eurasian studies, the analysis of energy production, transportation and consumption has come to occupy a paramount position in both academic and policy discussions of the Caucasus and Central Asia. The related body of literature produced in recent decades has typically been concentrated in three general areas: (1) the political economy of resource-rich states, or the association between hydrocarbon wealth, authoritarianism and economic development in the countries of the Caspian Basin (Sabonis-Helf 2004; Franke, Gawrich, and Alakberov 2009; Jones Luong and Weinthal 2010); (2) energy security, or the alleged primacy of access to or control over oil, natural gas and electricity supplies and transshipment routes in regional international relations (Karagiannis 2002; Starr and Cornell 2005; German 2008); and (3) various and sundry iterations of the New Great Game theme, or the representation of local energy reserves as the focus of continual geostrategic competition among the major global powers (Edwards 2003; Nuriyev 2007; Kubicek 2013).

Yet, relatively few systematic studies have examined the natural gas sector in those former Soviet republics most heavily dependent on external supplies for basic domestic or industrial necessities such as heating, cooking and electricity generation.[1] The present inquiry seeks to draw insights from the application of comparative institutional analysis in contemporary political science to gas policies in two resource-poor, low-capacity states – Armenia and Georgia – by examining the role of international and domestic influences on energy sector performance in transitional societies (Bunce 1999; Jones Luong 2002; Jones Luong and Weinthal 2006; Closson 2007, 2009). Conventional approaches tend to identify Armenia as an energy 'outsider' due to its exclusion from regional infrastructure projects, while Georgia has received much attention as a pivotal transit corridor for the Baku-Tbilisi-Ceyhan and Baku-Tbilisi-Erzurum oil and gas pipelines since their activation in the mid-2000s (Papava 2005). As a result, less recognition has been given to the impact of gas sector reform upon end consumers in these two countries, and thus the welfare of their citizenry.

Policy assessments have often emphasized the significance of technology upgrades in increasing the cost-effectiveness and reliability of gas distribution in Central Eurasia. Yet, it is necessary to consider other types of exogenous influences upon sourcing and adoption of measuring devices by national industries and their resultant effect upon energy sector performance. At the international level, foreign assistance for capacity building in the energy sphere has also been the result of interpersonal contacts and diplomatic interactions. In Armenia, identity-related factors such as diaspora relations and genocide-recognition policies have played a role in technology imports in the gas industry. In Georgia, insurmountable foreign debt and deterioration of infrastructure have motivated previous governments to sanction legal monopolies over the gas distribution system by major regional suppliers such as Kazakhstan and Azerbaijan – sometimes with the brunt of adjustment costs being borne by the public. At the same time, domestic state and non-governmental actors including energy regulators, private companies, producer cooperatives and organizations representing ethnic minorities may seek to offset reliance on foreign technology inputs by contributing to the enhancement of local industrial capacities. Thus, activities that promote energy development at the societal level may arise in response to conditions of dependency, inefficiency or citizen need inadvertently fostered by state energy policies. The contrasting trajectories of this process in both countries, and its attendant consequences for their citizens, invite further investigation.

The analysis presents empirical data collected in Vanadzor, capital of Lori Province (*marz*) in northern Armenia, and Tbilisi, Georgia, beginning in summer 2011, as well as national-level information drawn from secondary sources, in order to investigate the dynamics of resource dependence in contemporary Caucasian societies. These complementary spatial domains help capture similar conditions in the two states and within-case variation between subregions, where high levels of poverty, neglect by central authorities and lack of infrastructure strongly affect gas accessibility in the population, and administrative centres from which policies and practices related to gas distribution originate. In addition, the study makes use of materials such as trade publications, business plans and technical-assistance reports, supplemented by interviews with informants in the field. These are employed to examine the effect of multiple actors upon the technology–performance nexus in the Armenian and Georgian natural gas systems and to compare their relative implications for energy sector development from 1991 to the present. The examination of these cases is presented in two sections. The first considers the international context in which the introduction of measurement technologies has taken place, as a result of political and economic conditions and of the conduct of diplomacy between government representatives, public or private firms and interest groups. The second identifies influential domestic societal actors in each country setting and the role they have played in addressing conflicts of interest that arise between governments, regulatory agencies, industries and consumers. The concluding section presents a comparative summary and interpretation of how interactions between institutions affect energy performance in both states.

Theoretical foundations and research design

This qualitative historical analysis of the natural gas sector in the two energy-dependent nations of the South Caucasus seeks to make two disciplinary contributions. First, it introduces and tests an original model of energy sector development that incorporates theories of interaction between formal and informal institutions in political science (Helmke and Levitsky 2004). In this instance, *formal* actors are defined as state officials, ministries, public agencies or industries that are legally authorized to administer energy policies or programmes. *Informal* influences may include personal connections, ethnic affiliations, ideological preferences, or local arrangements and practices among individuals or organizations normally not involved in energy policies that become active in resource-related issues. The research question considers how contacts and associations between these structures positively or negatively influence the relationship between measurement technology and gas sector performance.

Second, the study seeks to expand upon the method of 'paired comparison' commonly employed in political studies. This involves the structured assessment of two crucial country cases guided by previously established theoretical assumptions and concerns (Tarrow 1999, 2010; Gisselquist 2014). The version of that approach applied in the present study is a 'most similar systems' research design, which relies upon the logic of 'common paths and foundations'. Here, the investigator selects cases that exhibit generally shared characteristics, presumably allowing one to control for error variance and infer cause and effect by isolating the most relevant factors that impact upon the dependent variable – the 'method of difference' (Bunce 1999, 16; Tarrow 1999, 9; Gisselquist 2014, 478–479). Armenia and Georgia have followed similar pathways, from small socialist republics lacking domestic fuel reserves and highly dependent on centrally supplied resources via shared pipelines. Citizens and state-controlled industries in both countries initially consumed a vast quantity of non-competitive public goods. Metering devices for gas consumption were not installed in the Armenian residential sector until the late 1990s.[2] Similarly, household gas supplies in Soviet Georgia were unmetered; fees were collected based upon a flat rate for per capita usage (Merklein & Associates 1997, 3; UNECE 2005, 2). A virtual collapse of energy distribution networks, accompanied by widespread loss, waste and theft, occurred after independence. This was followed by their gradual restoration and privatization, with external support, in the ensuing decades. In addition, both countries continue to exhibit a high degree of dependence upon and penetration of domestic markets by foreign providers. Lastly, they have pursued comparable efforts towards the institutionalization of standards governing energy supply and use, including technologies necessary for the accurate recording and measurement of popular consumption.

Living and working in both countries over a period of several years provided a unique vantage point from which to observe these conditions. In particular, being embedded in the difficult economic setting of Armenian and Georgian cities enabled recognition of the socio-political context of energy technologies beyond the purely mechanical aspects of metering equipment. Further, as will be seen below, it allowed one to identify more unusual combinations of actors and interests that have become involved in the process of gas sector development.

The theoretical scheme displayed in Figure 1 identifies four variables representing three different sets of associations. The first set, XY, signifies the conventional understanding in energy policy of a direct positive correlation between advances in technological inputs for the measurement of consumption and increased efficiency of domestic supply and distribution in both commercial and residential sectors. An assumed increase in accuracy and reliability has also been typically associated with the successful implementation of 'unbundling' or market-oriented reforms, as has been promoted by Western foreign aid institutions (US Agency for International Development, International Monetary Fund, World Bank and European Bank for Reconstruction and Development) since the early 1990s (Merklein & Associates, Inc. 1996, 1997; Hagler Bailly, Inc. 1997, 1998; AED 1999). These policies are predicated on the intuitive logic that the monetary value of a good is inherently linked to the precise determination of the amount consumed ('volumetric pricing'), thus generating incentives for its efficient use and conservation. In sum, this linkage is defined in the present study as *energy sector development*.

However, this simple bivariate relationship does not capture the larger international context in which new technologies are often introduced, including diplomatic interactions and the exchange

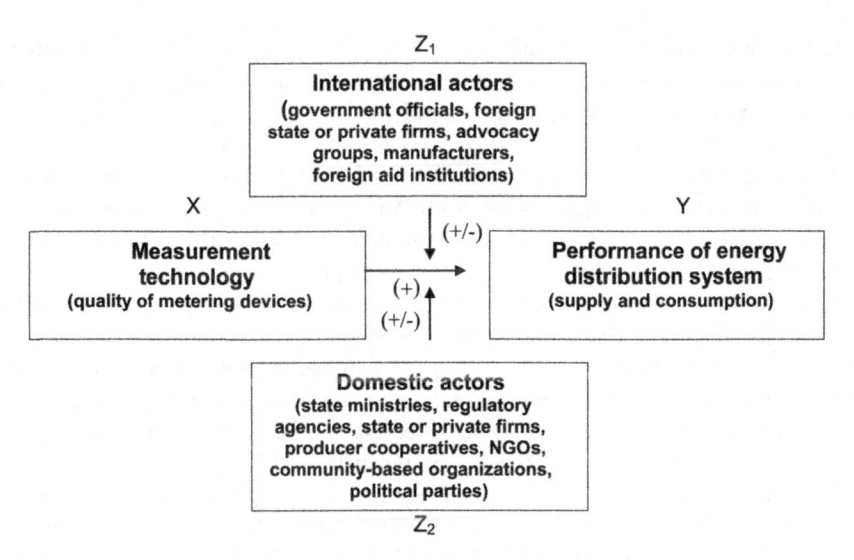

Figure 1. Model of international and domestic influences on energy sector development.

of information and resources between government representatives, state and private energy firms, equipment manufacturers, advocacy groups and foreign aid agencies (Z_1XY). Finally, the relationship between technology and performance is additionally affected by domestic influences (Z_2XY), including the activities of state ministries, regulatory agencies, private firms, producer cooperatives, non-governmental or community-based organizations, and political parties. To include these elements is to recognize the functioning of public utilities such as natural gas services as aspects of a transitional social system in which a variety of actors and institutions are engaged in decision making regarding national energy policy. It therefore additionally reflects the dynamic of responses to elite decisions from within civil society, which are often made in the context of significant intervention in weak or struggling states and economies by international forces.

Yet, it is also necessary to consider the potential pitfalls involved in the comparative method identified by positivist political scientists, namely the lack of 'degrees of freedom' in small-N case studies and the resultant failure or inability to identify alternative explanations for an observed outcome (Geddes 1990; King, Keohane, and Verba 1994, 43–46). The present study seeks to move beyond these limitations. By disaggregating the intervening variables into their constituent parts, one can identify different types of formal and informal actors and structures that have pursued complementary or competing interests and strategies, often in repeated interaction with one another. These actions or behaviours in turn serve as mechanisms that can be isolated and traced across time, thus indicating the logical and empirical links between explanatory and dependent variables (Tarrow 1999, 10–11, 2010, 238–240). This additional specification, combined with attention to 'dual-process tracing', introduces a greater number of observations within a case than if each correlate were treated simply as a single unit of analysis. The application of this framework to the two natural gas economies of interest is demonstrated in the following section.

Case studies

Armenia

International influences on gas sector development

A fundamental characteristic often attributed to the situation of contemporary Armenia is its high level of dependency upon foreign aid and technical assistance, and especially the role of the global diaspora in contributing financial resources in the form of private transfers or labour remittances – constituting as much as 20% of GDP in 2006 – to support economic and human development in the republic (Policy Forum Armenia 2010, 28). Yet, these relationships have seldom been examined in regard to the importation of measurement technology in the national energy sector. Following independence in December 1991, the economic free-fall engendered by the 1988 Spitak earthquake, the Nagorno-Karabakh War and the blockade imposed by Azerbaijan and Turkey rendered both government and citizens increasingly unable to purchase services. Comprehensive gas deliveries were restored by the majority-Russian-owned ArmRosGazprom (HayRusGazArd) through an agreement between the Ministry of Energy and Natural Resources, Itera International Energy and Gazprom in August 1997, which eventually gained a controlling interest (constituting 80–100% of shares) over the national energy sector (EBRD 2008, 185–186). The renewal of a vertically integrated supply arrangement with Russia thus facilitated the adoption of metering, billing and fee collection requirements for individual consumers.[3]

This linkage is further demonstrated by the manner in which publicly owned and private energy firms and manufacturers in the United States,[4] Iran,[5] France and the Slovak Republic have served as primary suppliers of measuring devices to the Armenian gas industry since the resumption of domestic service in the late 1990s (INOGATE 2012). As a result, these products, along with their positive or negative technical specifications, have often saturated the market alongside locally manufactured devices (Khitarov 2009, 2010). The prominent role of France as a patron of Armenian energy development was consolidated as early as 1988, when the predominantly government-owned Gaz de France established cooperation with the former ArmGazprom state concern based upon its long-standing relations with the Soviet gas industry. This was followed by the founding of the ArmFranGaz joint venture headed by Hayk Balasanian, member of the Permanent Bureau of the Union of French Citizens Abroad (UFE-SA), Armenia section, in 1994, which specialized in conducting feasibility studies on restoring the national gas supply infrastructure. It also demonstrated a motivation for seeking lucrative shares in the Armenian gas industry as a quid pro quo for the delivery and installation of new equipment (Asbarez Armenian News 1997; Sénat 1998, 23, 53).

The trend continued in early 1996, when Gaz de France, then chaired by French-Armenian public figure Jacques Deyirmendjian, was awarded a tender as lead contractor for the USAID and Technical Assistance to the Commonwealth of Independent States (TACIS) pilot project, Technical Support for the Restructuring of the Gas Sector in Armenia (Merklein & Associates 1997, 16). The terms of reference for its objectives included the upgrading of gas equipment manufacturing enterprises and improvement of production processes. However, a sharp divergence in preferences emerged between the market-reform agenda promoted by the donor community, and Gaz de France along with minister of energy and natural resources Gagik Martirosian. The latter party advocated minimal streamlining of the existing system to increase operational efficiency, rather than the objective of full privatization of state enterprises, which had been decreed in December 1995 by prime minister and liberal economist Hrant Bagratian. Nevertheless, during the same year, USAID arranged the delivery of an assistance package containing 2200 household gas meters and industrial units to local distributors to enable accounting methods for newly established services (Marjanyan 2004, 42).

In the wake of the approval of a bill recognizing the 1915 Armenian Genocide by the French Parliament in May 1998, a delegation of senators led by the chairman of the France-Armenia Friendship Group, Jacques Oudin, and accompanied by representatives of major French-based electronics firm Schlumberger Enterprises and Gaz de France, conducted a state visit in Yerevan hosted by the Union of Manufacturers and Businessmen (Employers) of Armenia. The engagement resulted in the signature of a contract with Schlumberger representatives for the importation of a reported 120,000 metering devices. In addition, Gaz de France extended a partnership offer with ArmRosGazprom in a meeting with president Levan Ter-Petrossian, prime minister Armen Darbinian, and Gagik Martirosian (Asbarez Armenian News 1998; Sénat 1998, 23).[6] In the same month, on the basis of a project on metering, billing and collections completed by USAID two years previously, the newly established National Institute of Standards (SARM) under the Ministry of Economy approved a plan for the installation of Metris 250 diaphragm meters produced by Schlumberger in the residential sector (Hager Bailly 1998, 10, 38, 44).[7]

The embargo on oil and natural gas supplies imposed by Azerbaijan during the Karabakh War has also motivated the central government to develop a domestic capability for gas technology production with assistance from foreign partners. Seeking to draw upon the experience of other post-socialist states in Central Eastern Europe, policy makers initiated commercial diplomacy with Slovakia, which subsequently recognized the genocide in December 2004. In the late 1990s the five-member industrial enterprise of the HayGazArd State Concern, reassembled from the Soviet-era ArmTransGaz Association, operated a Gas Meter Joint Venture Enterprise with the Slovak Khiran Joint Stock Company. Based in Yerevan, and with branches in Idjevan and Vanadzor, this firm specialized in the production of metering equipment, pressure regulators and spare parts (Merklein and Associates 1997, 7).[8]

Such industrial and diplomatic connections have been further reinforced by the work of the ARMES energy consulting firm and the Forum of Armenian Associations of Europe (FAAE), which was founded by the Yerevan-born leader of the Slovak ethnic-Armenian community, Ashot Grigorian and which maintain offices in both countries.[9] In an interview with national energy expert and World Bank Renewable Energy Project coordinator Ara Marjanyan,[10] it was confirmed that after its initial registration in September 1996, ARMES 'was engaged in [some] activities in Armenia related to gasometers [sic]' during the national energy crisis, as Grigorian utilized his émigré status and professional experience to assist with the restoration of supplies.

In summation, these contacts and associations have consolidated a mutually reinforcing dependency between external actors that have provided political and economic support for Armenia since independence, and predominant national energy industries, including the implementation of gas metering via imported equipment designs. Thus, as detailed below, the impetus for potential generation of indigenous solutions to gas sector problems may arise from prevailing national conditions of foreign-sponsored development.

Domestic influences on gas sector development

The present-day Armenian gas sector constitutes a legal private monopoly that operates with little or no oversight from either the state energy administration or the regulatory agency for public utilities (Hrayr Maroukhian Foundation 2013, 61–62). These conditions ultimately affect the extent to which the population accepts metering standards introduced by both foreign donors and domestic administrators, and the activities or strategies pursued by societal actors in return. The primary domestic institution concerned with representing citizen energy rights in post-Soviet Armenia was essentially a creation of the state rather than civil society. Its present incarnation, the Public Services Regulatory Commission (PSRC), was first established by presidential decree in April 1997 to address the immediate need to reactivate supplies. It did not assume formalized status until the ratification of the Energy Law in March 2001 (Marjanyan 2004, 18). Its primary competencies in the natural gas sphere include the issuing of licenses for the supply and delivery of services, as well as the consumer model for purchases (PRSC 2012). Significantly, according to the Law on the Commission Budget, as of 2004 its operations are funded directly from the state treasury based upon an annual estimate of maintenance costs and monetary requests submitted to the Ministry of Finance for regular approval, rather than accrued from independently collected taxes and fees (PRSC 2004; Bjork et al. 2006, 2). Secondly, it defines market rules in coordination with the Ministry of Energy rather than in a separate capacity (ERRA 2001; EBRD 2009, 184). Nevertheless, existing legislation defines it as an 'autonomous entity' not subject to interference by any governmental body. Although the PRSC is empowered to set rules and conditions for quality of service that require energy utilities to register consumer complaints, it has no oversight over internal procedures for addressing grievances. But its greatest limitation lies in the realm of anti-monopoly enforcement, for which it shares overlapping responsibilities with the comparatively under-staffed and under-funded State Commission for the Protection of Competition. Because both structures lack independent policy-making functions or legal prerogatives for quality control or prevention of abuses, it essentially plays the role of de facto interlocutor with monopolist firms in determining the price of goods and services (Hrayr Maroukhian Foundation 2013, 49, 75, 81). The ultimate relevance of the PSRC to popular gas consumption lies in the essential dilemma posed for effective regulation of utilities and protection of end users in a market dominated by a foreign energy provider sanctioned by state authorities. This issue is ultimately reflected in ongoing consumer and industry concerns regarding quality of service and implementation of standards for gas pricing. Given the essential role of ArmRosGazprom in the introduction of metering devices in the residential sector, the lack of accountability of firms, inspectors and laboratories creates conditions in which the extortion of fees from citizens – typically through tactics such as extracting charges or fines for replacement of allegedly faulty equipment – has become a side-effect of energy reform (Hrayr Maroukhian Foundation 2013, 61–62).

The frontier of innovation in Armenian energy development is thus arguably being delineated by the phenomenon of community-based organizations. These constitute a hybrid between structures with otherwise unrelated functions and agendas, such as cultural associations representing national minorities, private firms and international non-profit organizations or advocacy groups, as a strategy of pooling otherwise scarce resources to implement independent projects or policies. Among the most significant private companies that have recently assumed the role of 'broker' by forming associations with a broader range of societal actors is A-2 Ltd, an electronics developer and manufacturer. Founded in May 1990 as an outgrowth of the Yerevan branch of the USSR Central Scientific Research Institute ('Agat'), which produced radar and guidance systems for long-range missiles, it is presently a leading designer of thermoregulators for industrial meters. According to interviews conducted by the author with Arkady Khitarov, elected president of the Pontic Greek community (the second-largest ethnic minority in Armenia as of the 2002 census) and director of the Vanadzor branch of A-2,[11] the current structure of Greek representation in Armenia consists of nine individual NGOs unified under the umbrella Elpida (Union of Greek Public Organizations of Armenia) since 1997. In regard to financial resources, Elpida has a considerably closer relationship with the international non-profit organization World Council of Hellenes Abroad (SAE)-Periphery of the former USSR than with the Greek national government. Its current Regional Coordinator Ivan Savvidis, a Pontic Greek business leader of Georgian origin, has also served in the Legislative Assembly of Rostov Oblast and as a deputy to the Russian Federation State Duma. Vanadzor is also the site of its most important institutional feature, an Educational and Scientific Centre established in July 2009, which receives funding through the Embassy of Greece in Armenia. The main office houses a computer training and research centre that has received certification from the National Technical University of Athens and specializes in electronics and software engineering. However, while minimal Greek funding is provided for the technical centre, these finances support the physical facility rather than its research and development activities, which are currently sponsored by the Armenian government. Its current business plan seeks to address two prominent deficiencies in both domestically produced and foreign-manufactured measurement devices installed in the territory of Armenia: the inaccuracy of readings due to extreme seasonal temperature changes; and the infeasibility of manual data retrieval from devices located in remote mountainous areas (Khitarov 2010). Joint projects that have been initiated in cooperation with A-2 include the replacement of outmoded mechanical gas counters with electronic hardware, the development of wireless data-retrieval systems, and the fulfilment of certificates awarded by ArmRosGazprom for electronic upgrades of existing Russian-manufactured devices (Union of Greek Public Organizations of Armenia, 2013). These activities ultimately aspire to benefit private and industrial users, as well as to generate possible economic opportunities for the small Greek community in the northern provinces.

Finally (as is also discussed in the study on Azerbaijan in this volume), it is necessary to consider other local responses to negative externalities that have emerged as a consequence of government-sanctioned energy development, in which the unaccountability of public utility administrators has affected the relationship between citizens and the state. During preparations for the tendentious presidential elections of February 2008, the Yerevan-based Transparency International Anti-Corruption Center reported an effort by the incumbent Republican Party of Armenia (Hayastani Hanrapetakan Kusaktsutyun, HHK) to supplant the policy of free installation of gas meters previously pursued by local representatives in the politically influential Avan Community (Hamaynk'), whose prefect and HHK member Taron Margarian was re-elected the same year (TIAC 2008).

More recently, the conduct of the local territorial production and operational services in enforcement of metering regulations has fostered citizen grievances with the private gas monopolies as well as the state regulator. In 2005, SARM initiated a policy of conducting mandatory laboratory evaluations of household meters at five-year intervals. Following the most recent sequence, implemented over a 10-month period in 2010, ArmRusGazprom determined that slightly less than 3% of the over 80,000 inspected units showed signs of external interference (Arminfo News Agency 2010). However, the lack of independent monitoring of the testing process creates incentives to engage in dishonest practices toward consumers. Recently formed civil society organizations that provide legal representation and consumer protection services have increasingly intervened in such incidents. The Anti-Corruption Advocacy and Assistance Centre, originally launched by USAID through a contract with US-based international development firm Casals and Associates and currently directed by the civil rights advocacy group Armenian Young Lawyers Association, operates multiple branches nationwide. This network has been successful in providing mediation and support for citizens in Gyumri, Kotayk and Tavush Provinces (*marzes*) and the Yerevan capital district that have been subject to fines for unverified claims of meter tampering or unnecessary replacement fees by inspectors and department staff (AAC 2011, 2012; AYLA 2012a, 2012b). However, despite the benefits provided in terms of protecting the welfare of end users, it is unclear whether such measures have significantly affected the general condition of the licensee and billing system in the Armenian gas sector.

Georgia

International influences on gas sector development

In the case of Armenia, the traditional role of Russia as sole energy provider was central to the reconstruction of the national gas industry in the late 1990s. In Georgia, the hegemonic presence of Russian energy suppliers in the Caucasus has driven the pursuit of diversification, including alternative sources of technology inputs from a wide range of American and European manufacturers. The absence of reliable technologies for measuring consumption levels of imported Russian gas also played a primary role in the conclusion of new commercial agreements with alternative regional suppliers, in particular the major Caspian energy producers after 2005. The location of the main gas metering station on Russian territory prevented Georgian officials from accessing data on the actual volume of imports, rendering them unable to verify either the quality or the total amount consumed. Further, despite the gradual reconstruction of the gas sector into the mid-2000s, residential services were characterized by endemic non-payment, meter tampering and offering of bribes to inspectors in exchange for waiving or under-reporting of fees. As a result, between 1996 and 2002, Gazprom alleged that the Georgian gas industry had accumulated a massive debt, approaching USD 91 million. These conditions were combined with institutionalized corruption within Russian-Georgian industrial and business groups that maintained a vested interest in a lack of credible accounting and reporting in order to maintain access to the flow of rents (Jervalidze 2006).

A major catalyst for the introduction of foreign-made metering devices in the post-Soviet period was the discrepancy in equipment specifications and accounting standards between Russian and Georgian distributors at the Sioni border-crossing point for main gas pipelines. A fact-finding mission conducted by the International Gas Consulting Company in May 1998 recommended US-manufactured Sonic Flow Meters and Super-Flo computerized flow regulators to replace those previously installed at the Red Bridge (Krasny Most) and Gardabani stations on the borders with Armenia and Azerbaijan (Burns & Roe Enterprises 1998, 79). At the same time, a notable rift emerged concerning the recommendations of foreign advisors and the directors of the Production and Technical Departments of the Gardabani gas-fired thermal power plant. The administrators sought funding from USAID for the installation of separate metering facilities that would remain under their jurisdiction. This indicated a resistance to the formal coordination of measurement standards with officials of the national distributor, standard practice in the US commercial gas industry (Burns & Roe Enterprises 1998, 85).

In December 2004, after receiving a guarantee of restored supplies from Russian Gazprom daughter enterprise GazExport following a recent debt dispute, the former state distributor TbliGaz commenced the installation of new meters produced by the Russian–Italian joint venture LukAgip in the Vake district of Tbilisi, which were purchased by the company rather than consumers at a price of GEL 45 (USD 25) per unit. However, by January of the following year, this activity provoked a backlash among subscribers, who demanded the return of old units that had been dismantled by company inspectors. Presumably, the policy of replacement was based upon a commercial deal rather than necessity due to malfunctioning equipment (Daily News 2004, 2005).

In April 2005, negotiations were conducted between the Austrian and Georgian Ministries of Foreign Affairs to plan and finance an evaluation of the state-owned Tbilisi gas distribution network by a team of leading engineers employed by the energy service provider Wien Energie. This was reciprocated with a visit by a delegation of seven local experts hosted by Vienna Gas Company (United Nations Economic and Social Council 2005). The results of the exchange established an agenda for the urgent rehabilitation of the existing city metering system, which was characterized by the absence of technical standards, ease of tampering, and lack of regular calibration of individual units. The following month, the Tbilisi City Council hosted an international workshop sponsored by the United Nations Economic Commission for Europe (UNECE), Current State and Prospects for the Rehabilitation of the Local Natural Gas Infrastructure. Over 50 participants from Bulgaria, Estonia, the Russian Federation and Ukraine attended the meeting, as well as a representative of the Organization for Security and Cooperation in Europe. The assessments and recommendations of the delegates set in motion pursuit of funding, installation of updated equipment and assistance with drafting of new energy legislation.

The eventual bankruptcy of TbliGaz in December 2005 led to the signing of a memorandum between Georgia and Kazakhstan for the purchase of the decrepit capital distribution network by the state-owned KazTransGaz, followed by the formation of KazTransGazTbilisi in May 2006

(Reuters 2005; Daly 2009). Beginning in spring 2007, the company directorate commenced a policy of removal, inspection and replacement of existing Chinese-manufactured metering devices in the main entrances of residential apartments, and imposed payment of mandatory service fees to enforce compliance with the accounting system. These policies were advertised as a functional necessity given the preceding conditions of widespread theft among the population. However, the lack of involvement of third parties in the evaluation process has fostered periodic allegations of abuse. As related to journalists by Manana Kakhabrishvili, a resident of the Varketili micro-district (Suvarian 2008):

> The representatives of the company visited all families ... [and] verbally warned us to change the meters. And if we refused, we will be fined or the gas will be cut. ... [We] have to take old meters to the office of KazTransGaz for a technical examination. We have to write a notification that our meter does not work or does not work properly. If their experts conclude that the meter was damaged, the subscriber will be fined with the price equal to 300–500 cubic metres. Besides that, we are told to buy and install new meters with our own expenses.

In October 2008, the national regulatory agency announced that the practice of extracting obligatory fees was a violation of state laws governing the determination of tariffs for natural gas services; the cost must be absorbed by the company. The agency also attempted unsuccessfully to impose financial penalties for these policies. Yet, due to delays in implementation, the decision to enact new rules governing the use of metering devices did not enter into legal force until July 2009. Thus, KazTranzGaz representatives announced that as of 10 August, fines would be demanded from consumers who had not replaced meters determined to be malfunctioning or damaged. Ultimately, these conflicts fostered a resort to traditional practices of bypassing and non-payment by subscribers, ending with the eventual replacement of the Kazakh management board due to outstanding debts by the company.

Domestic influences on gas sector development

Perhaps the most significant domestic energy actor in Georgia since independence is the Georgian National Energy and Water Supply Regulatory Commission (GNERC), which was established in 1997.[12] While the GNERC was originally instituted as a publicly recognized civil association that functioned without direct government supervision, subsequent legislation altered its status to that of intermediary between central authorities and the energy industry (Dzidzikashvili 2010). These provisions define it as an autonomous regulatory body authorized by constitutional and municipal law, funded through taxes and fees paid by regulated entities rather than the state budget, and not attached to any other agency (GNERC 2007). Since 1999, its responsibilities specific to the gas sector include the issuing of licenses for transport and distribution, regulation of supply systems, monitoring of compliance with licensing terms, and administering penalties for violations (Hagler Bailly 1999; Dzidzikashvili 2010). The most significant function of the GNERC in reconciling government and commercial interests with the needs and rights of citizens is its role in the setting of tariffs for natural gas services and consumption. According to law, these are to be calculated through an independently determined methodology officially registered with the Ministry of Justice (Hagler Bailly 1999). These provisions further entail an obligation to protect the end user from price increases imposed by state or private monopolies (Transparency International Georgia 2008).

Yet, shifts in state energy policy were introduced during the past decade, in which the United National Movement (Ertiani Natsionaluri Modzraoba) party, led by president Mikhail Saakishvili, sought the rapid privatization and sale of strategic energy assets in order to maximize revenues generated by foreign direct investment. These reforms altered the legal status of the GNERC, introducing potential conflicts of interest between the government and those bodies empowered to represent the welfare of natural gas consumers. First, two amendments to the Law on Electricity and Natural Gas introduced in December 2005 transferred responsibility for determining the natural gas balance and market rules from the GNERC to the Ministry of Energy, reducing its independence (Transparency International 2008). Secondly, after the deregulation of foreign gas supplies in January 2006, the GNERC lost oversight over pricing of imports, which became the sole purview of the Georgian Oil and Gas Corporation established through a merger of former state enterprises. The Georgian Oil and Gas Corporation also assumed the role of government representative in all negotiations with foreign suppliers, further limiting public knowledge of the tariff-setting process (Jervalidze 2008).

Despite these political tensions, the GNERC has taken some initiative in addressing the task of altering and upgrading the technical specifications of existing meters to better serve consumer needs.[13] Independent studies conducted by GNERC's Natural Gas Department have revealed flawed methods for calculating gas losses by distribution licensees, and a negative effect of extreme cold temperatures at high altitudes on the accuracy of readings, with a resultant discrepancy between administered tariffs and actual rates of consumption (Namgaladze 2008, 2009). These findings have been used to advocate for the rights of end users and exert pressure upon distributing companies and the National Agency of Metrology, Technical Regulations and Standards to resolve these issues.

A significant example of the formation of voluntary associations to address gas technology issues in Georgia was the Permanent Commission Foundation convened by the General Directorate of TransGaz in April 1998 (Burns & Roe Inc. 1998). Its primary purpose was to monitor and assess the functioning and performance of existing distribution infrastructure (pipelines and metering stations) and measuring devices, as well as the open dissemination of information to public and private organizations. Its offshoot Ecology and Underground Metal Communications NGO, EcoEngineering, played a leading role in organizing the May 2005 UNECE workshop attended by private-industry representatives and public-interest groups, as well as local administrative officials and scientific experts (UNECE 2004). Based upon a preliminary assessment of the dire condition of the Tbilisi gas distribution system, Ecoengineering chairman Ivane Zazashvili, in coordination with the database manager of the UNECE technical cooperation programme Gas Centre, also arranged the donation of pipeline leakage detection equipment by Gaz de France, which had previously made significant investments in the Armenian gas industry (UNESCO 2005).

The negotiated acquisition of the rural gas transport system by the State Oil Company of the Republic of Azerbaijan (SOCAR) in 2008 is further representative of the extent of external intervention and reliance upon foreign technological inputs in contemporary Georgia. The presidential programme Gas in Every Village, initiated in 2010, expanded the national transmission network into settlements that had lacked access, surpassing even Soviet standards of comprehensive gasification. A relatively under-examined dimension of the activities of SOCAR and its partner firms is their impact upon the diverse ethnic and religious communities of the Georgian regions (*mkharebi*), which continue to exhibit a perceptual divide between state and society despite a decade of efforts towards electoral and constitutional reform. In 2008, residents of the Telavi and Marneuli Districts (raioni) in Kakheti and Kvemo Kartli, respectively, charged that the Telavgas and Marneulgas distributors purchased by Wissol Petroleum Georgia had introduced drastic increases in tariffs. This was combined with obligatory replacement of meters that had successfully passed previous laboratory inspections, at an inflated price of GEL 240 (USD 135), with threats to disconnect service as a penalty for noncompliance (Mtsivlishvili 2008). These events fostered plans to organize a community protest. As expressed by resident Elene Beruchashvili to the NGO Human Rights Centre:

The inhabitants of my district paid over GEL 100 back in 2005 when the district was first gasified. ... [We] installed the new meters which were sanctioned by an inspection lab at the time. No one from Telavgas had demanded to change the meters till the spring of 2008. No one said we had to pay more than we had already spent. We have been experiencing problems with Telavgas ever since it was bought by Wissol.

In several villages in Guria, SOCAR Georgia Gas has implemented the relocation of functioning meters from the inside to the outside of residences to simplify inspection. While this service is performed free of charge, residents are obligated to fund replacement of malfunctioning devices, while others have alleged the imposition of fees totalling GEL 250 GEL (USD 141) for removal and testing without their consent. Independent journalists described company actions as 'violence' which imitated the earlier conduct of KazTransGazTbilisi (Rezonansi 2009; Gogelia 2011).

A distinctive trend is the manner in which popular discontent regarding mandatory evaluation and replacement fees has overflowed into the sphere of opposition politics. In autumn 2008, the Georgian Labour Party (Sakartvelos Leiboristuli Partia, SLP) held a news conference and protests that called for expulsion of KazTransGaz and nationalization of assets in response to discriminatory price hikes which allegedly benefited the Saakashvili government. In January 2009, party representative Paata Jibladze introduced a petition to prohibit obligatory charges for replacement of meters. In July, a rally was held at the GNERC office to protest SOCAR policies. In the same month, National Democratic Party (Erovnul-Demokratiuli Partia, EDP) MP Guram Chakhvadze established a special commission to provide assistance to subscribers and reduce fines for new meters from GEL 600 to GEL 125 (USD 400 to USD 70), which was described as 'an act of violence and swindle' by the provider. Most recently, demonstrations organized by the EDP and SLP were held at the offices of KazTransGaz and the GNERC in the months preceding the 1 October 2012 parliamentary election, demanding that the cost of replacement meters be absorbed by the company rather than by citizens (Rustavi 2 2008, 2009a, 2009b, 2009c; Channel One Georgia 2009, 2012). However, it is not clear whether these actions have elicited a direct response from former or incumbent officials, given their absorption into general pre-election public discourse.

Results and interpretation

Table 1 presents a chronological summary of data derived from the two case studies detailed above. Each observation identifies a chain composed of linkages between international and domestic actors that occurred in each country, for a total of 25 interactions. The respective columns identify the state, year of the event, actor types, influence upon energy sector development and estimated direction of its impact (positive, neutral, or negative) from 1991 to present. The criteria for evaluating these outcomes lie in whether the behaviours and interests of formal and informal institutions involved in gas policies were convergent or divergent. Four categories indicate the effectiveness or ineffectiveness of prevailing rules and procedures: *complementary*, where informal factors facilitate or reinforce existing arrangements; *accommodative*, where they contribute to compromise and reduction of tensions between differing interests; *substitutive*, where they carry out functions that formal structures are unable to perform; and *competitive*, in which they challenge or reject ineffectual policies (Helmke and Levitsky 2004, 728–730).

Of the 13 interactions examined in the case of Armenia, diaspora-related contacts during the 1990s served to complement state gas policies in the majority of observations. An exception is the second chain, in which a French state-owned firm and the Ministry of Energy unsuccessfully sought to maintain socialist-era standards in opposition to both Western aid agencies and the prime minister. In addition, the joint business projects pursued by A-2 and Elpida/ERC in Armenia since 2009 have played a substitutive role by developing more advanced and efficient devices that provide an alternative to foreign technology imports.

Table 1. International-domestic interactions and energy sector development since 1991.

State	Year	International–domestic interactions	Influence on energy sector performance	Direction of influence
Armenia	1994	Foreign state firm–foreign advocacy group–domestic state firm	complementary	+
	1996	Foreign aid agency–foreign state firm–domestic state ministry	accommodative/ competitive	±
	1996–present	Foreign private firm–foreign advocacy group–domestic private firm	complementary	+
	1998	Government officials–foreign private firm–foreign state firm–NGO	complementary	+
	1998	Government officials–foreign private firm–foreign state firm–domestic private firm	complementary	+
	1998	Foreign aid agency–domestic state agency–domestic state ministry–foreign private firm	complementary	+
	2008	Political party–government officials–consumers–NGO	substitutive/ complementary	±
	2009–present	Community-based organization–foreign advocacy group–domestic private firm–producer cooperative	substitutive	+
	2010–2012	NGO–regulatory agency–foreign state firm–consumers	substitutive	+
Georgia	1998	Foreign aid agency–foreign private firm–domestic state firm	accommodative/ competitive	±
	1998	Domestic state firm–domestic private firm–producer cooperatives–government officials	accommodative	±
	2004	Foreign state firm–foreign private firm–domestic private firm–consumers	competitive	–
	2005	Foreign state ministry–domestic state ministry–foreign private firm–domestic state firm	complementary	+
	2005	NGO–foreign aid agency–government officials–foreign private firm	complementary	+
	2005	NGO–foreign aid agency–foreign state firm	complementary	+
	2008–2012	Regulatory agency–government officials–foreign state firm–political parties–consumers	substitutive/ competitive	±

In contrast, of the 12 interactions analyzed in Georgia, interests between actors were complementary in only half. In the first chain, formed in 1998, state-owned plant directors bargained to receive external funding to avoid the oversight of metering practices recommended by US advisors. In the second and third chains, formed in 1998 and 2004, producer cooperatives played a mediating role between the Georgian government, state industries and the public, while gas consumers challenged metering deals reached between foreign suppliers, state distributors and joint enterprises. Complementary relations include activities of state ministries and energy-related NGOs that helped arrange legal, technical and financial support from foreign governments and donor agencies for the rehabilitation of the Tbilisi gas distribution system in 2005. At the same time, the role of identity-related factors such as the diaspora in supplying foreign technical assistance is not evident in the Georgian case. Georgia also exhibits little equivalent to the hybrid functions of Armenian firms and ethnic community-based organizations in developing independent technical innovations.

In four instances from 2010 to 2012, Armenian citizens sought third-party intervention by the NGO sector for legal advice or resolution of payment disputes due to the inability of the PRSC to enforce consumer protection. Conversely, the relative independence initially enjoyed by the Georgian regulator in terms of financial autonomy, power to define market rules and calculation of tariffs has allowed it to play a greater role in representing consumer interests.

Lastly, the strongest contrast between conditions in both countries is the extent to which metering policies have become politicized. In Armenia, the ruling party has utilized free installation of meters in the capital to cultivate electoral support among its constituents. In contrast, in six instances between 2008 and 2012, Georgian opposition parties incorporated popular discontent with the metering practices of KazTransGaz and SOCAR into their challenge to incumbent governments. Georgian citizens have also devised informal forms of substitution and resistance such as collective refusal of payment, formation of special committees, and demonstrations in competition with formal energy administrators.

Conclusion

While the effective measurement of energy consumption in former Soviet states has been a central concern of the international policy community, its larger social and political context has seldom been addressed in academic treatments of Eurasian energy issues. The present study has sought to identify dependency and innovation in metering technology as the essential link between macro-level structural issues of gas sector performance and its impact upon citizens of post-socialist systems that have experienced various challenges in providing resources to vulnerable populations. The analysis presented above seeks to account for the larger variety of actors and institutions that participate in decision making on gas sector development in the resource-poor states of the South Caucasus. In particular, the Armenian case demonstrates how ethnic identity can interact with political influence in a manner that solidifies economic dependency while inspiring local innovation. Conversely, the relative absence of these variables in Georgia underscores the constraints and costs of liberalization and diversification away from Russian providers via replacement by Caspian gas monopolies. At the same time, to address the question of generalizability and scope conditions (or the need to account for the presence of similar phenomena across a greater number of societies), the present theoretical approach might be extended and applied to a larger sample of energy-dependent former Soviet states, such as the Eastern European/Slavic Republics (Ukraine, Belarus and Moldova). In sum, these preliminary findings suggest the potential for a comparative institutional perspective to augment conventional approaches and contribute new insights to the study of regional energy policies, which incorporates the role of more complex interactions that occur within the standard technology–performance relationship.

Acknowledgements

The author would like to give recognition to Arkady Khitarov, head of the Vanadzor branch of A-2 Ltd and chairman of Elpida (Union of Greek Public Organizations of Armenia), for providing the initial inspiration for this study.

Notes

1. The centrality of gas-fuelled appliances in these economies is further underscored by their relative affordability, often fostering conversion in economically vulnerable households.

2. This stands in sharp contrast to the electricity sector, where metering was traditionally concentrated in individual households, which fostered a distinctive policy of relocating devices to common sites to combat tampering (i.e., turning back the counters of mechanical meters by hand) long before privatization of power supplies was initiated.
3. An initial attempt at accounting for household gas consumption was made with a restart programme implemented from 1995 to 1996 that installed master meters to record collective usage in several villages and relegated responsibility for fee collection to municipal authorities. However, this effort was unsuccessful due to disputes among residents regarding payment for unequal rates and the inability to enforce compliance.
4. The major role of global energy exporters in providing technology to Armenia is also exemplified by the joint US–Russian plant operated by Emerson Process Management/Rosemount and Metran Industrial Group in Chelyabinsk Oblast.
5. The burgeoning cooperation between Armenia and Iran in securing an auxiliary to Russian gas and technology supplies during the past decade is exemplified by the joint venture Gaz Souzan Armenia, based in Najafabad Industrial Zone in Isfahan, which since 2005 has become a major supplier of diaphragm meters and pressure regulators to the Armenian market.
6. These diplomatic linkages were further reinforced beginning in spring 1999, when Gaz de France (and initially the US branch of Schlumberger) extended an offer to finance construction of the Meghri-Sardarian section of the Iran-Armenia Natural Gas Pipeline as part of a consortium including Gazprom and the National Iranian Gas Company.
7. The AL 250 diaphragm meter is another type of flow-measurement device commonly used since the 1990s, which operates upon the principle of differential pressure of fluids or gases entering and filling separate valves within the unit.
8. The signing of a bilateral cooperation agreement between the government of Armenia and the Committee for Standardization, Metrology and Certification of the Slovak Republic in September 1997, followed by an Economic Trade and Scientific-Technical Cooperation instrument in February 2000, served to bolster these activities. During the administration of state tests of national metrological standards implemented by SARM in the mid-2000s, a certain proportion of evaluation procedures were conducted by its counterpart in Slovakia. At the turn of the past decade, the former Premagas Slovakia (now a subsidiary of Elster Group) was active in the supply of diaphragm meters to the Armenian market, as well as the installation of joint assembly lines for equipment production in both Armenia and Iran.
9. The FAAE subsequently facilitated the formation of the subsidiary Forum of Armenian Businessmen in Europe, which at its first annual meeting declared its objectives to be the 'creation of close ties between Armenian businessmen for future collaboration, the necessity of developing communication systems, the establishment of economic relations with Armenia and to develop collaboration of similar institutions for future investments'.
10. In correspondence dated 31 July 2013.
11. The first of these interviews were conducted between 5 and 18 July 2011.
12. The GNERC presently operates under the 20 November 2007 amendments to Article 4 of the Georgian Law on Electricity and Natural Gas, and Article 2 of the Law on Independent National Regulatory Authorities, enacted 15 October 2002.
13. At the same time, the participation of national-minority NGOs in energy development as observed in Armenia is not apparent in the Georgian case. For instance, according to a report on the social service and development programmes administered by British Petroleum in cooperation with Mercy Corps during the construction of the Baku-Tbilisi-Ceyhan and Baku-Tbilisi-Erzurum pipelines in 2004, the leadership of the Federation of Greek Communities of Georgia was unfamiliar with its activities, despite the fact that they traversed the Pontic and Urum settlements of Tsalka District.

References

AAC (Anti-Corruption Advocacy and Assistance Center). 2011. "Gas Meter Laboratory Test Results reviewed after Yerevan AAC intervened." 21 February. Accessed July 7, 2013.

AAC (Anti-Corruption Advocacy and Assistance Center). 2012. "Gyumri Regional Department of ArmRusGasArd resign its Claim." 8 January.

Academy for Educational Development. 1999. *Armenia Energy Training Program: Contract No. LAG-1–00–98–00011–00, Task Order Two Technical Report: Natural Gas Transmission and Distribution Loss Reduction Strategies*. 4 August.

Armenian Young Lawyers Association. 2012a. "AAC Protected the Citizen's Rights". 8 August. Accessed 2013. http://ayla.am/en/2012/08/08/aac-protected-the-citizens-rights/

Armenian Young Lawyers Association. 2012b. "AAC Against Public Service Entity." 8 May. Accessed 2013. http://ayla.am/en/2012/08/05/aac-against-public-service-entity/

Arminfo News Agency. 2010. "80198 Gas Meters Checked over 9 Months." 29 November.

Asbarez Armenian News. 1997. "Gas Consortium is Largest Venture of Recent Years." 11 September. Accessed 2013. http://asbarez.com/34276/gas-consortium-is-largest-venture-of-recent-years/

Asbarez Armenian News. 1998. "French Senate to Ignore Pressures on Bill." Monday, July 6. Accessed 2013. http://asbarez.com/36346/french-senate-to-ignore-pressures-on-bill/

Bjork, I. M. et al. 2006. *Armenia: Report on The Status Of The PSRC Produced In Conjunction With The CIS Regulatory Benchmarking Report, 2006.* Produced for ERRA by Pierce Atwood, supported by USAID, June.

Bunce, V. 1999. *Subversive Institutions: The Design and Destruction of Socialism and the State.* Cambridge, MA: Cambridge University Press.

Burns and Roe Enterprises, Inc. 1998. *Final Report, Emergent Work In Georgia: Development Of Gas Pipeline Inspection, Leak Detection and Emergency Response Protocols,* Republic Of Georgia, September 22. Accessed June 2013. http://pdf.usaid.gov/pdf_docs/PDABR508.pdf

Channel One Georgia. 2009. "National Democratic Party Accuses Khaztransgaz for Infringing Customers' Rights." 29 June 13:15. Accessed July 6, 2013. http://1tv.ge/news-view/5597?lang=en

Channel One Georgia. 2012. "Labor Party Held Protest Outside GNERC." 1 July 17:04. Accessed June 29, 2013. http://1tv.ge/news-view/5670?lang=en

Closson, S. 2007. "Short-Circuiting Reform: Informal Politico-Economic Networks in Georgia's and Kyrgyzstan's Electricity Sectors." *Visiting Research Fellow Papers.* Bishkek: American University of Central Asia Social Research Center. Accessed May 2013. http://src.auca.kg/images/stories/files/Closson_eng.pdf

Closson, S. 2009. "State Weakness in Perspective: Strong Politico-Economic Networks in Georgia's Energy Sector." *Europe-Asia Studies* 61 (5): July, 759–778.

Daily News. 2004. "JSC Tbilgaz Decides To Make Order In Gas Consumption Accounting." December 8. Accessed June 30, 2013. http://www.sarke.com/cgi/search/search.asp?Page=1&Search=vake+gas+meters&x=0&y=0

Daily News. 2005. "Tbilgaz Says It Will Return Dismantled Meters to Consumers." January 24. Accessed June 30, 2013. http://www.sarke.com/cgi/search/search.asp?Page=1&Search=vake+gas+meters&x=0&y=0

Daly, C. K. 2009. "Analysis: Kazakh Investment in Georgia's Energy Sector." UPI.com. 9 April. Accessed July 9, 2013. http://www.upi.com/Business_News/Energy-Resources/2009/04/09/Analysis-Kazakh-investment-in-Georgias-energy-sector/UPI-81991239300029/

Dzidzikashvili, M. 2010. *Georgian National Energy and Water Supply Regulatory Commission: Commission Structure and Authority.* National Association of Regulatory Utility Commissioners-Kentucky Public Service Commission First (Introductory) Partnership Activity, May 17–21. Accessed 2013. http://www.narucpartnerships.org/Documents/05%20dzidzikashvil%20english.pdf

Edwards, M. 2003. "The New Great Game and the New Great Gamers: Disciples of Kipling and Mackinder." *Central Asian Survey,* 22 (1): March, 83–102.

Energy Regulators Regional Association. 2001. "Energy Law of the Republic of Armenia." 11 April.

European Bank for Reconstruction and Development. 2008. *Armenia Country Profile.* Accessed 2013. http://www.ebrd.com/downloads/legal/irc/countries/armenia.pdf

European Bank for Reconstruction and Development. 2009. *B-b. Observers to the Treaty establishing the Energy Community: Georgia Country Profile.* Accessed 2013. http://www.ebrd.com/downloads/legal/irc/countries/georgia.pdf

Franke, A., A. Gawrich, and G. Alakberov. 2009. "Kazakhstan and Azerbaijan as Post-Soviet Rentier States: Resource Incomes and Autocracy as a Double "Curse" in Post-Soviet Regimes." *Europe-Asia Studies* 61 (1): January, 109–140.

Geddes, B. 1990. "How the Cases You Choose Affect the Answers You Get: Selection Bias in Comparative Politics." *Political Analysis* 2: 131–50.

Georgian National Energy Regulatory Commission. 2007. *Law of Georgia on Electricity and Natural Gas, Chapter I, General Provisions.* Accessed 2013. http://www.gnerc.org/uploads/law_of_georgia_on_electricity_and_natural_gas__updated_version.pdf

German, T. 2008. "Corridor of Power: The Caucasus and Energy Security." *Caucasian Review of International Affairs* 2 (2) Spring: 64–72.

Gisselquist, R. M. 2014. "Paired Comparison and Theory Development: Considerations for Case Selection." *PS: Political Science & Politics* 47 (2), 477–484.

Gogelia, N. 2011. "Problems with Gas Meter Inspection", BeyondTbilisi.ge, Transparency International Georgia, April 22. Accessed 2013. http://beyondtbilisi.ge/en/content/problems-gas-meter-inspection

Hagler Bailly, Inc. 1997. *Georgia: Oil & Gas Sector Reform Program: Assessment of the State of Commercialization in the Oil and Gas Sectors of Georgia Final Report.* 27 August.

Hagler Bailly, Inc. 1998. *Natural Gas Distribution Commercialization Project: ARMENIA: Final Report,* NIS Institutional Based Services Energy Efficiency and Market Reform Project Contract No CCN-Q-OO-93–00152–00, Delivery Order No 15, September.

Hagler Bailly, Inc. 1999. *Tbilgazi Gas Distribution Company Tbilisi, Georgia: Information Memorandum.* September.

Helmke, G., and S. Levitsky. 2004. "Informal Institutions and Comparative Politics: A Research Agenda." *Perspectives on Politics* 2 (4): 725–740.

Hrayr Maroukhian Foundation. 2013. *Monopolies in Armenia.* Friedrich-Ebert-Stiftung, Yerevan, February.

INOGATE. 2012. "Armenia: Energy Sector Review." Energy Portal: Energy Cooperation between the EU, Eastern Europe, the Caucasus and Central Asia. Accessed 2013. http://www.inogate.org/index.php?option=com_inogate&view=countrysector&id=113&lang=en

Jervalidze, L. 2006. *Georgia: Russian Foreign Energy Policy and Implications for Georgia's Energy Security.* London, UK: Global Market Briefings, Institute for the Analysis of Global Security.

Jervalidze, L. 2008. *Georgia's State Energy Policy in the Natural Gas Sector.* Transparency International Georgia, 29 February.

Jones Luong, P. 2002. *Institutional Change and Political Continuity in Post-Soviet Central Asia: Power, Perceptions, and Pacts.* Cambridge and NY: Cambridge University Press.

Jones Luong, P., and E. Weinthal. 2006. "Rethinking the Resource Curse: Ownership Structure, Institutional Capacity, and Domestic Constraints." *Annual Review of Political Science* 9: 241–63.

Jones Luong, P., and E. Weinthal. 2010. *Oil is Not a Curse: Ownership Structure and Institutions in Petroleum-Rich Soviet Successor States.* Cambridge and NY: Cambridge University Press.

Karagiannis, E. 2002. *Energy and Security in the Caucasus.* New York & London: RoutledgeCurzon.

Khitarov, A. 2009. Бизнес-проект: "Организация регионального научно производственного-учебного центра" [Business Project: Establishment of a regional scientific-production training center]. Union of Greek Public Organizations of Armenia, Vanadzor.

Khitarov, A. 2010. "Business Plan for Development of Measuring Natural Gas Consumption Devices." Union of Greek Public Organizations of Armenia, Vanadzor.

King, G., R. O. Keohane and S. Verba. 1994. *Designing Social Inquiry: Scientific Inference in Qualitative Research.* Princeton, NJ: Princeton University Press.

Kubicek, P. 2013. "Energy Politics and Geopolitical Competition in the Caspian Basin." *Journal of Eurasian Studies* 4 (2), July 2013, 171–180.

Marjanyan, A. H. 2004. *Overview of the Armenian Utility Sectors: Power and Gas Sectors.* Ameria Consultancy, Yerevan.

Merklein & Associates, Inc. 1996. *Republic of Armenia: Petroleum Sector Development Gas Sector Restructuring MIS System.* May.

Merklein & Associates, Inc. 1997. *Republic of Armenia: Organization and Structure of the Natural Gas Sector: Review and Recommendations,* Energy and Infrastructure Division Office of Energy, Environment and Urban Development Bureau for Europe and the New Independent States, U.S. Agency for International Development, January.

Mtivlishvili, G. 2008. "Telavi Inhabitants Accusing Wissol in Extortion", Humanrights.ge, September 30. Accessed June 30, 2013. http://www.humanrights.ge/index.php?a=main&pid=7360&lang=eng

Namgaladze, D. 2008. "In-process Losses in Natural Gas Distribution and Transportation Systems." Georgian National Energy and Water Supply Regulatory Commission, 27 June-3 July.

Namgaladze, D. 2009. "Problems of Metering Natural Gas Used by Population", Georgian National Energy and Water Supply Regulatory Commission Natural Gas Department. Accessed July 17, 2013. http://www.narucpartnerships.org/Documents/Presentation%20namgaladze_en.pdf

Nuriyev, E. 2007. *The South Caucasus at the Crossroads: Conflicts, Caspian Oil and Great Power Politics.* Berlin: Lit Verlag.

Papava, V. 2005. "The Baku-Tbilisi-Ceyhan Pipeline: Implications for Georgia." In *The Baku-Tbilisi-Ceyhan Pipeline: Oil Window to the West,* edited by F. S. Starr and S. E. Cornell, pp. 83–102. Washington and Uppsala: CACI and SRSP.

Policy Forum Armenia. 2010. *Armenia-Diaspora Relations: 20 Years Since Independence*. State of the Nation Series. August. Accessed June 30, 2013. http://www.pf-armenia.org/sites/default/files/documents/files/PFA%20Diaspora%20Report.pdf

Public Services Regulatory Commission of the Republic of Armenia. 2004. "Unofficial English Translation: The Law Of The Republic Of Armenia On The Regulatory Body For Public Services." 17 January. Accessed July 9, 2013. http://www.psrc.am/download.php?fid=1341

Public Services Regulatory Commission of the Republic of Armenia. 2012. "HTSKH-i patmut'yuny (PRSC Story)." Accessed June 29, 2013. http://www.psrc.am/am/?nid=18

Reuters. 2005. "Georgia will Sell Capital Gas Net to Kazakhstan Kaztransgas." Tbilisi, December 26. Accessed May 31, 2014. http://www.kase.kz/news/show/185532

Rezonansi. 2009. "SOCAR at'visebuli qazakhet'is met'odebi klientebt'an urt'iert'obis (SOCAR Assimilated The Kazakh Methods Of Customer Relations)." 15 July.

Rustavi 2 Broadcasting Company. 2008. "Labor Party Rallies at Gas Distribution Company." 30 October. Accessed June 30, 2013. http://www.rustavi2.com/news/news_text.php?id_news=28538&pg=1&im=main&ct=4&wth=0

Rustavi 2 Broadcasting Company. 2009a. "NDP Accuses Gas Distribution Company of Swindle". 10 July.

Rustavi 2 Broadcasting Company. 2009b. "Labor Party Rallies Outside the Regulatory Commission." 7 July. Accessed June 30, 2013. http://www.rustavi2.com/news/news_text.php?rec_start=176&rec_start_nav=22&id_news=32510&pg=1&srch_w=&im=main&srch=1&ct=0&wth=0&l=0&ddd=

Rustavi 2 Broadcasting Company. 2009c. "Labour Party Accuses Kaztransgas of Terrorizing Subscribers." 15 January. Accessed June 30, 2013. http://www.rustavi2.com/news/news_text.php?rec_start=144&rec_start_nav=11&id_news=29728&pg=1&srch_w=&im=main&srch=1&ct=0&wth=0&l=0&ddd=

Sabonis-Helf, T. 2004. "The Rise of the Post-Soviet Petro-States: Energy Exports and Domestic Governance in Turkmenistan and Kazakhstan." In *In the Tracks of Tamerlane: Central Asia's Path to the 21st Century*, edited by L. Daniel Burghart and Teresa Sabonis-Helf, 159–86. Washington, DC: NDU Press.

Sénat. 1998. *France-Arménie: accompagner une renaissance (visite du 29 juin au 4 juillet 1998) Rapport de groupe interparlementaire d'amitié n° 25 - 15 décembre 1998*. Accessed 2013. http://www.senat.fr/ga/ga-25/GA-251.pdf.

Starr, F. S., and S. E. Cornell, eds. 2005. *The Baku-Tbilisi-Ceyhan Pipeline: Oil Window to the West*. Washington and Uppsala: CACI and SRSP.

Suvarian, N. 2008. "Kaztransgas-Tbilisi" Makes Subscribers to Again Change Meters." Humanrights.ge, 6 December. Accessed June 11, 2014. http://www.humanrights.ge/index.php?a=main&pid=7478&lang=eng

Tarrow, S. 1999. "Expanding Paired Comparison: A Modest Proposal." *APSA-CP: Newsletter of the Organised Section in Comparative Politics of the American Political Science Association*, 10 (2): Summer, 9–12.

Tarrow, S. 2010. "The Strategy of Paired Comparison: Toward a Theory of Practice." *Comparative Political Studies* 43 (2): 230–259.

TIAC (Transparency International Anticorruption Center). 2008. "Gas Meters are Installed Free of Charge in Avan Community of Yerevan by the Republican Party of Armenia (HHK)." 2 September. Accessed 2013. http://transparency.am/monitor_2008.php?id=84

Transparency International Georgia. 2008. *State Policies of Georgia in the Energy Sector: Tariffs on Electricity and Gas*, 26 March.

Union of Greek Public Organizations of Armenia. 2013. "Education and Research Center (ERC)." Accessed June 30, 2013. http://greeks.am/?page_id=132

United Nations Economic and Social Council. 2005. *Economic Commission for Europe Committee On Sustainable Energy, Working Party on Gas and Gas Centre, Workshop on the Current State and Prospects for Rehabilitation of the Local Natural Gas Infrastructure in the city of Tbilisi, Tbilisi (Georgia), 18–19 May 2005*. 30 June.

United Nations Economic Commission for Europe. 2004. *Meeting of the Extended Bureau of the Committee on Sustainable Energy*, ECE Gas Centre, Geneva, 9 December. Accessed June 30, 2013 http://www.unece.org/fileadmin/DAM/ie/se/pdfs/exbur/klef049decex.pdf

United Nations Economic Commission for Europe. 2005. "Georgian Gas Industry." 15th Session of the Working Party on Gas & Round Table on Balance between Market and Regulation, 18–19 January, Geneva. Accessed June 30, 2013. http://www.unece.org/fileadmin/DAM/energy/se/pdfs/wpgas/countries/georgia_zaz.pdf

Flows of oil, flows of people: resource-extraction industry, labour market and migration in western Kazakhstan

Philipp Frank Jäger

Department of History, Humboldt-Universität zu Berlin, Germany

Twenty years after independence the labour market of western Kazakhstan is strongly oriented towards the resource-extraction industry. The oil sector offers job opportunities not only in mining and exploration but also in connected services such as transport, security and food supply, and maintenance services. Based on a year of ethnographic fieldwork in the region, I argue that the resource-extraction industry provides a blessing for the working population in terms of relatively high salaries; however, it represents a curse in terms of labour conditions. This article highlights, through the example of Aktobe province, workers' attitudes towards and their agency within the oil sector that influences migration choices. The research suggests that money earned in the oil sector can work as a catalyst for migration and urbanization.

Introduction

While most Europeans are aware of oil as consumers, for citizens in western Kazakhstan processes around oil touch many levels of their everyday lives. This is more than just fuel for cars; many have found jobs connected to the oil industry. While in Soviet times the local economy hinged on the agricultural production of the steppe area between the Caspian Sea and Aral Sea, particularly as a result of the Virgin Land Campaign,[1] nowadays agriculture has declined and given way to a fossil fuel extraction-orientated economy. For the regional labour market the oil and chrome industries play a significant role not only in extraction but also in the large service sector surrounding it.

During Joseph Stalin's industrialization drive, mines and heavy industry complexes were founded all over the country and extended, such as Ust-Kamenogorsk (eastern Kazakhstan, lead and zinc), Karaganda (central Kazakhstan, coal), and Aktobe (western Kazakhstan, chrome). In independent Kazakhstan citizens now tie their expectations of economic development to this mineral resource wealth. This resource wealth and supporting infrastructure, however, is now exploited through complex arrangements between the government and private companies. The intersection between state aims and private businesses means that the use and benefit of the resources sometimes do not meet the hopes and expectations of the citizens.

In this article I focus on the relationship between oil, labour market and migration in western Kazakhstan, and how this influences people's hopes and expectations. I examine examples where people migrate in order to work in the resource-extraction industry and how people take decisions to migration in relation to regional economic developments. I also discuss how the oil business is perceived by the oil workers and what kind of alternatives exists for employment. Further, I examine my ethnographic material in relation to the global political and economic discourse of development and the difficulties migration presents.

I draw upon results from my fieldwork in Aktobe region in 2012. I conducted fieldwork in Aktobe city, provincial towns and villages strongly influenced by a transforming labour market and by migration. My methods were based on participant observation and semi-structured or open-ended interviews which I conducted in Kazakh and Russian. I gathered further data in informal talks with workers and their family in both languages. During my research I had the opportunity to speak with unskilled labourers who worked mainly as drivers, cleaning staff or storage workers, drillers and oil engineers. The majority were between 20 and 40 years of age.

My main research questions were oriented towards migrant's choice of work place. I intended to understand to what extent jobs in the resource-extraction industry attract migrants and how they evaluate the work places there. Do they prefer jobs at the oil stations or in the urban environment? In how far do migrants see a future perspective in working for an oil company? With these questions I intend to contribute to the discussion of regional development from an anthropological point of view.

I applied the method of multi-sited ethnography (Marcus 1995) in order to follow the migrants to the places where they and their household members live. My research intentionally focused on migrants and their relationships with their families at home and among other migrants. I complemented this by conducting interviews with local politicians and mayors, and collected data about resource-extraction industries from the available literature. I was unable to conduct more extensive research with the companies engaged in resource extraction because in my experience they were sceptical towards foreign (Western) researchers and their political agenda (in my opinion due to the Zhanaozen incident; see below).

Perspectives on the 'resource curse'

In such contexts, focus is often turned to the 'resource curse'. However, the experiences of my informants[2] in Kazakhstan have led me to question this notion and its focus. Academic discussions of resource-driven growth in Central Asia often refer to the 'resource curse' (among others, see Ross 1999, 2012; Auty 2004; and Alayi 2005). McNeish and Logan (2012, 10) give a striking explanation of the term:

> The term resource curse is now commonly applied to describe how countries rich in natural resources are unable to use that wealth to boost their economies, and how, counter-intuitively (if one discounts imperialism), these countries have lower economic growth and development outcomes than countries without an abundance of natural resources.

Because of this paradox, Behrends, Reyna, and Schlee (2013, 6) speak about a 'crazy curse'.

The political scientist Michael Ross who has written about the relationship of resources and development in Third World countries highlights the strong connection between the changes in a country's oil revenues according to the world oil price. State authorities need to plan prudently in order to secure financing for central projects when oil prices shrink and evade squandering surplus money when oil prices are higher. Secrecy also appears to be a problem: rulers of oil states are likely to use their national oil company's (NOC) budget as an always-available resource for their expenditures (Ross 2012, 6). Considering this point, it becomes debatable if the state's investment in the new capital Astana can be seen as a kind of squandering resources.

Ross (2012), however, warns that if a country is increasingly dependent on oil, not only does money pour in, but also new threats appear. At the financial level the state becomes more dependent on oil revenues and less on taxes. This development makes an oil-founded government more sensitive about investors into the resource extraction sector and less responsive to the concerns of its tax payers (5). In Kazakhstan this process has been even more severe because all the country's oil fields and formerly state-owned companies were sold to foreign companies at a bargain while many industrial companies had to close because of the economic transition (Ostrowski 2010, 48).

Observing the economy at the macro-level, it cannot be said that Kazakhstan's oil boom has an appeal to the country's population. Although the resource-extraction industry has a significant impact on the reduction on unemployment, the positive influence ends at Aktobe province's borders. The balance of migration between Aktobe and other provinces stabilizes around zero (Aktobe oblysynyn statistika departamenti 2011, 56). This may be caused by the conditions of work and living in the West that stay opaque for citizens from other parts of Kazakhstan. One point to consider is that working at an oil corporation is not regarded as prestigious for Kazakh families, while travel and information costs are also high (Aldashev and Dietz 2011, 11). Without regional knowledge it is complicated to find an affordable living space and capacity in childcare institutions. Additional difficulties are faced by female household members when only the husband has a job offer in the resource-extraction industry. Household income may be less than before migrating to Aktobe, even though a male household member may earn more at an oil station than he earned before in another province. The demand for workers can be satisfied inside the province by the rural population migrating to the urban centres.

Not only are investments in the extractive industries more sensitive, but also popular discontent is considered a threat. The events in Zhanaozen, I argue, are an example of how protests reveal the 'curse' for the economic and social implications it has, and threatens the government's control over its own presentation of the benefits of the sector (cf. Sakal, 2014). Asking about the political processes of the 'resource curse' has become particularly relevant since the Zhanaozen incident on December 16, 2011, on the anniversary of the 1988 riots in Almaty, which were seen as the first public resistance against Soviet rule in Kazakhstan. In the town of Zhanaozen in Mangystau province at least 15 people were killed and over 100 injured as a long-lasting protest by oil workers escalated in December 2011 (Demytrie 2012). Until today, the precise background of the events is unclear, but there is a strong indication that the protests threatened companies and a government unwilling to allow the legitimacy of labour movements. While the state hastily sent more security staff and pushed money into programmes to improve the 'political literacy' of the population[3] in order to silence the riots, the deeper causes of the situation remain unchanged. Instead of raising the question of a local population's political empowerment, the citizens were stigmatized as uneducated roughnecks who have to be civilized. For over one-and-a-half years before the riots, oil workers in Zhanaozen were engaged in a labour dispute over labour conditions and salary. The protests are a proof that citizens express their entitlement on the resource wealth.

'In Kazakhstan we have all kinds of resources,' said Temirkhan to me, 'but nevertheless we are still poor.' In his mid-50s, Temirkhan works seasonally in Aktobe as a day labourer. Formerly he worked for Tengizchevroil[4] at an oil station near the Caspian Sea. He learned a bit of English at the company and gained insight about the procedures at his working place. All he has left from his job is his Tengizchevroil working suit which he still wears for his jobs in Aktobe. He quit his job at the transnational oil company (TOC) for medical reasons. The long working shifts at the stations were hard for him to endure. Temirkhan, remembering the early 1990s, told that he was full of hope and expectations when Kazakhstan threw off Moscow's paternalism. Now he is disappointed about more recent results. He blames the TOCs for just picking out the pearls and not caring about anything else. Temirkhan considers the government as too weak to encounter the TOCs at an equal level. 'And when we protested, we were shot down,' he added embittered. People like him are sensitive to the processes going on.

Many oil workers believe that their state sold out the country's wealth. Temirkhan expressed these thoughts: 'They sold Baikonur to the Russians, Kashagan to ENI[5] and Atyrau to the Chevroil.[6] Soon nothing is left over for us.' A statement like this shows deep frustration. The workers and their relatives feel locked out of the processes in which the terms of trade between their government and the TOCs are negotiated. While Astana makes profitable deals, western Kazakhstan has a low priority in the pecking order. Although western Kazakhstan's cities are developing, significant income does not reach local households, since the salaries for most employees of subcontractors are kept at a low level.

The harsh government crackdown during the Zhanaozen events has perhaps resulted in no recent public protests. As a result, the Zhanaozen incident broadened the gap between politics and the local population. The political sphere is widely perceived as a dirty game with its own rules. Even the younger generation has turned away disappointed. Although recently TOCs like CNPC[7] invested in the social sphere (equipping libraries, renovating schools).[8] Such activities often originate as a result of pressure from local authorities belonging to the presidential party Nur Otan, rather than from the direct demands of the local population.

Oil extraction affects not only change in a country's economy and politics. Oil's influence can be seen in the society as well, especially in developing countries. In this respect, Behrends and Schareika (2010, 84–85, original emphasis) claim that 'the impact of oil can and must also be considered with regard to socio-cultural and therefore very heterogeneous and context specific *meaning* or *significations* attributed to various aspects of oil production by the involved actors'. At this place anthropology can make a contribution to the resource course discourse. The authors underline that in particular anthropology's 'theoretical and methodological strength' can contribute to this new field (85–86; cf. Weszkalnys 2010).

Ethnographies like Yessenova's (2012) can shed light on the effects of the 'resource curse' at the local level or argue against economist's generalizations. This study shows the interdependences between migration and the oil sector by analysing migrants' attitudes and agency towards working opportunities. Their opinions may differ greatly from the perspective of the central state or the provincial political powers. The government treats oil primarily as a strategic resource that should be a central topic in foreign policy. Oil money is used for prestigious projects; it does not reach the villages out on the steppe. In the eyes of the rural population they stay behind while oil is pumped to the West – and oil money to Astana in the east.

Attention has to be paid to the meaning actors attach to oil and their own lives when working the resource-extraction industry. While it can be summarized that the exploitation of oil is mainly seen to be positive, which perhaps reflects the Soviet fascination with technical achievements, the significance for individuals and local groups has to be captured in detail by anthropological research. Aspects of Kazakh culture have to be taken into consideration at this point, which will be analysed in this article.

The oil industry in western Kazakhstan

Together with Atyrau province, Aktobe province profits from the recent oil rush. Unemployment rates went down continuously from 13.7% in 1998 to 4.9% in 2011. This percentage is the lowest in the whole republic, the national average being 5.4% (Boranbayeva 2009, 2012; Smailov 2012, 6). This positive development is caused mainly by the work created in and around the resource-extraction industry. While many Soviet-era local light industry factories closed, production concentrated on heavy industry connected with the locally extracted chrome. In this article I will concentrate on the oil and gas industry because this sector has developed rapidly after Kazakhstan's independence. Chrome extraction[9] was already well-established in the Soviet period and was later privatized and modernized step by step with significant smaller impacts on the local labour market.

As a resource-rich country, Kazakhstan played a decisive role in the energy supply of the Soviet Union. The Kazakh Soviet Socialist Republic expanded to become its third largest energy-producing republic (Dahl and Kuralbayeva 2001, 429). Beside other resources like coal, copper, lead, zinc, iron ore, manganese, titanium, chromium and uranium, Kazakhstan has a significant share of the world reserves in oil and gas (Kaiser and Pulsipher 2007, 1300). Kazakhstan holds 3.2% of world reserves in oil, ranking ninth among states (Palazuelos and Fernández 2012, 29). After the first oil discoveries in the 1950s on the Mangyslak Peninsular, smaller oil companies were established like Mangistauneftegas (in 1963), Uzenmunaigaz (in 1964) or Aktobemunaigaz (AMG), which began oil production in 1967 (Ostrowski 2010, 30–31).

Kazakhstan's post-independent years were characterized by unrealistic expectations in how far the production could be pushed, considering the technical difficulties in the Caspian Sea region. The discovery of the Kashagan oil field in 2000 turned out to be the largest oil find in the late 20th century, comparable only with the Prudhoe Bay discovery in Alaska in 1968. This shifted Kazakhstan to the first league of oil producers globally, but made clear that large foreign investment would be required to exploit the technically difficult field. The scheduled beginning of production in 2008 was delayed for years, while the costs exploded (Brauer 2008, 2). It was only on September 11, 2013 that the operating consortium announced the opening of the first oil wells. Meanwhile the exploring TOCs are sceptical about the outcomes of Kashagan (also known as 'Cash-all-gone') project (Scheck 2013).[10]

AMG, the largest oil company in Aktobe province, was privatized in 1997. Soon after the takeover of 60.3% of stakes by the Chinese state-owned oil and gas corporation CNPC, first tensions with the local population arose, which cumulated in public protests when CPNC fired a total of 2000 employees in April 1999. In the year 2000 workers demanded the cancellation of the CNPC contract (Ostrowski 2010, 126). Press reports complained that AMG wanted to limit the use of the Kazakh language at the workplace and forced the workers to sing the Chinese national anthem. As the planned investment measure was not taken, CNPC was first critiqued by the provincial government, later by Astana. As Kazakh Prime Minister Kasymzhomart Tokayev intervened and foreshadowed complications for Sino-Kazakh relations, CNPC promised to reinstate some of the sacked workers and allocate US$1 million as a financial aid to boost the local rural economy (Yermukanov 2004).

Erlan, who works at AMG and migrated from a village to Alga, has mixed feelings about his employer. On the one hand he rates the 'Chinese bosses' as 'zhadnyi' (Russian, 'greedy'), and states that they cannot be trusted. On the other hand, he admits that Chinese staff concentrate on work and are not afraid of the harsh conditions at the oil and gas stations in distant regions. In his point of view, the younger locals are looking for an easy life and are not ready to give their best at the stations. This perception is also mentioned by Ostrowski (2010). While at the beginning of the oil rush unskilled labourers could immediately find employment in the oil branch, now subcontractors look out for specialists who can hardly be found locally. Engineers for the oil and gas sector are trained in Almaty and Astana or the Institute of Oil and Gas in Atyrau, which had already been established in the Soviet period.

In the past few years the working climate has not improved, while CNPC strengthened its grip on the company by raising their stakes to 85.42% of shares. CNCP not only gained new licences for exploring and drilling in the Aktobe region and southern Kazakhstan (conducted by bought local companies), but also it started to build oil and gas pipelines to China. The market access by the takeover of local companies was a kind of win–win situation for the Chinese and Kazakhstani governments. CNPC ensured an immediate start of their operations on the bought companies' assets and resource fields, and Astana could justify Chinese engagement by referring to saved workplaces toward a local population that tends to be extremely sceptical towards China. Large investments doubled the crude production from 65,000 barrels per day in 2001 to 122,000 barrels per day in 2009, establishing AMG as the fourth large domestic oil and gas corporation in Kazakhstan (Palazuelos and Fernández 2012, 30). The most important site in Aktobe province is the Zhanazhol oil and gas field where AMG recently invested in the improvement of their gas production.[11]

For the province's most important oil and gas field Zhanazhol, no literature on the labour force is available. But Yessenova (2012, 106) portrays the reorganization of work at the Tengiz oil field, where Kazakh subcontractors cut down services like the provision of transportation and accommodation while keeping salaries at a minimum. The example of the 2004–05 riots at Tengiz village shows that the workers have not been able to have their grievances addressed. At the time nearly 3000 workers of the Senimdi Kurylis and other subcontractors started a labour dispute. Instead of negotiations, violence erupted in which domestic and foreign workers as well as managers and the police were involved. The state authorities tried to persuade the workers to stop the strike after they worked out a Memorandum of Understanding that suggested a higher minimum wage. During this labour dispute the Chevron TOC, which is the major player at the Tengiz oil field, only observed the processes. They refused to take part in the labour dispute, pointing out that it is a matter for the subcontractors and that the strike took place in the public area of Tengiz village rather than on corporate territory (Yessenova 2012, 107–108).

Village life and the challenges of the changing rural economy

In order to understand rural–urban migrants' views and opinions about work in the resource-extraction industry, I have traced their mobility back to the former collective farms and gain an overview about the situation in the villages today. Several push factors lead to a significant stream of migrants from the villages. Migrants mentioned often referred to three issues: lack of work, lack of educational possibilities and lack of infrastructure in their home villages. While elderly people often decide to stay on their privatized farms, the younger population are willing to move to urban centres. Migrants indicate that the lack of infrastructure and work intensified rural–urban migration. In Soviet times the state had offered not only a basic supply system, but also cultural events like concerts, public celebration of holidays and rural cinema. After independence this system broke down, kindergartens closed and rural clubs were disbanded. The rural situation remained problematic for a long time while cities developed. Some urban areas like Karaganda went into decline, losing citizens when the large industrial factories restructured and laid off workers, but the western Kazakhstan towns of Aktobe, Aktau and especially Atyrau – which Prime Minister Serik Balgymbayev in 1999 called the 'oil capital' (Ostrowski 2010, 91) – quickly developed.

In the past five years the state has begun to invest in rural education by repairing old school buildings and reopening kindergartens. This is financed not directly by oil money but also by credits from international banks given to the state in expectation of future oil royalties. The schools have been well-equipped with computers and electronic learning tools. Teachers have also been sent to regional qualification seminars. But the improvement of rural education favours rural out-migration, because the school leavers attain an improved education and a majority want to gain vocational and professional qualifications, which lead them away from the village. Depending on families' financial means, almost all teenagers except those willing to continue their parents' animal breeding attend professional schools with dormitories in the regional centres or leave for Aktobe, where accommodation has to be privately organized.

Thus, the main reason for out-migration is a lack of job opportunities in the rural areas. My informants estimate that the village sphere is limited to agriculture. Almost all farms work on a subsistence level. The farms are unable to use additional workforces effectively. They lack resources like water and capital as well as a means of production to broaden their family assets into agribusiness. The farms I visited during my fieldwork relied heavily on older Soviet infrastructure. Animal breeders told me that they prefer buying used machinery from farmers migrating out than investing in modern equipment which they cannot repair themselves. They use revamped Soviet equipment until it finally breaks and is non-repairable. Due to the lack of base capital and securities, banks refuse to give credit.

The only income is the salary of villagers in public services (administration, healthcare and education institutions). Several times I stayed at the houses of school teachers who bred at least some cows and sheep as a basic source for their daily diet. Animal breeders only make money by selling animals, which leads to a situation in which only a limited amount of money can be spent, because family farmers lack the opportunity to bring large numbers of their animals onto the market. This means that there is little chance for a service sector in the village economy.

The only opportunities are smaller shops, mainly selling alcohol and cigarettes. In some cases villagers form a transport company, providing taxi or bus services, often as an extension to live-stock farming. Although in Kazakhstan some limited social welfare is offered, most rural house-holds cannot access it because they are considered self-reliant rural farms as long as they keep animals.

Opportunities and constraints of working in the energy sector

For the rural population, jobs in the resource extractive industry offers an opportunity to find work. The salary there is higher than any position in a village would give them. To find an access is not complicated as Kuat, who works as a security guard at Zhanazhol, told me. He finished school at a remote village near the Russian boarder and joined the army. The security work is his first job which required only basic army training. For Kuat his job is just a transitional solution earning money for his future plans. He is looking for a better salary than the 40,000 Tenge (approximately US$220) he is working for and a job in the city of Aktobe. He considers his job at the oilfield as boring and unsatisfying, while dreaming of the entertainment and recreation the city offers.

The Zhanazhol oil and gas field and smaller oil stations of Aktobe province are located in the open steppe far from urban centres. The oil companies may not solely rely on the population of these sparsely inhabited regions and have to invite workers from other parts of the province, mainly the provincial capital Aktobe and a smaller town located between Aktobe and the oil fields. The companies organize bus transport to the fields, which attracts migrants to the settle-ments along their routes. I meet oil workers migrating seasonally to urban centres because their villages were cut-off from the traffic routes by snow- and sandstorms as well as by flooding from melting snow.

Many tasks necessary to oil production are outsourced to subcontracting companies. These are a constant topic of dispute, as Ostrowski (2010) has shown. In the 1990s, the first local sub-contractors were at a disadvantage when competing with the larger and more experienced inter-national subcontractors. Local authorities continuously targeted the non-Western subcontracting companies, claiming that they violate labour laws, do not provide proper equipment and have much worse working conditions than Western companies (Ostrowski 2010, 95–96). In August 2000 the government intervened by impeding the work of foreign non-Western subcontractors and introducing a quota for the foreign workforce. In this way national companies became more competitive. Foreign companies reacted by hiring more local workers. The foreign subcon-tracting companies have learned to navigate in a volatile political environment, registering as Kazakh companies and using various feints to veil their data (Ostrowski 2010, 117).

In the eyes of the locals, not every subcontractor is the same. Zhanna, an unmarried woman in her mid-50s, underlines that she could find a job at a subsidiary of Schlumberger[12] by several years of service as waitress. Her company offers better working conditions, especially the number of working hours and accommodation. She supports relatives and friends to find jobs in resource extraction-related services. She is satisfied with her situation, but she sees no possibility to improve her situation by working directly for Schlumberger or one of the TOCs.

Due to the high competition local companies are permanently exposed to the danger of bankruptcy. Workers emerge as sufferers in this system. Their salaries are held back when the companies confront financial problems and then fall away without compensation if the subcontractor becomes insolvent. Workers are not able to complain about their subcontracting company. The typical employment form is a one-year contract. 'Inconvenient' workers' (i.e. people who complain) contracts will simply not be extended. Against this background, workers prefer to work for international subcontractors. Working there opens their eyes to the benefits of Western (and Eastern) employees, who not only earn up to 20 times as much but also receive insurance and social benefits (Ostrowski 2010, 88). At the local level there exists an understanding that specialists should be well paid. However, the population widely disagrees with the salary disparities and the fact that the TOCs' interest in training local experts is very limited.

The majority of workers are employed by subcontracting companies. They work in a one-year contract which threatens not to be renewed if they complain, have trouble with the boss or even simply if the economic situation worsens. In this setting the workers have to try to improve their employment situation. Only a few of them can find permanent work directly at TOCs or NOCs. The majority looks to other economic spheres. But in order to gather information about this, they have to use their recreational shift time in Aktobe or the regional centres.

Due to job uncertainty in subcontractor companies and the hard environmental conditions, workers look out for other jobs when they have earned a certain amount, which in the ideal case allows them to build a house on the outskirts of Aktobe. How to obtain a new house or flat are important considerations for a parents' household before planning a marriage. Working at the oil and gas stations mainly attracts singles. Usually the stations work on two 12-hour shifts over an unbroken period of 14 days. Family fathers and mothers complained about jobs at the oil stations that require leaving their families for longer periods.

Some employees build up savings in order to open up their own business, such as a kiosk or a taxi service. Most workers look for employment in a company in Aktobe or a regional centre in the profession for which they gained diplomas, but the labour market is highly competitive. To get a job there, working experience in one of the oil stations is only of limited interest. Especially when a person has a certain social capital and networks (professional, neighbourhood or religious), they have opportunities to find a higher salary in the informal sector instead of the isolated work at the stations.

Due to working shift models which comprise 14 or 28 days of work and a rest period of the same duration, oil workers have time to find additional freelance work. Those with a car are able to work as taxi drivers. They earn around US$3–4 for a short ride in the centre. Some also offer trips to regional towns. Although the state tried to regulate and curtail private taxi rides, the official measures have only partly been successful. The private taxi drivers' origin plays a role here. I observed that drivers born in the city and connected in their neighbourhood 'defended' their nearby taxi hotspots against rival migrant taxi drivers who have to evade the micro-districts and look for clients driving along the main roads or at the parking lots of large shops.

Nevertheless, young adults working for the oil industry do not tend to boast about their jobs. For them it can also be a painful experience, taking a job as an oil worker after having studied and being unable to find a skilled job. In one case I met a young man who studied law in Almaty, which is regarded as the cultural and educational capital of Kazakhstan. Altynbek's family only recently resettled from the regional centre of Khobda to Aktobe. Lacking networks in the city he failed to find a job as a lawyer, despite his qualifications. In his position Altynbek earns less money and gains less social prestige than the white-collar work as a lawyer would have brought him. He took a job as an oil worker purely because of the salary connected to it.

Among the Kazakh population work at the oil stations is conceived as male labour. Only in the service sector can women take positions in cafeterias or offices. The work at the stations is expected to be dangerous for a young woman's reputation. Often Kazakh parents do not allow adult unmarried daughters to work in the open steppe because of the fear sexual harassment by the mostly male colleagues there. In Aktobe, meanwhile, the labour market for young women is overcrowded. In a situation where men become the main breadwinners, young women are supposed to take care of the household and the children completely. Combined with the care of elderly family members, women have no promising perspective for a career.

For young women in the 20s and 30s their complicated economic situation is frustrating. They are in fear of losing their professional skills and knowledge attained through their studies. Without a job they are expected to fulfil their role as the keeper of the household, as Kazakh parents-in-law often expect. When they intend to return to work after the children start school, these women mostly depend on their husbands' standing in business to find a job for them.

Women find work in the public service sector like administration, education, libraries or hospitals. These jobs are more likely to be available, but badly paid. As I collected data in the Aktobe municipal job agency, I talked without exception only to women of the cleaning staff, the consultants, the department managers and the director. As I talked to a friend, a retired policeman, he told me that in his opinion this is caused by the fact that in the job centre there is no possibility to gain bribes. True or not, the leading positions in the administration where resources are managed and strategic decisions are taken are mostly covered by men.

The problem of higher unemployment rates among women is not limited to Aktobe province. During my research I met women without work who just did not register as unemployed because relatively little money is paid (around US$40 a month) and they did not find the bureaucratic hassle worth their while. In other cases women willing to find work extended their maternity leave up to one year in which they gained a bit more public support (around US$60). Nevertheless it can be said that the significantly higher unemployment rate of women in Kazakhstan seems to be a structural problem in the ongoing period of economic transformation. This cannot be solely explained by the impact of the resource-extraction industry.

The work at the oil stations is a topic for all the family, not just the workers themselves. A Kazakh pensioner, Mayramgul, gives a perspicuous view about what are the elder generation's attitudes toward work in the resource-extraction industry today in which companies with nebulous foreign owners operate, driven by the global economy. Two of Mayramgul's three sons work for AMG. She asks a rhetorical question how just it is that Chinese specialists earn US$2000 while her sons earn US$200. She also raises an issue about their responsibilities. Living in the regional town Alga all her life, she felt the Communist party and the large chemical complex located there caring for the inhabitants. In her opinion the current government on various levels is being bought by the TOCs in order to close its eyes. These companies are just looking for profit and are not caring at all about social issues. The town stays '*bez khozaina*' (Russian, 'without a master'). Although the elder generation experienced Russian paternalism, nevertheless there was a head who could be addressed in case of trouble and intermediated between conflict parties.

Such perspectives should not be treated as embittered phrases of old nostalgics. Mayramgul's views express how many feel. In such an environment trust in companies engaged in resource extraction cannot grow. As pensions are small and older people are connected to the economic situation of their children's household, they are concerned about working conditions. Moreover, a cultural conception of the multigenerational Kazakh household plays a significant role. In an ideal household elderly parents should live with their youngest son and his children. While the grandfather is respected as the symbolic head of a household, his son is expected to deal with household matters. A son living half the time at an oil station means he is not able to take care of his parents.

Urban migration and employment opportunities

Working in the oil sector is not the only way migrants can earn money. The urban environment offers other opportunities to find work. Many work in the construction sector, which attracts thousands of workers to Aktobe. Working in construction has many benefits. Jobs are usually easily accessible and do not require diplomas or knowledge about the local market. In this way jobs in construction are especially interesting for migrants. The main motivation working in this sector is the salary, which is twice as high as in the education sector and many more times what can be earned through agricultural work. Construction workers earn an equal amount of money as workers in the processing industry without the need to be introduced and trained in how to use machinery.

As oil companies are investing in new facilities in the city there has been a boom in people seeking accommodation. Connected to this the city administration has to give new construction orders for streets, supply facilities and public services like schools or hospitals. Oil sector taxes are reinvested into the infrastructure. Nevertheless the provincial government has difficulties in coping with the speed of the boom. In this sense Aktobe is not comparable with Astana with its progressive building strategy, and makes more the impression of 'firefighting' an unbearable supply situation. In the Soviet era Aktyubinsk[13] never was expected to exceed half a million inhabitants.

While private homes are mainly built by migrant families themselves, construction workers build the oil industry's administrative centres, commercial centres and multi-storey housing complexes. The number of employees in the province working in the construction sector almost doubled from 2007 to 2011 (Boranbayeva 2012, 62), counting only those officially employed by construction companies, not the additional thousands of seasonally hired helpers. In a regional comparison, it turns out that the salary in the construction sector could even be higher than in Russia (An and Becker 2013, 51). This situation is not expected to calm down, at least in the next five years. As Aktobe is supposed to grow further, the demand for living space is likely to remain high.

Many young families lack the necessary financial base to afford a living space in Aktobe. The average salary (US$430 in 2011) is not often reached by migrants (Boranbayeva 2012, 8). The small salary of both parents often just allows for the renting of a small flat. In 2012 the average rent for a one-room apartment was between KZT40,000 and 60,000 (US$250–370). Although the average income per person rose enormously, living expenses also rose sharply over the past five years. The high rental price does not allow for the saving of money that could be used to buy a flat or build a house. Problems arise when a young couple wants to have children and the mother stays at home and does not earn an income.

Well-paid jobs are sparse and often not publicly announced. A manager in the city employment centre complained that companies do not announce available job positions. The offers at the centre are mainly for unskilled and low-skilled jobs like cleaning staff or night watchmen, which are remunerated with only KZT30,000–40,000 (US$190–250; job offers at the employment bureau). To some extent, job offers are announced in newspapers, but a large portion of positions are allocated via networks around a company. This can be the personal networks of the manager or employees, but also professional networks with business partners. Without the right contacts, migrants are left behind.

To deal with the problem of living space in Aktobe, migrants adopt a variety of strategies. First, people move to the city together with their parents. By pooling family resources, an extended family is able to buy a flat or build a house. To gain private credit, working colleagues and clan affiliations also play a role. In this case a young couple is expected to care for the older parents in all respects. Especially daughters-in-law should resign from work to care for the children and the spouse's parents. Second, people are renting a flat together with others. This new version of the Soviet *kommunalka* should be seen only as a temporary form.[14] The rental system by private landlords functions without a contract and offers the possibility to live without registration. This option is attractive especially to cyclic migrants, who in this way may save themselves a lot of bureaucracy and can still take advantage, for example, of childcare services in rural places where their children live (with their parents or other family members). Third, some rent a *dacha*. *Dacha*s were holiday homes in Soviet times. After the end of the Soviet Union, the bureaucratic control of *dacha* settlements loosened and some areas were abandoned due to the breakdown of the water supply. *Dacha*s near the centre of Aktobe were reconstructed to full-scale houses with water and gas supply. Although these buildings do not have the status of permanent houses and cannot be registered as an official address, de facto several hundred houses have become primary living space in this way. This development is tolerated by the authorities, but the inhabitants live in constant fear that the plots might be torn down. Other *dacha*s just remain huts in which the poorest migrants find a refuge.

As discussed above, a household's hope for stable and profitable jobs is one of the main reasons to move to the city. The other main reason lies in educational possibilities for children. Not every family is able to find a stay for its daughters and sons in the city. So the beginning of a study programme often marks a time when a family migrates. Without money earned in the oil sector, such moves would be unthinkable. In this sense, the resource-extracting economy can be regarded as a motor of development of Aktobe province. But not every migration biography is a success story. For thousands, a home in the city and a regular job remains a pipedream. They are only able to stay temporarily in the city when they are invited for short-term work or wait in the streets for work as day labourers. The rising costs of living diminish their chance to acquire living space in the city.

Almost all of my informants working in the energy sector hoped to transfer to employment in another field. The search for another job turns out to be problematic. Personal contacts are necessary to find a job in the informal labour market. In the formal labour market, either the salary is minimal or the entry obstacles are high. Employers often emphasize that post-Soviet diplomas and certificates are meaningless. During the early independence period, many education institutions opened, which gave out diplomas according to their individual programme. Meanwhile the state has liquidated at least half of these private institutions because of the low quality of their curriculums.

In this situation, opening up your own company seems a fitting solution. On the one hand, the fast developing market promises profits, and, on the other hand, a business-person is threatened by an opaque system of regulations. An individual shop can be opened easily and small trade flourishes in Aktobe, carried out by a proportionally high number of migrants, not only from the villages but also from other parts of Kazakhstan. The new shopping centres offer compartments in various sizes for shop owners. The low-wage service jobs in and around these trade centres such as security, cleaning or the cafeteria staff are also mainly occupied by migrants.

Alternatives to the city

Not every migrant is able to acquire proper housing in Aktobe. Failing to get a job in the city, unable to pay the rents for the flat or being afraid of the criminality at the *dacha*s, these are just some possible reasons why migrants sometimes turn their back on Aktobe again. But this does not mean that they return to the villages they come from. Some migrants do not have the possibility of going back because their villages were entirely dissolved for environmental reasons – mainly the lack of water and the extension of desert areas – as in the south of the province. Around the nearly extinct Aral Sea, the environment has worsened to a degree in which people's health is seriously affected. While pastures were lost to the desert, the water supply for the population has become problematic. In Khlebodarovka, a village about one hour away from Aktobe, I encountered a unique case: members of a community from the southern Shalkar region who abandoned their village and resettled entirely. The Shalkar region reaches the northern coast of the drying out Aral Lake, an area which was affected by desertification. Some brought their animals with them, which by communal legislation excluded the possibility of moving to the city.

An increasing suburbanization can be witnessed around Aktobe in which settlements in a one-hour radius around the city benefit. Khelobarovka is not the only example. Smaller villages are now also revived again after losing large parts of their core population in the early independence era. While land for building in general is provided for free in Aktobe, the awarding process has become highly bureaucratized in recent years. Payments and bribes have become the norm in order to get preferred land in a realistic time-frame. In villages, on the other hand, construction land is offered immediately by mayors. They consider a higher population level profitable, so help each other in a system of mutual support. Building regulations in the villages are minimal in relation to the city. It is even possible to get benefits from the public housing programme. A young teacher in a village school next to Aktobe was given a house free of charge within the framework of a new programme in order to attract teaching staff to villages. Although her salary is minimal compared with those in the private economy, it covers living expenses, while the earnings of her husband working in the oil sector can be invested in constructing their own house later. Official residence and other benefits are measures through which village administrations actively court young specialists.

In a strong continental climate, energy is a deciding factor in selecting a place of residence. The main criterion is whether a gas supply is available, which allows cooking and heating during the long and cold winter with temperatures down to –40°C. The provincial government is eager to extend gas connections after gaining advantageous conditions from AMG. Where no gas is available for heating, coal or dung is used. Formerly the supply with fuel and basic commodities was a central concern of the Soviet administration. Now the continuously rising price for coal and its transport costs make it difficult to secure heating. This leads to a situation in which prevailing disparities let some villages double or triple their size, while others seem to dissolve. In summary, while in the Soviet period a maximal utilization of land for agricultural development was a central concern, nowadays the far away villages bleed out. In the main, only elderly people stay there. On the other hand, the villages near economical centres – mainly Aktobe – are growing.

In the situation of strong growth another model is to work as a freelance, skilled worker. Serik, in his mid-30s, is an example of a former oil worker now freelancing. He worked for several years for KMG as a welder but quit his job because he wanted to work a more convenient timetable and to spend more time with his wife and three children. Living in Khlebodarovka he works in the suburbs of Aktobe as a freelance welder at private construction sites. He can lay the gas supply from the communal pipeline to the house and connect it with a heater. Although this work is also offered by the gas company, Serik is immediately available and works more cheaply in clandestine employment. Important for this kind of work are his personal networks to other freelance construction workers. They support each other by giving recommendations to gain orders from private households which hire additional workers according to their own skill in construction. In the summer peak season in construction work, he is able to earn more than KZT100,000 (US$620), which counts as a top salary in comparison with the average wage of a craftsman in the larger companies in Aktobe (around KZT30,000, US$180).

The regional centre of Alga (20,000 inhabitants), one-and-a-half hours by car from Aktobe in a southerly direction, is also growing. After the Alga chemical plant was closed in the early 1990s, many of the former workers – especially the highly qualified technical staff – migrated to Russia. Unemployed workers had begun to produce their own food at the *dacha*s or opened up their own business. In the past 10 years the economic situation improved. The town administration now has the funds to repair and reconstruct public facilities, while small trade is developing. Only a small part of Alga's inhabitants have been able to find work in the newly opened distillery. The largest employer is the oil industry. A middle-aged woman in one of the multi-storey buildings in the centre of Alga said that every second adult in her house works for the oil company. In comparison with the city, rentals here at KZT15,000–20,000 (US$90–120) for a one-room flat are less than half the price of Aktobe property.

Money earned by oil workers is spent in Alga, a town in which a small service sector with a bazaar and small shopping buildings could be opened. The town of Alga offers kindergartens, a complete school education from the first to the 11th class, a hospital, public space for recreation and a cultural infrastructure. The larger oil companies organize transport for their employees from Aktobe via Alga to the stations in and around southern Zhanazhol.

Erlan is one of Alga's oil workers. He lived in a *sovkhoz* in the Alga Region where he had just finished his professional education as a farm machine driver when the village's collective farm was abandoned. As he looked around for work in 1992 he found employment as a driver at AMG in Zhanazhol. After five years working for AMG he settled in Alga and started a family. His stable salary allowed him to build a house in a development area to the south of Alga.

Erlan had chosen Alga as a compromise, an affordable site to build his family's home, giving his children an opportunity for a good education, and relocating his household at a transit point between his working place and the city with its supply offers. His example shows a common pattern of a provincial towns' development. Because many people take similar decisions, Alga is enjoying modest growth, opening new perspectives for a new local service sector. Nevertheless, due to social problems like female unemployment, or criminality and tensions between locals and migrants from the villages, it cannot be claimed that a real 'renaissance' is taking place in Alga.

Considering migrants' choices

The differentiated migration processes can be understood through Cohen and Sirkeci's approach on security. A household living in a remote mining town is completely dependent on the resource-extraction industry. A household in Aktobe or a nearby settlement, on the other hand, is more flexible to react to internal and external influences. Household members bound in non-economic contributions like housework, education, child and elderly care (Cohen and Sirkeci 2011, 77) have the opportunity to take up (part-time) employment in a diversified city economy. When in remote areas a person has an opportunity to take on a job, for example a mother whose children enter school freeing up part of her day, it is often not possible to reorganize her labour into wage labour outside the household.

My ethnographic evidence corroborates Cohen's and Sirkeci's argument. Young mothers noted that Aktobe's economic surrounding allows flexible return-to-work activities according to their possibilities. One of my informants, Kamshat, could begin a job in a public service two to three afternoons a week as an advisor for the electronic service of the municipal administration. Kamshat coordinated with her husband to pick up their son at the kindergarten during her working days and to look after the home and her parents-in-law on her days off. She compared her situation with those of her friends in Alga who could not get such favourable job opportunities. It is important to note here the gendered mobility (the family car mostly used by the father) and a gendered timescale (night-time work is not considered morally proper for Kazakh women).

Analysing the marital status of my informants I can state that the less a person is bound to a family the more likely he or she is willing to accept a job in the resource-extraction industry. The more household obligations puts pressure on a person, the less he or she is willing to work longer periods outside home. Especially mothers of younger children are excluded from work at the oil stations. From another perspective single men are able to collect money for their marriage celebrations. In this perspective Kazakhstan is similar Kyrgyzstan where Madeleine Reeves (Reeves 2012, 110) observed that massive resources are pumped into an elaborate ritual economy. These expenses may increase the social capital of a household, allowing it to claim a better stand at a migration destination or bridge gaps between way stations of household's members' mobility. Economic capital can be transferred into other types of capital that may influence a household's future economic situation.

Especially in urban sectors of the economy, personal networks are decisive. The broader is a migrant's network, the faster he or she gains access to a desirable job in the city. Networks an oil worker accesses at a station are of lesser significance because colleagues' backgrounds and origins differ greatly. Work in the energy sector can be regarded as a waiting loop for better possibilities. But not everyone is able to hold onto his or her livelihood in the city of Aktobe. Migrants who cannot find a satisfying job move on to provincial towns or villages in the suburbs.

What my observations show is that migrants use work in the resource-extraction industry as a catalyst for migration. Available and well-paid jobs in the resource-extraction industry offer migrants the opportunity to earn money to intensify their household's migration. In a situation where property costs and rentals have risen sharply, a solid financial base is required before moving to the city. Working in an urban environment gives migrants more options, better abilities to react on economic possibilities, better access to social networks and a better future perspective.

Conclusions

For the middle and young generation, those who participate in oil extraction, the oil industry is a prism through which they critically observe their hopes and expectations clashing with the neoliberal economic order. The main discourse of the middle generation targets the sovereignty of the Republic of Kazakhstan. Spending their younger years in the USSR they experienced Russian paternalism. My informants (between 35 and 60 years of age), like Temirkhan, indicated that for them Kazakhstan's independence was more than a political move, it was a realization of their patriotic desire. Now it is a bitter experience to see how their fatherland is boxed in by powerful states like China and Russia, and the sense that Kazakhstan has become a ballgame in the world economy, in which mighty TOCs act like states inside the state, executing power on regional constellations in western Kazakhstan. They feel the natural wealth of their homeland was sold out and does not primarily serve Kazakhstan's population. The future after the oil rush remains uncertain.

The younger people aged 18–35 with whom I met, like Altynbek, complained about difficulties in coping with the situation. First, among the younger generation the main discourse is around the expectation of realizing a prosperous life through education. But their illusion breaks immediately as they experience an educational system in which money for bribes is more important than academic achievement. Second, the imagination of job opportunities does not fit the labour market, which is increasingly concentrated around the resource-extraction industry. The few jobs outside this main economic direction can only be attained by good connections rather than personal qualifications, which deeply frustrates the younger generation.

As I have shown in this article, work in the oil sector is both an opportunity and a risk for local development. While a portion of the local population finds jobs in the oil branch, it remains questionable how sustainable is the economic boom. Workers can earn basic savings for their future. But beside the harsh working conditions at the oil fields, permanent jobs in the oil sector are limited and highly contested. Several groups are excluded from this development. One-year contracts are precarious. Only with stable work and salary expectations can the situation of families be bettered in the long run.

My ethnographic study shows that the resource-extraction industry has not offered long-term perspectives for migrants. Except for the few oil and gas engineers, the majority of workers are forced to work in disadvantageous conditions. In this context migrants see working at the oil stations as a transitional period before they can find another job. For them work in the resource-extraction industry appears as a catalyst for migration from the villages to Aktobe. But the resource-extraction industry overshadows other economic activities in the region so that it remains hard to find other employment. Further social and economic problems are likely to appear when the first years of the boom have ended and the construction sector scales down opportunities for work. An improvement of the rural supply and transport infrastructure might reduce the push factors of rural–urban migration. The future will show whether Kazakhstan's business with natural resources will in the long-term have a positive or a negative influence on the region. Riots like the Zhanaozen incident are alarming signs and recommend reconsidering the national strategy. The residents of western Kazakhstan no longer want to be excluded from the dealings between the government and the TOCs.

What is seen in the case of western Kazakhstan is a coincidence of turbulences of a general economic transformation and a fast-developing resource-extraction industry. This study showed that in this environment migrants find no reliability in the oil and gas sector. Permanent struggles between oil workers, subcontractors and the TOCs reduce the attractiveness of working in this field. Migrants dream of their own business or a job in a trusted institution that allows them to take their fate into their own hands. Migrants see temporary jobs in the resource-extraction industry as a means to an end.

Notes

1. The Virgin Land Campaign was a large-scale project initiated by Nikita Khrushchev to increase cultivable land. The initiative was presented in 1954 and targeted 'virgin' and 'idle' land mainly in western Siberia and northern Kazakhstan. Western Kazakhstan was included in the campaign in the early 1960s. The campaign turned out to be problematic because of mismanagement and the misallocation of resources, which reduced the crop. The climatic conditions were also simply not favourable enough to secure continuous large harvests (see http://www.sjsu.edu/faculty/watkins/virginlands.htm, accessed September 17, 2013; and Merl 2002).
2. All names of informants have been changed.
3. See the Zhanaozen municipal homepage: http://www.zhanaozen.gov.kz/ru/gorod_obshestvo/gorod_obshestvo_molod_politika/ (accessed June 11, 2014).
4. Tengizchevrol was founded in 1993 as a joint venture between the American Oil Giants Chevron (50%), ExxonMobil (25%), the Kazakh NOC KazMunayGaz (20%) and the Russian LukArco (5%). It is the largest oil company in Kazakhstan: http://www.tengizchevroil.com/about/overview (accessed on August 2, 2014).
5. Ente Nazionale Idrocarburi (ENI), an Italian energy company
6. An American oil company.
7. China National Petroleum Corporation (CNPC), a state-owned Chinese oil company
8. For a description, see: http://classic.cnpc.com.cn/en/cnpcworldwide/kazakhstan/ (accessed on June 11, 2014).
9. The chrome reserve's exploitation began in the 1930s (Tazhibayev et al. 2002, 100). Today the Aktobe ferroalloy plant and mining sites in the province are owned by Kazchrome, which employs about 18,000

people in the region. Kazakhstan is the world's third biggest producer of chrome. The mining sites are concentrated in the Aktobe region. While domestic demand is low, Europe, the United States and, increasingly, China buy chrome from Kazakhstan. The reserves are appreciated for their high-grade chromite ore and a low content of undesirable ore constituents (Levine 2011).

10. The Wall Street Journal Online titled an article on April 18, 2013: 'A $30 Billion Hole in the Caspian Sea': http://online.wsj.com/articles/SB10001424127887324050304578412760496098192.
11. CNPC website: http://classic.cnpc.com.cn/en/cnpcworldwide/kazakhstan/ (accessed on June 11, 2014).
12. A large oilfield service company. The headquarter is located in Houston, Texas.
13. The Russian colonial name. The Kazakh name Aktobe (Ақтөбе) means 'white hill'. The city was founded 1869 as a Russian military fort on the Eurasian steppe (Bisembayev 2006, 215–216).
14. A *kommunalka* was a common appearance in the early Soviet Union. Due to a lack of sufficient living space workers had to share a flat with others in which every family inhabited one room and shared the bathroom and kitchen. While the situations improved in the post-war period, *kommunalka*s until today exist mainly in St Petersburg and Moscow.

References

Aktobe oblysynyn statistika departamenti. 2011. *Aqtobe obylysynyn demokrafijalyk zhylnamalygy. Statistikalyq žinaq*. Aktobe: Aktobe oblysynyn statistika departamenti.

Alayi, M. A. 2005. *"Resource Rich Countries and Weak Institutions: The Resource Curse Effect."* Accessed July 10, 2013. http://are.berkeley.edu/courses/EEP131/fall2006/NotableStudent05/Resource%20CurseM_Alayli.pdf

Aldashev, A., and B. Dietz. 2011. *Determinants of Internal Migration in Kazakhstan*. Working Papers, No. 301. Regensburg: Osteuropainstitut.

An, G., and C. M. Becker. 2013. "Uncertainty, Insecurity, and Emigration from Kazakhstan to Russia." *World Development* 42: 44–66.

Auty, R. 2004. "Natural resources and Civil Strife: A Two-staged Process." *Geopolitics* 9 (1): 29–49.

Behrends, A., and N. Schareika. 2010. "Significations of Oil in Africa or What (more) can Anthropologists Contribute to the Study of Oil." *Suomen Antropologi* 35 (1): 83–86.

Behrends, A., S. P. Reyna, and G. Schlee, ed. 2013. *Crude Domination. An Anthropology of Oil*. New York: Berghahn.

Bisembayev, A. A. *et al.*, ed. 2006. *Istoriya Aktyubinskoj Oblasti*. Aktobe: Oblastnoj centr istorii, etnografii i arkheologii.

Boranbayeva, A. O., ed. 2009. *Aktyubinskaya oblast' v cifrakh 1991-2008. Statisticheskij spornik*. Aktobe: Department statistiki Aktyubiskoj oblasti.

Boranbayeva, A. O., ed. 2012. *Aktobe oblysy 2011 zhyly. Statistikalyq zhylnamalygy*. Aktobe: Aktobe oblysynyn statistika departamenti.

Brauer, B. 2008. "Der Streit um das Kaschagan-Ölfeld: Ressourcennationalismus oder Emanzipation auf Kasachisch." *Zentralasienanalysen* 2: 2–9.

Cohen, J. H., and I. Sirkeci. 2011. *Cultures of Migration. The Global Nature of Contemporary Mobility*. Austin: University of Texas Press.

Dahl, C., and K. Kuralbayeva. 2001. "Energy and the Environment in Kazakhstan." *Energy Policy* 29: 429–440.

Demytrie, R. 2012. "Kazakhstan: UN's Pillay urges Zhanaozen riot Inquiry." BBC, News Asia, Accessed September 19, 2013. http://www.bbc.co.uk/news/world-asia-18816018

Kaiser, M. J., and A. G. Pulsipher. 2007. "A Review of the Oil and Gas Sector in Kazakhstan." *Energy Policy* 35: 1300–1314.

Levine, R. M. 2011. "The Mineral Industry of Kazakhstan. 2009 Minerals Yearbook." United States Geological Survey. Accessed September 17, 2013. http://minerals.usgs.gov/minerals/pubs/country/2009/myb3-2009-kz.pdf

Marcus, G. E. 1995. "Ethnography in/of the World System: The Emergence of Multi-Sited Ethnography." *Annual Review of Anthropology* 24: 95–117.

McNeish, J.-A. and O. Logan, ed. 2012. *Flammable Societies. Studies on the Socio-Economics of Oil and Gas*. London: Pluto.

Merl, S. 2002. "Entstalinisierung, Reformen und Wettlauf der Systeme 1953-1964." In *Handbuch der Geschichte Russlands*, edited by Stefan Plaggenborg. Band 5, 1. Halbband. Stuttgart: Hirsemann.

Ostrowski, W. 2010. *Politics and Oil in Kazakhstan*. London: Routledge.

Palazuelos, E., and R. Fernández. 2012. "Kazakhstan: Oil Endowment and Oil Empowerment." *Communist and Post-Communist Studies* 45: 27–37.

Reeves, M. 2012. "Black Work, Green Money: Remittances, Ritual, and Domestic Economies in Southern Kyrgyzstan." *Slavic Review* 71 (1): 108–134.

Ross, M. L. 1999. "The Political Economy of the Resource Curse." *World Politics* 51 (2): 297–322.

Ross, M. L. 2012. *The Oil Curse. How Petroleum Wealth Shapes the Development of Nations*. Princeton: University Press.

Sakal, H. B. 2014. "Natural Resource Policies and Standard of Living in Kazakhstan." *Central Asian Survey* doi:10.1080/02634937.2014.987970.

Scheck, J. 2013. "A $30 Billion Hole in the Caspian Sea?" *The Wall Street Journal*. Accessed June 11, 2014. http://online.wsj.com/articles/SB10001424127887324050304578412760496098192

Smailov, A. A., ed. 2012. *Kazakhstan in Figures. 2011*. Astana: Agency of the Republic of Kazakhstan on Statistics.

Tazhibayev, M. K. *et al.*, ed. 2002. *Encyklopedia 'Aktobe'*. Aktobe: Otandastar-Poligraphija.

Weszkalnys, G. 2010. "Re-Conceiving the Resource Curse and the Role of Anthropology." *Suomen Antropologi* 35 (1): 87–90.

Yermukanov, M. 2004. "A thorny Road to Sino-Kazakh Partnership." *China Brief* 4 (14). http://www.jamestown.org/single/?tx_ttnews%5Btt_news%5D=3834#.VHdtODGG_jI]

Yessenova, S. 2012. "The Tengiz Oil Enclave: Labor, Business, and the State." *Polar. Political and Legal Anthropological Review* 35 (1): 94–114.

Notes on the moral economy of gas in present-day Azerbaijan

Tristam Barrett

Division of Social Anthropology, University of Cambridge, Cambridge, UK

Most residents of Baku, Azerbaijan, retain a positive view of the state restructuring of the gas distribution network and do not object to the principle of paying for gas at its 'market price'. They are, however, very critical of the street-level officials (*gazoviki*) of the state-owned gas company, who often defraud residents in elaborate schemes. This article highlights the neighbourhood-level impacts of broad technological changes in the domestic gas distribution system, arguing that they have permitted new forms of exploitation by *gazoviki*. By examining the terms in which citizens have responded to such scams, it is possible to relate these commentaries to locally prevailing and culturally patterned understandings of moral economy and governance. Popular critiques both of malfeasance in the gas network and of wealth accumulation as a result of Azerbaijan's hydrocarbon boom are discursive attempts to restore a moral order that citizens increasingly worry has been abandoned.

Introduction

A local version of the Prometheus myth has a shepherd flicking his cigarette into the hillside near Baku in the 1950s. The gas locked into the porous shale rock burst into flames and has burnt ever since, in a place now known as Yanar Dağ,[1] or Fire Mountain. It is a fitting monument to the immense hydrocarbon wealth that transformed this landscape into a centre of Soviet industry and now makes Azerbaijan a significant energy supplier in the world's political economy. In recent years the Yanar Dağ has been 'privatized' and visitors can pay a few *manat* to take tea in the heat of its flames. The appropriation and exploitation of this national symbol – Azerbaijanis consider theirs to be the 'land of fire' – seems fitting testament to the informal and moral economies of domestic gas supply that are the topic of this article.

The big story in Azerbaijan over the last 20 years is hydrocarbons. The oil industry itself contributes half of the country's gross domestic product, and transfers from the State Oil Fund account for 60% of the state budget (EIU 2012). The vast sums of oil money flowing into the country have given rise to ambitious infrastructural projects and sweeping reforms of formerly Soviet institutions, such as the domestic gas supply network.

While these oil-boom developments have permitted the formation of a new middle class and corresponding aspirations, a significant number of citizens remain locked into what might be termed a continuing economy of post-socialism. These people do not have prospects in the capitalist-style economy that is springing up in Baku, which offers well-paid jobs to a new middle class and opportunities to participate in a flourishing consumerist lifestyle – from shopping and foreign travel to private gyms and healthcare.

Those in the residual economy depend primarily on low wages and social transfers from the state. A recent report by the International Labour Office (2012, vii) identifies high youth unemployment and increasing income disparities: 'the share of low-wage earners has ballooned since 2000, reaching 40% of the population in 2010'. Furthermore, many citizens depend on a more or less Soviet model of social safety net that provides pensions to categories of people considered unable to work (notably retired persons, those with disabilities and war veterans). Pensions account for three-quarters of spending on social transfers and cover 46% of the population, so they remain an important contributor to household finances.

Considering the importance of infrastructure to ideas of Soviet social modernity (Collier 2011) and of hydrocarbons to present-day wealth, transformations in the domestic energy regime seem an ideal site to explore the political subjectivities of those who have so far not made gains in the new Azerbaijan. Such a line of inquiry would get at people's ideas about the nature of the political community and of their place in it. In a transformed economy, are public services viewed as a right or a commodity? Are utilities still part of an enduring 'substantive' or moral economy in which economic transactions are embedded in and bear the moral weight of attachment to other areas of social life – or are they a commodity, the exchange of which implies little moral evaluation? Interactions between street-level bureaucrats (Lipsky 1980) and the public have received little scholarly attention in Azerbaijan or in Central Asia more generally. The present study is the first to examine such interactions around an infrastructure network in Azerbaijan.

Nevertheless, a stimulating scholarly literature (e.g. Humphrey 2003; Alexander 2007; King and Stuckler 2007; Collier 2011; Kharkhordin and Alapuro 2011; Rogers 2012) has explored the social ramifications of fundamental infrastructural changes in the former Soviet space. In Russia, social scientists have shown that the privatization efforts of the 1990s failed to appreciate that enterprises were thoroughly integrated into the substantive economies of Soviet citizens. This led to occasionally catastrophic effects when public heating systems, for instance, were disconnected from the industrial enterprises that fuelled them. Unsurprisingly, Russians responded to these privatizations and the marketization of utilities with opprobrium.

A significant finding of my research, however, is that in Baku, reactions to the marketization of the gas network have been notably more muted. Indeed, residents from all walks of life have greeted many changes favourably. Instead of bemoaning increased tariffs or the metering systems that now measure household consumption, as might be expected when markets are introduced into a formerly socialist society, the real and frequently articulated source of popular dissatisfaction seems to be with the behaviour of the gas company's low-level functionaries (*gazoviki*, gasmen), with whom many residents have conflicts.

In this article I therefore look at the changes in the gas supply regime, at the behaviours of *gazoviki* that have been empowered by these changes, and at the kinds of commentary produced by citizens who are subjected to these behaviours. My focus is on the gas supply system of Baku and the Abşeron Peninsula, which encompasses the city's surrounding regions and suburbs. This gas network is the largest in the country and serves about 650,000 customers. Considering the extent of academic and journalistic interest in the geopolitics of hydrocarbons, the domestic energy sector in Azerbaijan is under-researched. Natural gas, though, is the most utilized energy source in Azerbaijan, and gas supply is thus a useful lens through which to examine the domestic aspects of the country's state-driven, hydrocarbon-fuelled development model and its implications for the daily lives of its citizens. It also throws light on the workings of power in Azerbaijan. The domestic supply infrastructure for gas connects households and communities to state structures; and it engenders regular contact with officials who administer connections, collect payments, and recover debts. Nevertheless, this is a difficult topic to research because of a lack of publicly available information and the caginess of those involved in the sector. I base the arguments in this article on fieldwork in Azerbaijan over a two-year period between 2009 and 2011 and follow-up interviews with residents of Baku during the first part of 2013. Interviews were conducted in a mix of Russian (my working language) and Azeri, with the aid of a good friend who was invaluable when conversation inevitably drifted into Azeri. My interviewees were householders from different parts of Baku with diverse educational and occupational backgrounds, ranging in age from mid-thirties to late seventies. Those who evinced the most difficulty with *gazoviki*, however, were invariably from the lower rungs of society. This sample is not statistically representative, but is indicative of local experiences of the domestic gas sector in Baku, Azerbaijan's major urban settlement. I organize this article as follows. In the first part, I discuss the state of utility infrastructure in the context of the hydrocarbon boom of the past decade, and how the domestic gas network is set up. I argue that contemporary institutional and infrastructural arrangements are reflective of a broader state-led development model that essentially constitutes a reworking of the Brezhnevite state to accommodate certain features of market economy. I then go on to discuss Baku residents' accounts of their dealings with low-level officials of the state gas company. These demonstrate how changes in the pricing and measuring of gas consumption have produced new and unsettling relations between gasmen and citizens, in which consumers now bear the cost of malfeasance directly. Finally, I relate the moral commentaries of Baku residents to a popular model of authority that informs understandings of who can legitimately appropriate and redistribute public goods. Criticisms of gasmen, and of the hydrocarbon economy more generally, must be related to this cultural understanding of state authority.

Ultimately, I argue that recent institutional and technological developments in the domestic gas supply infrastructure have not implied a fundamental transformation either in the logic of state provision or in citizens' understandings of the state. However, recent technological changes to the consumer end of the domestic gas supply network have resulted in new relationships between certain state officials (*gazoviki*) and consumers. The resultant conflicts reveal the disjuncture between entrenched understandings of the state as a moral community, a form of *khozyaistvo* (Rogers 2006), and the rent-taking practices that actually underpin the workings of the Azerbaijani state.

Azerbaijan's domestic gas supply infrastructure

Far from the dark predictions of a decade ago, which warned of 'increasing risk of systematic collapse' (World Bank 2005, 7) of the electricity and gas sectors, the restoration of Azerbaijan's infrastructure networks is something of a success story. Although the republic as a whole may not have universal and continuous access to utilities, in Baku at least the gas and water shortages and rolling blackouts that characterized the immediate post-independence period are but memories in the minds of most.

At the time of independence Azerbaijan inherited an extensive gas network, but the interdependence built into Soviet infrastructure meant that this collapsed alongside the all-Union economy. Azerbaijan's agricultural sector suffered when cheap, subsidized natural gas for heating greenhouses was cut off in the early 1990s (Yalçın-Heckmann 2010, 59), and attempts to supply the domestic network with gas drawn from Azerbaijan's developing offshore oil and gas fields actually exacerbated the deterioration of infrastructure through the volume of unprocessed gas entering and corroding the pipelines.

The situation changed radically in 2005 when the hydrocarbon industry took off in earnest with the opening of the Baku-Tbilisi-Ceyhan (BTC) oil pipeline. Long-term international investment in Caspian oil had been secured as early as 1994, but it was the BTC pipeline that finally secured a direct route to European markets. In 1999, the Shah Deniz gas field was discovered, and since it came on stream in December 2006 it has become the main source of natural gas for both export and domestic consumption. Its development by British Petroleum has permitted

Azerbaijan to achieve full energy independence and become a net exporter of natural gas through the South Caucasus Pipeline, which runs parallel with the BTC pipeline. Further development of the Shah Deniz gas field, due to be completed in 2018, is expected to double gas production (EIU 2013).

Hydrocarbons are crucial to Azerbaijan's economy and have fundamentally determined the post-Soviet development of its state. The stratospheric GDP growth rates in the early years of the recent oil boom (almost 35% in 2006 after the BTC pipeline came on stream) have enabled the government to pursue a development agenda without needing to be accountable either to international donors or its own citizenry. Because oil production peaked in 2010, natural gas is taking an increasingly important role in Azerbaijan's hydrocarbon economy, leading commentators to announce a new Great Game for gas in the Caspian (EIU 2013). In June 2013 the route was decided for a Southern Gas Corridor that will export gas to the European Union. This will see gas exported from the second stage of the Shah Deniz offshore gas development through the Trans-Anatolian and Trans-Adriatic Pipelines. In Azerbaijan, it is hoped that this will permit the country eventually to act as a broker between European demand and significantly larger gas reserves in Turkmenistan. Gas and the infrastructure to capture, process and transmit it are therefore increasingly taking over the role of oil in connecting Azerbaijan to the world system.

The government of Azerbaijan has accepted financial and technical assistance from international development organizations to rehabilitate infrastructure networks and set tariffs according to market prices, but it has resisted pressure to open domestic energy to the private sector.[2] The government's State Programme for Development of the Fuel and Energy Sector in Azerbaijan for 2005–2015 covers the rehabilitation and development of oil, gas and electricity systems, but does not focus on the institutional and market reforms that development assistance organizations consider necessary for the development of the energy sector.

Development assistance has therefore focused on strategic planning and investments in infrastructure, including projects to develop a policy and regulatory framework, set up a tariff regime, and rehabilitate power plants (European Commission 2006, 15ff.). According to the World Bank (2013, 12), these recent 'investments in energy generation, transmission, and distribution capacities have resulted in notable improvements in the quality of utility services'. The modernization and improvement of infrastructure remains one of the government's main stated budgetary priorities, as demonstrated by the fact that actual budget allocations are almost entirely in the area of infrastructure investments (5).

At least until recently, the domestic gas network operated as follows.[3] The gas sector is a vertically integrated monopoly. Whilst oil and gas are formally under the purview of the Ministry of Industry and Energy, informally the national oil company SOCAR is the main actor both in policy formation and in the petroleum sector as a whole (Kjærnet 2010, 7). SOCAR acts as the single buyer of natural gas for delivery to the domestic market, handling up to 10 billion m^3 of gas annually. The gas is then sold at wholesale prices to various companies under the umbrella of SOCAR, including AzəriKimya, the country's petrochemical facility, and Azəriqaz.

The state-owned company Azəriqaz is the sole supplier of gas to the domestic market in Azerbaijan, supplying natural gas to over 1.5 million households and managing the associated infrastructure for gas transmission and storage. It also supplies natural gas to all of the country's fossil fuel power plants, operated by Azərenerji. Azəriqaz was founded in 1992 on the basis of the former regional gas administrations (such as Bakgaz in Baku) and has gone through a number of incarnations since independence. In May 1996, in an experiment in privatization, it was established as a state-owned closed joint stock company. It was subsequently re-established by presidential decree in July 2009, when it became a subsidiary of SOCAR under its present director, Əkbər Hacıyev.

These institutional developments are a good example of the state-led development model that Azerbaijan, along with the other resource-rich countries of the Caspian littoral (Kazakhstan and Turkmenistan), has chosen to pursue. The rehabilitation of utility infrastructure is a frequently reported government priority, and the president makes regular pronouncements on the subject. Continuing involvement of the state in the utilities sector has the effect that, despite institutional changes and aborted experiments in privatization, citizens still feel that utilities are very much part of their dealings with the state. One of my neighbours echoed most residents of Baku in his admission that he had never really taken notice of the administrative changes around utility provision: for him, as for many others, he knows that he gets a bill each month and payment is collected on behalf of the state. As far as consumers are concerned, then, when dealing with Azəriqaz they are dealing with the state and its officials.

Yet there are differences between the Soviet period and now. In the planned economy, most households in Azerbaijan were connected to the gas supply network, and consumption was estimated and billed at a prescribed ratio according to household size. Improvements to the physical infrastructure have been accompanied by a radical transformation of this logic of 'prescriptive norms' (Collier 2011) into one that seeks to measure and price consumption, so that payment is now made according to the amount of gas the consumer actually uses.[4] Gas tariffs have been brought in line with market prices (so-called 'true economic value'), and all connections are now metered.[5]

Despite these changes to the way consumers operate within the gas supply network, the actual pipeline infrastructure that brings gas to consumers continues to impose the logic of planned consumption according to which it was first laid. The age, capacity and integrity of the gas distribution infrastructure produce bottlenecks in the system that have undermined subsequent infrastructural and institutional changes. Although the gas network is no longer formally divided into different regions (*rayonlar*), according to which a certain amount of gas would be provided to each *rayon* and street, the deterioration of the infrastructure means that gas passing through the system cannot flow at the pressures it was designed for, and gas supply still operates under a so-called 'regime' in which gas is rationed to each region. Thus, even when a household is connected to the mains, there is no guarantee that gas will be supplied. The German utility company E.ON Ruhrgas has completed a feasibility study and concept note on rehabilitating and upgrading the Baku and Abşeron gas supply system. But the development of a final gas supply master plan is contingent on the completion of a general urban plan for Baku, which has not yet been finalized.

At present, in the absence of the intended overhaul of the gas supply infrastructure, institutional changes have not led to significant de facto change in how households are supplied. The present system remains something of a hybrid, a largely Soviet edifice with tweaks to measurement and valuation that expose a fundamental shift in the way of thinking about utilities, if not in the mode of their provision.

Gazoviki and citizens: a telling relationship

'Now with smart cards it's a lot better.'
'That's why they are being taken down!'
From an interview with residents, 27 August 2013

In addition to metrification of consumption and increases in tariffs, new smart meters and cards introduced in Azerbaijan since 2007 have changed how people pay for gas. Following a pilot project in the second city of Gəncə, smart meters have been rolled out in the capital and are intended to be provided to all connections in Baku by the end of this year. (Officially, over half the population is now on the smart metering system – Trend.az, 'Azerbaijan's Gas Operator Continues Installation of Smart Counters', 9 September 2013.) These prepaid smart meters and cards allow consumers to pay for their metered consumption in advance. Meters are installed at customer connection points, and payment cards can be topped up at banks, special ATM machines, and on the Internet. Many residents have welcomed them for their increased convenience and as a boon for consumers, who were used to greeting with suspicion the gasman who came to the door to collect payment. In a telling statement of how readily many Azerbaijanis have come to accept the equation of value with price, a friend tells me that 'now we understand the value of gas'.

Despite general public acceptance of the system there are still conflicts over utilities. Some even erupt into public mobilizations, such as in the Baku village of Nardaran, on the Caspian coast north-east of Baku. This slightly embellished account by one of my interviewees, a scrap dealer in central Baku with family connections in the area, reveals that even these protests are not about the principle of paying for utilities:

> In Nardaran, they broke the electricity meters. They didn't want to pay electricity and gas and water because they said that they don't have sufficient money to live. So they all decided not to pay. But in a week the situation was settled. I myself went there on the 19th of April, before Novruz, they were blaming and fighting the procurator of the republic and Ilham [Əliyev]. Electricity, gas, water. They were waving pistols openly, whoever came they said they would shoot. ... The question is not that they didn't want to pay; it was that they *didn't have* the money to pay [interviewee's emphasis].

Nardaran is perhaps an exceptional case, having become something of a hot spot for protest actions and with the dubious reputation among Bakuvians of harbouring a population of fearsome Islamists. The unrest in Nardaran frequently makes the national press, with utility debts and gas stoppages commonly cited as the motivating factors (Turan 5 December 2009; Contact 27 August 2009; RFE/RL 16 February 2011). But there is something else going on here as well. As one of my interviewees from Nardaran attests, 'At the end of the month they will come to take money for gas and electricity and we expect some events. It happens very frequently.'

'They' are the *gazoviki* or gasmen. These are street-level gas company officials who come to people's doors to service connections and obtain payments from customers. They are the primary interface between consumers and the gas company, and because the gas company is state-owned, they are to all intents and purposes considered by citizens to be another aspect of their dealings with the state. A regular fixture of life in the Soviet period, present administrative arrangements vest considerable power in these street-level officials, who can now calculate bills on the basis of meter readings and cut off non-paying households. On the basis of local accounts of relations to *gazoviki*, I propose that conflicts over utilities are not about their price or the principle of paying. Rather, local actions are taken against the malfeasance of the gasmen, who use their powers to fiddle the bills, collect false payments and unfairly cut off gas supplies, leaving the population uncertain and unhappy about how much and whom they are paying. This account of stoppages orchestrated by street-level bureaucrats tells quite a different tale of power and its legitimation than that of the politicians in Siberia who engineer energy stoppages to establish their legitimacy, and therefore electability, as local big men (Humphrey 2003).[6] In Baku, the perceived illegitimacy of *gazoviki* and their actions helps cast light on local notions of legitimacy that continue to inform citizens' understandings of the state in the post-Soviet period.

The following scam – recounted in conversation with a good friend and her neighbour, both in their mid-fifties and nowadays making ends meet by giving private tuition – gives a sense of the machinations of these *gazoviki*. It also shows the distress and moral outrage that the unrestrained behaviour of certain *gazoviki* provokes in residents. The scam involved a gasman fiddling bills that would be presented monthly on the basis of projected gas consumption. By creating a leak in the pipe, generating an inflated estimate, and then closing off the leak again, the gasman could obtain an amplified estimate of projected consumption and ask for payment on that basis. (As far as I could establish, the gasman or his superiors could subsequently submit the actual consumption records and pocket the refunded difference between estimated and actual consumption.) All this was done with a veneer of respectability – bills and receipts were presented to the customers – even if there was considerable disquiet from the constant smell of gas in the courtyard! Once, having just paid a gas bill, my interviewee recounts how the gasman nevertheless disconnected her:

> I asked Mikayil [the interviewee's neighbour] to call him, and I said, 'I paid you, why did you close it off?' And he said, 'It's a good thing I did, I do as I wish' [Rus. *tak khochu, tak delayu*]. ... He began to play with the gas meter and Mikayil shouted to try to stop him, and do you know what he said? 'I am playing with her nerves' [Az. *onun nervini oynadıram*]. This is how they work. They come and wrap people around their fingers. It is a trap. They leave people without gas and for that reason no one messes with them, and they are not punished for it.

In this case, my friend had good contacts and managed to get the gasman sacked (but before their complaint could be put through official channels). He was subsequently beaten up by another group of neighbours. Nevertheless, this story demonstrates the considerable autonomy gasmen enjoy under the oversight regime within which they operate. In another incident a gasman kept his job despite having been caught red-handed cheating an elderly woman out of AZN 73 (about USD 100).

The *gazoviki*'s bilking of residents occurs within a form of administration in which various state functions are informally franchised out to actors at the interface between the public bureaucracy and its citizens. In a system known within the sociological literature on Russia as administrative rent-taking (Oleinik 2011, cited in Humphrey 2012a, 23), these actors are able to extract profit by exploiting their positions as gatekeepers within the public bureaucracy. This sketch of the functioning of the Azerbaijani state is congruent with analyses of late-Soviet bureaucratic practice in Azerbaijan (Zemtsov 1976; Vaksberg 1991; Derlugian 2003) and in the Caucasus more generally (Avtorkhanov 1979), which emphasize an entrepreneurial character that seems to have persisted into the post-Soviet period. Indeed, on the basis of research into the experiences of Turkish businesspeople in Azerbaijan, Pınar Bedirhanoğlu (2013) considers corruption in Azerbaijan not an aberration, but part and parcel of a system of rule, which she links to the – in my experience frequently ironically employed – Azeri term *hörmet* (respect):

> '*Hörmet*,' in its classical meaning, refers to a hierarchical power relation between master and subject, in which, by giving presents in different forms such as money or goods, the subject is meant to recognize the respectful authority of the master, and the master in return takes care of the subject's well-being. Consequently, rather than referring to a non-hierarchical monetary exchange for personal gain, as the conceptualisation of 'bribe' would imply, '*hörmet*' is a reflection of underlying power relations.

The notion of *hörmet* is a useful one because it links corruption to local ideas of patronage and the enacting of relations of authority and respect (Sneath 2006) that need to be considered as part of the workings of the Azerbaijani state. In so doing, *hörmet* offers a more complex and satisfactory understanding of corruption in Azerbaijan than provided in the present academic and international development literature. But it also draws attention to the presumption that such relations ideally take place within an encompassing moral framework, similar to the Soviet idea of the state as a *khozyaistvo*, which I discuss in the next section. If this is the case, then when it comes to accounting for the operations of *gazoviki* the idea of *hörmet* does not seem to accurately reflect their situation.

The practices of *gazoviki* (as well as other groups of officials in the public bureaucracy) operate according to a different logic from that presupposed by *hörmet*. While patronage is based around authority figures that are able to *direct* flows of resources to their clients, the power of petty functionaries stems from their ability to *block and unblock* such flows, as obligatory nodes within a bureaucratic system. From numerous accounts of citizens' interactions in the public bureaucracy, it is clear that low-level officials are unavoidable in a citizen's quest to obtain documents or rights, and that they need to be bribed to obtain the services to which people are legally entitled. These practices may be justified by reference to *bereket* (Az. 'blessing', an Islamic notion that a good deed is rewarded many times over), or by not wishing to bring bad luck by arguing over money regarding a child's birth or registration. But the subjects of these interactions do not consider them to be anything other than bribes. There is no sense in which these low-level officials are considered to be acting as a master taking care of his subject's well-being.[7] From their own perspective, these officials may feel entitled to extract revenue from citizens in order to bring their wages up to a level that accords with their own sense of status (see Humphrey 2012b for a comparable discussion of inequality justified through the idea of 'fairness').

The public bureaucracy around gas is no exception to the generalized system of administrative rent-taking described above. In a positive sense, the system can help people to 'get things done'. If a person doesn't own a registered property, for instance, a connection can be made and registered to a person's name upon payment of an unofficial fee. But it can also operate negatively. *Gazoviki* have considerable scope for punitive forms of entrepreneurship because as key passing points in the gas distribution network they hold what Timothy Mitchell (2011) has referred to as the power to stop or sabotage the flow of gas within the system. Unlike in Soviet times, this malfeasance does not come at the expense of the anonymous state but hurts people directly.

This use of the power of stoppage seems to be a qualitatively new phenomenon within the gas sector, not least since its victims are individual householders. In the Soviet-era second economy, state assets were subject to misappropriation but would be redistributed into personal networks. The present-day informality that has colonized the public-utilities sector seems to be a departure from this Soviet logic. Most significantly, the *gazoviki*'s capacity for exploitation is premised on changes to the way in which gas is valued and billed: the metrification of household gas consumption means that gas bills will vary and are therefore ripe for unscrupulous practices that were not possible in the Soviet period when a standard tariff was charged based on household size.

Anecdotes of the malfeasance of *gazoviki* are common currency among residents of Baku, and reinforce the sense that the people who work in the gas and electricity system are thieves. The government's efforts to combat this malfeasance – such as through smart metering and banning of taking payments at the door – have been well received, if not wholly successful. Still vested with the power of stoppage, *gazoviki* have in some cases exacted reprisals against consumers. A resident of Buzovna recounts:

> We had people come to collect [bill payments] from our homes and in recent months we haven't paid them and have given it to the bank instead. But though we pay the bank they [the *gazoviki*] demand money from us. We don't give and they torture us in different ways. ... They threatened other relatives of mine in the same way elsewhere. They told another relative, they said with this smart card you will still pay us because we will provide a very small amount of gas and you will die without gas, so you will have to pay us a bribe to get gas. And I often go to them and they don't have gas, just tiny amounts, it takes two, three hours to boil a kettle. But they don't pay. My relative said, 'If you want to give gas, give, if not, don't, but we won't pay you any more.' She answered them like that and sent them away.

This has even occurred with smart cards. The following anecdote, drawn again from Nardaran, sums up the situation.

> Smart meters were installed, and they showed that we used less gas [than used to be taken in payment], but it doesn't suit the gasmen. They left us without gas. And we were made to call them back. They

destroyed the devices and we again pay them, and on the computer it is written that payment hasn't been made to the state. We pay them. They don't let us pay the state.

These examples point to how changes in how resources are valued, as well as in the technologies by which they are measured, have fundamentally affected the social relations that form part of the socio-technical assemblage of gas provision. The change from the normative consumption regime envisaged in Soviet urban planning has created new opportunities for gasmen to turn a profit by exploiting their position as brokers and potential saboteurs of the utility system. Further technological changes, introduced to ease this situation – payment in banks and the introduction of smart meters and billing – were not accompanied by institutional changes, and gasmen were thus able to resort to strong-arm tactics in an attempt to keep their particular avenues of profit open.

This situation has resulted in the paradox that although the public overwhelmingly approve of the new utility system there are numerous complaints and protests over utilities in and around Baku. People accept the market principle that consumption is measured and billed according to use; many are even relieved that the new smart meter and bill payment system prevents corruption, and take it as a sign of improvements in the country as a whole. But the continued excesses of certain gas officials create discontent among those who are subject to them. To understand why this discontent seldom boils over into anti-government protest even though the enduring constant has been state ownership and oversight of the gas distribution network, we need to look at how local discursive understandings of legitimate power intersect with the abuses of these state functionaries such that the discussion of corruption in the provision of gas is restricted to criticisms of the gasmen.

The state as a moral economy

E.P. Thompson (1971) set the paternalist 'moral economy' of Tudor England against the emerging 'political economy' of Adam Smith that gradually achieved hegemony over the course of the eighteenth century. English peasants and townspeople, Thompson argued, would defend the moral economy in actions to set and enforce what they considered to be a fair price on grain. While Thompson focused very much on the actions of the poor in defence of the moral economy, it is equally important to consider the paternalist relations in which peasants' ideas of fairness were embedded. In the following section I aim to further sketch out the cultural understandings of patronage and fairness that inflect Azeri understandings of the state as just such a form of moral economy, and which certain sectors of the population feel is being eroded.

In former-Soviet contexts, social scientists have observed the presence of a moral economy in difficult times. This moral economy was based not so much on a principle of egalitarian fairness as on hierarchical relations of personalized largesse around the remnants of former state institutions that had already been *khozyaistva*, or 'domains of management'. To be *khozyain* implies stewardship of a domain, as in the *selskoe khozyaistvo* of a smallholding, the *kollektivnoe khozyaistvo* of a state farm (*kolkhoz*), or the *narodnoe khozyaistvo* of the national economy.[8] The authority of a *khozyain* (pl. *khozyaeva*) – which Douglas Rogers (2006, 915) figures variously as a 'master, owner, administrator, boss, man of the house' – was founded on his ability to maintain patronage networks, barter goods and favours, and honour moral expectations that he would provide for his employees and the community at large (cf. Humphrey 1998). These and other comparable accounts of fiefdoms and suzerainties in post-Soviet Russia (e.g. Humphrey 1991; Verdery 1991) are frequently related to the economic crisis and de facto state collapse that Russia and other countries of the former Soviet Union underwent during the 1990s. Networks of patronage that had existed informally during the late Soviet period took on a new salience, because they became the only way of getting things done in difficult times. This popular sense of a moral economy based on patronage is crucial to understanding both the politics and the substantive economies of post-Soviet societies.

In its basic elements, Rogers's account sets out the *khozyaistvo* as a common domain that is ruled by or under the protection of a *khozyain*. The *khozyain* is bound by a set of obligations towards the community, which, so long as these obligations are honoured, accepts that he will use this position for personal gain. The authority of the *khozyain* is based on his ability to distribute goods and services. People can request favours from the *khozyain*, but this implies future obligations on their part and they may not always want to put themselves into his debt. To avoid this they may steal illicitly from the *khozyaistvo*, which is nevertheless legitimate because the *khozyaistvo* is considered a commonly held property. A *khozyaistvo* is thus a social, political, economic and moral configuration that contains within it a bundle of obligations and expectations, including of patronage, asymmetrical reciprocity, and the qualified legitimacy of personal enrichment on the part of both subject and patron.

Unlike in the cases of autonomous suzerainties (such as with the various mafia enterprises of 1990s Russia) or hierarchically integrated fiefdoms (such as collective farms and factories), informal relations with *gazoviki* are not predicated on patronage of clients. Although they are themselves integrated into a hierarchical system of patronage, to which they probably owe their employment, they are not *khozyaeva*. The wheeling and dealing of *gazoviki* does not involve the kind of social capital or prestige that is critical to the notion of *khozyain*. Instead, as suggested by Simon Kordonskiy (2008), such functionaries might instead be usefully considered members of a *sosloviia* – an estate or status group (in the Weberian sense) which extracts payments from those it considers to be legitimately below it (discussed in Humphrey 2012b, 310–312).

While the *khozyaistvo* ethos does not govern everyday public interactions with the petty bureaucracy (although it certainly operates in other domains of state and social life, such as in the regional Executive Authorities), it continues to exist discursively in the ways people talk about the state. Discussing an official from the Ministry of Taxes, a former police officer in Baku told me:

> He was a very kind, very nice person but his activity was to take as much money as he could from the budget. He was a good man. It doesn't matter that he takes. If he gives to people then he is a good man.

The predominant model of authority is personalized in this morally dubious figure of the *khozyain*, and the *khozyain* figure *par excellence* is the president of Azerbaijan himself. One of my interviewees, an elderly man who had been involved in managing an illicit (but informally sanctioned) factory or *tsekh* in the Soviet period, presented his account of former First Party Secretary Heydar Əliyev's dramatic return to the presidency in the early 1990s:

> Heydar came to his office, locked the head of the Supreme Court and his colleagues in there, locked them all in and then threw them out onto the street. In a month, they came to him and said, 'You shouldn't have done that, we've got a state; a state should have its norms. Norms, and a place where they are issued. Who will issue them if you have thrown out the head of the court?' [And Heydar responded,] 'These words, "*hökm etdi*" [Az. 'ruled', i.e. by a court], delete them. *Hökm etdi* isn't necessary. Only I make rulings. And now write not *hökm etdi* but *prigovoril* [Rus. 'sentenced']. But I will make the rulings [*hökm etdi*]. There is only one khozyain [Az. *bir dənə xozayin var*] – Heydar Əliyev.' And to the present day Heydar Əliyev remains.

While there is absolutely no reason to trust in the factual accuracy of this account, it remains a common trope among residents of Baku[9] and it provides important insight into how Azerbaijanis understand power as congealed around the singular figure of the president. As one interviewee put it: 'Everything depends on the president in our country. Baku is not as large as Moscow, and everything is in his palm.'

The idea of a *khozyain* is strong in people's imagination of the state, and the current president has not acted to dispel this notion. Indeed, his public actions reinforce the sense of a personalized dominion, with amnesties for prisoners and the practices of gift-giving and personal intervention that befit a *khozyain*. What we are beginning to see with *gazoviki*, however, is the breakdown of certain elements that constitute the state as *khozaistvo*. *Gazoviki* manage to interrupt the moral order, to the extent that they may prevent even the president's gifts from getting through to their intended recipients.

The president has declared numerous amnesties on utility debts (most recently in January 2012), and the government subsequently gifted 1 m^3 of gas to households when introducing smart cards. However, an employee of the gas company suggests that although consumers received this gift of gas in the Baku village of Mərdəkan, where she worked, consumers in other parts of Baku did not. This employee assumed that the gas that should have been credited to consumers was instead charged as normal and the difference pocketed by the gasmen. Another interviewee told me that regarding the amnesty on gas and electricity debts, the gasman had explained to her: 'This amnesty is for the president, not for you.' Thus, she concludes, 'although the government has several times cancelled all gas and electricity debts, the situation just repeats itself'.

The accounts of Baku residents relating to *gazoviki*, then, indicate a strong commitment to the model of the state as *khozyaistvo* and power figures as *khozyaeva*. They also relate a dismayed sense that this model of patronage is being eroded by the quite different logic by which minor state officials oversee provision and distribution. Criticisms of power holders frequently reveal an implicit defence of the state as a moral, if hierarchical, economy and a censorious attitude towards those who, in the local argot, 'eat without allowing others to eat' or who otherwise ignore their personal standing as *khozyaeva*. The former police officer describes working with a senior official:

> A son's friend was in the army and she wanted him to attend the wedding. Sabir [the official] arranged for him to come to Baku for ten days and even paid for her son's travel. I have great respect for all these people; they behaved according to human values [Rus. *po chelovecheski*]. Another official had to be replaced because he ate everything alone and didn't share his earnings. Today it is not like it was then: one ate and let others eat, but now one eats and doesn't let others eat [Az. *biri yedi ve digerlerinede icaze versinler yesinler*].

If we accept the notion of the state as *khozyaistvo* then we can see that moral opprobrium against the corruption of gasmen is designed to reaffirm citizens' understandings that they are participating in a certain kind of moral economy. The administrative rent-taking to which people are subjected is part and parcel of the workings of the Azerbaijani state; yet people criticize the misbehaviour of its officials rather than the system as a whole. Part of the reason for this is that this franchised system also operated in the Soviet period (although not in the gas sector), but back then its consequences were only indirectly felt because the misappropriation of anonymous flows of state production did not entail a direct and personalized extortion of money from individual householders. Even if the *khozyain* was in effect stealing from consumers *in general*, and thereby aggravating the notorious Soviet deficit economy, he was able to maintain prestige by redirecting the flow of goods in personalized interactions with *particular* clients.

The behaviour of the gasmen is keenly felt because their actions directly cost the residents. The *khozyaistvo* system depends on a conversion of the general into the particular, from generalized theft into personalized giving. The result is that commentaries about *gazoviki* focus on particular instances of improper behaviour rather than the broader system of administrative rent-taking on which that behaviour is predicated. The misdeeds of gasmen are thus considered aberrations from, not constitutive of, this idealized moral system. The actions of this 'well-organized band of thieves' cause distress, yet somehow they don't upset the notion of the state as *khozyaistvo* or the president as *khozyain*. By limiting criticism to outraged commentaries on individual incidents, the *gazoviki* (and figures like them) thus act to insulate the state itself from attack.

Concluding remarks

In this article I have used local commentaries on Baku's domestic gas supply network to examine how power and its legitimation are affected by changes in the technological and bureaucratic regimes within which they operate. Because during the Soviet period utilities were charged at a fixed tariff based on household size, gas supply seems to have been immune from the pervasive appropriation and redistribution that characterized other elements of the actually existing Soviet economy. But the post-independence introduction of gas metering that measures household consumption, rather than billing according to household size, created new relationships between gasmen and consumers. Vested with the new responsibility to both measure and bill consumption, and with the power to cut off supplies, gasmen were able to exercise a new and seemingly unfettered power of arbitrary stoppage over the domestic gas supply network. In so doing, they profited from either lack of effective oversight or administrative complicity, leaving citizens little access to the hierarchy above them and thus insulating it from both supplication and criticism. Subsequent government changes to metering and bill collection – smart metering and payment at banks – have been well received by residents because they mitigate this distressing situation. But gasmen have viewed these reforms as a threat and, because no corresponding changes have been made to the administrative regime, they have in many instances been able to sabotage the intentions behind the technological changes to the network.

The intrigues around domestic gas supply help refine a broader discussion of the nature of political authority in the Caucasus and in Central Asia more generally (cf. Grant 2009). By pointing to the way in which citizens accept certain circuits of appropriation and redistribution (the state as *khozyaistvo*) as legitimate and others (the expropriation and stoppage practices of gasmen) as illegitimate, my material shows how state power is embedded within a culturally patterned moral economy. Indeed, the illegitimate practices of gasmen act as a foil by which residents affirm – in its transgression – the model of *khozyaistvo*, which for them constitutes legitimate authority.

The *khozyaistvo* system, however, was dependent on the Soviet political economy in which circuits of appropriated state assets and personalized redistribution enabled *khozyaeva* to transform their position into a wealth in people (Rogers 2006, 920). In the present day, Azerbaijan is integrated into global market economy through the oil industry, leading to increased social stratification and an erosion of the ethos of *khozyaistvo* in daily life. Though there seems to have been little space for the *direct* exploitation of consumers within the Soviet gas supply system, the present-day impunity of gasmen points to the erosion of the *khozyaistvo* ethos in practice. As far as a moral economy of energy is concerned, popular critiques of malfeasance in the gas network and even of wealth accumulation as a result of the oil boom in Azerbaijan should not be considered as resistance to either marketization or personal enrichment, but rather as so many discursive attempts to restore the moral order of *khozyaistvo* that citizens increasingly feel has been abandoned.

Acknowledgements

My thanks to Caroline Humphrey, Maya İskenderova and especially Cara Kerven for suggestions and comments that improved my argument. Names have been changed to protect the privacy of those individuals who appear in this account.

Funding

Primary field research in Azerbaijan during spring 2013 was conducted with the support of CEELBAS.

Notes

1. A note on transliteration. Azerbaijani usage follows the Latin transcription adopted by the Republic of Azerbaijan in 1992. This follows the same pronunciation as Turkish with the exception of ə [æ] and ğ [ɣ]. I use Azerbaijani transcription except where an international form is more appropriate, such as the when referring to the Shah Deniz gas field [Az. Şahdəniz].
2. A brief flirtation with the privatization of Baku's electricity network between 2002 and 2006 to the Turkish company Barmek-Azerbaijan Electricity Distribution LLC ended in acrimony, with the director and seven company officials tried for abuse of power, embezzlement and negligence, and the electrical grid restored to the state-owned Bakıelektrikşəbəkə JSC.
3. I have been informally told that there have been further restructuring and centralization of the network, but have not been able to establish the particulars of these changes.
4. There is a special regime for internally displaced persons and refugees, who are given a substantial allowance, beyond which they must pay market rate.
5. In 2004 the retail gas price was increased from approximately AZN 6.5 to AZN 47.2 per thousand cubic metres. The price was further increased in July 2009 to AZN 100 (about USD 120) per thousand cubic metres (AzeriReport.com, 1 June 2009).
6. It also makes for interesting comparison with Michael Degani's (2013, 178) account of the 'grey-market labour and transactions that have … colonised [Tanzania's] ailing electricity infrastructure'. While in Tanzania the arbitrage and scams of electricity company officials can be seen as manifesting an ethic of 'entrepreneurial citizenship' (187), in Baku the activities of *gazoviki* are read as significant insofar as they index the moral health of the state.
7. The register of *hörmet* and *khozyaistvo* may nevertheless be employed at the next rung of administration. An informant reported to the state anticorruption department that hospital staff had solicited an AZN 600 bribe for a maternity stay in a public hospital. The line manager in the hospital summoned this young man and asked why he went over her head when he could have brought the issue to her and they could have arranged something (his behaviour was not *hörmetli* to a willing *khozyain*). She then made a show of her care by offering the service free of charge and even giving provisions to the new mother.
8. In Azeri, the national economy is rendered as *xalq təsərrüfatı*, while a smallholding would be *kənd təsərrüfatı* (village economy). The term *təsərrüfat* is more or less synonymous with the Russian *khozyaistvo* and contains similar implications of stewardship.
9. I have similar accounts that emphasize the singularity of Heydar Əliyev as an authority figure. When cleaning up Baku of the former *lotu* (Az. 'counts') or *vory v zakone* (Rus. 'thieves-in-law'), who were criminal authority figures in the informal network of Soviet power, he is said to have declared, 'There is only one mafia in Azerbaijan, it is me.'

References

Alexander, C. 2007. "Almaty: Rethinking the Public Sector." In *Urban Life in Post-Soviet Asia*, edited by Catherine Alexander, Victor Buchli, and Caroline Humphrey, 70–101. London: UCL Press.

Avtorkhanov, A. G. 1979. *Sila i bessilie Brezhneva: Politicheskie etyudy*. Frankfurt/Main: Possev-Verlag.

Bedirhanoğlu, P. 2013. "State-Business Relations in Azerbaijan Through the Eyes of Turkish Businesspeople." Manuscript submitted for publication.

Collier, S. J. 2011. *Post-Soviet Social: Neoliberalism, Social Modernity, Biopolitics*. Princeton, NJ: Princeton University Press.

Degani, M. 2013. "Emergency Power: Time, Ethics, and Electricity in Postsocialist Tanzania." In *Cultures of Energy: Power, Practices, Technologies*, edited by Sarah Strauss, Staphanie Rupp, and Thomas Love, 177–192. Walnut Creek: Left Coast Press.

Derlugian, G. M. 2003. "How Soviet Bureaucracy Produced Nationalism, and What Came of It in Azerbaijan." *Socialist Register* 39 (March 9), 1–21.

EIU (Economist Intelligence Unit). April 2012. "Country Report: Azerbaijan."

EIU (Economist Intelligence Unit). July 2013. "The Great Game for Gas in the Caspian: Europe Opens the Southern Corridor."

European Commission. 2006. "ENPI Strategy Paper 2007–13 for Azerbaijan." http://ec.europa.eu/world/enp/pdf/country/enpi_csp_azerbaijan_en.pdf

Grant, B. 2009. *The Captive and the Gift: Cultural Histories of Sovereignty in Russia and the Caucasus.* Ithaca, NY: Cornell University Press.

Humphrey, C. 1991. ""Icebergs", Barter and the Mafia in Provincial Russia." *Anthropology Today* 7 (2): 8–13.

Humphrey, C. 1998. "The Domestic Mode of Production in Post-Soviet Siberia?" *Anthropology Today* 14 (3): 2–7.

Humphrey, C. 2003. "Rethinking Infrastructure: Siberian Cities and the Great Freeze of January 1991." In *Wounded Cities: Destruction and Reconstruction in a Globalized World*, edited by Jane Schneider and Ida Susser, 91–107. Oxford: Berg.

Humphrey, C. 2012a. "Favors and "Normal Heroes" The Case of Postsocialist Higher Education." *HAU: Journal of Ethnographic Theory* 2 (2): 22–41.

Humphrey, C. 2012b. "Inequality." In *A Companion to Moral Anthropology*, edited by Didier Fassin, 302–19. Malden: John Wiley & Sons.

International Labour Office. 2012. *Decent Work Country Profile: Azerbaijan.* Geneva: ILO.

Kharkhordin, O., and R. Alapuro. 2011. *Political Theory and Community Building in Post-Soviet Russia.* Abingdon: Routledge.

King, L. P., and D. Stuckler. 2007. "Mass Privatization and the Postcommunist Mortality Crisis." In *The Transformation of State Socialism: System Change, Capitalism or Something Else*, edited by D. Lane, 179–197. London: Palgrave-Macmillan.

Kjærnet, H. 2010. "The State Oil Company SOCAR: A Microcosm of Azerbaijani Development?" *Caucasus Analytical Digest* 16: 5–7.

Kordonskiy, S. G. 2008. *Soslovnaya struktura postsovetskoy Rossii.* Moscow: Institut Fonda "Obshchestvennoe mnenie".

Lipsky, M. 1980. *Street Level Bureaucracy: Dilemmas of the Individual in Public Services.* New York: Russell Sage Foundation.

Mitchell, T. 2011. *Carbon Democracy: Political Power in the Age of Oil.* London, New York: Verso.

Oleinik, A. N. 2011. "O prirode i prichinakh administrativnoi renty: Osobennosti vedeniya biznesa v rossiiskom regione." *Politicheskaya Kontseptologiya* No. 2: 117–40.

Rogers, D. 2006. "How to Be a Khoziain in a Transforming State: State Formation and the Ethics of Governance in Post-Soviet Russia." *Journal for Comparative Study of Society and History* 48 (4): 915–945.

Rogers, D. 2012. "The Materiality of the Corporation: Oil, Gas, and Corporate Social Technologies in the Remaking of a Russian Region." *American Ethnologist* 39 (2): 284–296.

Sneath, D. 2006. "Transacting and Enacting: Corruption, Obligation and the Use of Monies in Mongolia." *Ethnos* 71 (1): 89–112.

Thompson, E. P. 1971. "The Moral Economy of the English Crowd in the Eighteenth Century." *Past & Present* 50: 76–136.

Vaksberg, A. 1991. *The Soviet Mafia.* London: Weidenfeld & Nicolson.

Verdery, K. 1991. "Theorizing Socialism: A Prologue to the 'Transition'." *American Ethnologist* 18 (3): 419–439.

World Bank. 2005. "Azerbaijan: Issues and Options Associated with Energy Sector Reform." Report No. 32371-AZ.

World Bank. 2013. "Azerbaijan Partnership: Program Snapshot." http://www.worldbank.org/content/dam/Worldbank/document/Azerbaijan-Snapshot.pdf

Yalçın-Heckmann, Lale. 2010. *The Return of Private Property: Rural Life after Agrarian Reform in the Republic of Azerbaijan.* Berlin: LIT Verlag.

Zemtsov, I. 1976. *Partiya Ili Mafiya?. Razvorovannaya Respublika.* Paris: Les Éditeurs Réunis.

Switching off or switching source: energy consumption and household response to higher energy prices in the Kyrgyz Republic

Franziska Gassmann[a,b] and Raquel Tsukada[a,b]

[a]*United Nations University - Maastricht Economic and Social Research Institute on Innovation and Technology, the Netherlands;* [b]*Maastricht Graduate School of Governance, the Netherlands*

The Energy Poverty Action Initiative of the World Economic Forum suggests that 'access to energy is fundamental to improving quality of life and is a key imperative for economic development'. This is particularly true in Central Asia, where winters are harsh and long. Changes in energy prices affect the purchasing power of households, hitting the poor in particular. The impact very much depends on a household's energy basket and the available strategies for switching to alternative energy sources. Using data from the 2011 Kyrgyz Integrated Household Survey, this article analyses the profile of household energy consumption and the impact of electricity tariff increases on the probability that households would switch to alternative energy sources. The results suggest that households would respond to an electricity price increase by increasing consumption of fuels; households would be likely to move away from electricity-only heating and towards stove-only heating.

Introduction

Several countries in Central Asia have been advised to reform their energy sector. In its 2011 report on Central Asia, the International Crisis Group recommended that Central Asian governments 'open the sector to market reforms by significantly decreasing state control and encouraging competition and external investment. Develop a timeline for bringing tariffs in line with market prices and design a targeted system of assistance for socially vulnerable populations' (2011, ii). A central component of such reforms is bringing electricity tariffs up to the cost-recovery level. This is deemed necessary for sustainable service provision and to enable infrastructure investments required in the sector.

According to microeconomic theory, the general result of a price increase is a decrease in demand through income and substitution effects. The response of consumers to an electricity tariff increase would be to reduce energy consumption ('switching off') as their purchasing power is reduced. According to the Energy Poverty Action Initiative of the World Economic Forum, 'access to energy is fundamental to improving quality of life and is a key imperative for economic development' (Energy Poverty Action (EPA), n.d.). Hence, reducing energy consumption below a certain minimum may hinder development. Consumers could also consider switching to alternative energy sources, when substitutes are available. Switching to alternative sources may however not always be desirable, nor physically or financially possible, particularly in the short term. Moreover, the alternative source could have undesirable side effects, such as health problems caused by indoor air pollution (Duflo, Greenstone, and Hanna 2008; Akhmetov 2013), reducing the household's well-being. Neither is it desirable that households climb down the energy ladder, i.e. downgrading from the use of efficient energy sources (electricity or modern fuels) to biomass fuels (firewood, dung, crop residues, etc.) (UNDP 2000). Understanding the consumption behaviour of households and constraints on their possible coping strategies is essential when designing energy policies such as a tariff increase.

The Kyrgyz Republic is no exception among the former Soviet Union countries when it comes to heavily subsidized energy tariffs and repeated reform attempts over the past two decades. After the collapse of the Soviet system the energy infrastructure deteriorated dramatically and countries were confronted with higher energy prices. Towards the end of the 1990s, several countries in the region started reforming their energy sectors and raised tariffs in order to make the sector financially viable and encourage efficient energy consumption. In 2003, however, electricity tariffs were still below cost-recovery levels in 14 of the 19 countries in Eastern Europe and Central Asia (Lampietti, Banerjee, and Branczik 2007).

Reforming the energy sector has been on the Kyrgyz government's agenda from as early as 1995. Over the years, the government has simplified the structure and increased the tariffs several times. Electricity tariffs were raised five times between 1999 and 2002 (USAID 2008); the number of tariff blocks was reduced from six to two in March 2003. Between 2003 and 2006, the tariffs remained unchanged. In May 2006, a unified tariff was introduced at KGS 0.62/kWh; this was increased to KGS 0.7/kWh in 2008. In 2008 the government also adopted a mid-term strategy for electricity tariffs, with the objective of achieving cost-recovery level in 2012. Besides the objectives related to the production and delivery of electricity, the strategy also said that by 2012 all electricity subsidies must be targeted to low-income consumers and provided through the state social benefit system (USAID 2008, 52). The latest reform attempt dates to January 2010, when electricity tariffs were doubled, and thermal power prices quadrupled. The aims of this substantial increase were to eliminate implicit universal subsidies and to introduce equitable cost-recovery tariffs. However, after the political unrest in April 2010, which was also an expression of the population's dissatisfaction with the tariff reform and which eventually led to the ousting of President Bakiyev, the government was forced to undo the increase in residential energy tariffs. Currently, electricity tariffs are still at a level below full cost recovery. USAID (2011) estimated the full cost recovery price for electricity at KGS 2.03/kWh (USD 0.044), implying a subsidy of KGS 1.33/kWh given the current tariff of KGS 0.7/kWh. It is estimated that implicit energy subsidies accounted for more than 4% of GDP in 2009 (Gassmann 2013).

Access to reliable and affordable energy is essential for a country like the Kyrgyz Republic, where winters are long and cold. The country is landlocked, and its climate is influenced by the Tien Shan and Pamir mountain ranges, which dominate the country. However, regions vary considerably in terms of climate. The south-western part in the Ferghana Valley has a subtropical climate, with very hot summers. The climate to the north of the mountains is temperate, while the areas high in the Tien Shan Mountains are characterized by a dry continental and even polar climate. It is not unusual for temperatures in these locations to stay below 0 °C for more than 40 days in the winter. Generating sufficient warmth is vitally important for survival.

From 2007 to 2009, electricity generation in the Kyrgyz Republic decreased significantly. Especially during the winter months, the Kyrgyz Republic lacks the capacity to meet energy demand, which is reflected in regular power outages (World Bank 2014). In 2011, only 11% of households never experienced an electricity outage. Some 62% were disconnected several times a year, and 10% at least once a week. The problem of reliability is much more dramatic in certain areas. In 13 of the 56 *raions* daily interruptions affected up to 49% of the local population.[1]

This article investigates the potential impact of electricity price increases on residential energy consumption in the Kyrgyz Republic. First, we analyse the energy consumption profile of households. Given that a great share of energy is used for space heating, we then investigate the determinants of households' choice of energy for heating, and analyse the probability that house-holds would switch to alternative sources[2] as a response to electricity price increases.[3]

The data used are based on the 2011 Kyrgyz Integrated Household Survey (KIHS). The KIHS is an annual survey implemented by the National Statistical Committee of the Kyrgyz Republic. The sample covers about 5000 households, representative at the national and regional levels. The survey collects detailed information on household demographics, including education, health, migration, individual employment, housing, land and livestock possession, and household incomes and expenditures. Although the KIHS is a rotating panel, whereby about one-quarter of the households are replaced each year, we refrained from using the panel data to estimate the impact of price changes on consumption in view of quality issues. Households are not tracked over time, e.g., in case they have migrated, and are simply dropped from the sample. In addition, other households are dropped randomly and replaced by new households in the subsequent year, leading to different replacement rates each year. It remains therefore unclear to what extent the panel subsample is representative (Esenaliev, Kroeger, and Steiner 2011).

The impact of energy reforms in Eastern European and Central Asian countries has been studied increasingly. One strand of the literature is concerned with distributional impacts and with policies to mitigate the negative impact on the poor. Studies of electricity price increases in Poland (Freund and Wallich 1997), electricity and thermal energy in the Kyrgyz Republic (Gassmann 2013) and gas in Armenia (Ersado 2012) find a disproportionally higher negative impact on the poorest households. To mitigate that effect, Price and Pham (2009), after analysing hypothetical scenarios of electricity reform in Albania and Bulgaria, recommend always includ-ing lifeline tariffs in any tariff scheme. Gassmann (2013) also analyses the effect of reducing sub-sidies, including lifeline tariffs, and she proposes introducing cash transfers to compensate the poorest households in the Kyrgyz Republic.

This article adds to another strand of literature on the impact of energy reforms, one which investigates household energy choices and household behavioural responses to energy price increases. A key question in this literature is *when* households would consider switching to alternative energy sources. Our article investigates the determinants of energy choice in the Kyrgyz Republic, with focus on energy for space heating, which accounts for a large share of residential energy consumption in Central Asian countries. Previous studies have focused on cooking fuels (Helteberg 2004, 2005). Our article also contributes to understanding the determinants and limitations of households' switching to different heating energy sources. It adds to the literature by bringing in evidence for the Kyrgyz Republic, in line with Silva, Klytchnikova, and Radevic (2009), who simulated the response of households in Montenegro to electricity tariff increases.

Energy consumption in the Kyrgyz Republic

Changes in energy prices affect the purchasing power of households. The effect depends on the magnitude of the price change, a household's energy basket, and its available strategies for switching to alternative energy sources. Studies on the potential removal of electricity subsidies estimate the expected real income loss to range between 2% and 16% for the poorest 20% of the population (IEA et al. 2010, Annex 4; Adenauer and del Granado 2011). Estimates for the Kyrgyz Republic indicate in general a real welfare loss of 5% for the poorest households if electricity tariffs are raised to cost-recovery levels (Gassmann 2013). Both the composition of the energy used and available switching strategies depend on the household's location, welfare level and demographic composition. It is therefore essential to know the energy consumption basket for different households (see also Kraudzun, 2014, this issue).

Household energy consumption profile

The first question in reforming energy tariffs must be, What are the most common energy sources used by households? Access to electricity is close to universal in the Kyrgyz Republic (see Table 1), although service provision may not always be reliable.[4] The second-most commonly used energy source is solid fuels, used by over 60% of households.[5] Since the use of multiple energy sources is rather common in the Kyrgyz Republic, an electricity tariff increase would probably have no linear effect on consumption; households would rebalance their energy basket by mixing several sources. After all, they have been doing this already. Irrespective of the location, households often rely on more than one energy source, as we see in Table 1.

An assessment of energy sources by location reveals significantly different profiles of energy use. Provision of (district) central heating and piped gas is concentrated in flat areas, reinforcing the idea that natural barriers still hinder service delivery in other terrains in the Kyrgyz Republic. These services are heavily concentrated in the country's capital. Bishkek stands out in the use of central heating and piped gas, followed by a few users scattered in other urban areas across the country. Despite the wide availability of electricity, the incidence of households using fuels is very high. Over 50% of households, even among the richest in the nation (see the upper quintiles of the income distribution), rely on fuels.

Solid fuels are crucially important alternative sources of electricity in the Kyrgyz Republic. The basket composition of fuel consumption varies considerably across geographical locations. Firewood and coal are equally the most prevalent fuels used for heating or cooking purposes, except in Bishkek (see Table 2). Between 2007 and 2010 the consumption of coal increased to almost 60% (Slay 2011, 16), although it can effectively be used only in detached homes. It is also interesting that corn is especially prevalent in the southern regions (Jalalabad and

Table 1. Per cent share of households with positive expenditures on energy sources.

	Electricity	Central heating	Piped gas	Fuels
Total	99.7	15.7	26.7	60.5
High mountain areas	99.8	0.9	1.0	81.9
Semi-mountain areas	100.0	1.8	1.5	59.6
Flat areas	99.6	19.9	34.3	57.9
Bishkek	98.7	57.1	76.5	15.5
Other urban areas	99.9	15.2	34.5	54.4
Rural areas	99.9	2.3	7.3	77.5
Issyk Kul	99.9	2.8	0.3	58.2
Jalalabad	100.0	3.8	14.8	65.4
Naryn	99.5	2.0	0.4	78.2
Batken	99.8	2.2	12.7	85.1
Osh	100.0	5.5	20.3	80.4
Talas	100.0	0.8	0.6	63.7
Chui	100.0	14.1	23.1	64.3
Bishkek	98.7	57.1	76.5	15.5
Quintile I	99.8	5.6	16.0	67.3
Quintile II	99.8	6.0	16.2	69.3
Quintile III	99.9	14.2	24.0	61.2
Quintile IV	99.4	20.4	32.1	58.1
Quintile V	99.5	32.2	45.1	46.4

Source: KIHS (2011).
Note: Since households may use multiple energy sources, shares do not add up to 100%. Quintiles at household level, based on total household expenditures per capita. Only a few areas in the Kyrgyz Republic are provided with central heating (Bishkek, parts of Chui Valley, Naryn Town and Osh City, and a few other places).

Table 2. Per cent share of households using solid fuels for heating or cooking.

	Wood	Coal	Dung/peat	Corn
Total	65.8	65.6	31.3	12.6
High mountain areas	81.3	86.5	66.6	1.9
Semi-mountain areas	87.9	64.6	53.4	24.9
Flat areas	60.0	63.1	23.1	11.7
Bishkek	7.6	17.4	0.2	0.0
Other urban areas	55.0	57.4	9.7	5.8
Rural areas	89.1	84.6	49.9	19.3
Issyk Kul	84.9	59.8	37.7	0.2
Jalalabad	76.0	70.3	35.1	20.0
Naryn	62.0	85.4	83.9	0.1
Batken	90.9	90.0	44.3	7.1
Osh	84.4	84.7	48.8	35.3
Talas	68.7	70.7	38.1	0.0
Chui	75.5	75.7	14.4	1.3
Bishkek	7.6	17.4	0.2	0.0
Quintile I	77.1	73.4	39.6	16.0
Quintile II	73.0	73.7	37.9	16.7
Quintile III	69.9	71.1	29.3	13.1
Quintile IV	61.1	61.1	28.3	9.8
Quintile V	47.9	48.6	21.4	7.0

Source: KIHS (2011).
Note: Since households may use multiple energy sources, shares do not add up to 100%. Quintiles at household level, based on total household expenditures per capita.

Osh – the Ferghana Valley is very fertile and used for agriculture and crops). Dung on the other hand is very popular in Naryn, a very mountainous region with lots of livestock.

The preference of households for either firewood or coal does not differ sharply by income distribution (lower panel in Table 2). Apart from the richest quintile, the proportion of households using one or another fuel remains balanced within the same income quintile. As the energy ladder theory foresees, it is clear that as households become wealthier the use of non-modern fuels tends to decrease.

According to the International Energy Agency, energy security requires uninterrupted availability of energy, at an affordable price.[6] Analysis by type of energy shows that overall the largest energy expenditure as a share of the total household expenditure is on solid fuels (on average KGS 3957, approximately USD 85, per year), followed by electricity (KGS 2737, approximately USD 58).[7] This certainly varies with the household's actual energy consumption basket, and thus Table 3 cannot provide either availability or affordability information for assessing household energy security in Kyrgyzstan. However, given that the electricity price is fixed across the country at a single tariff (KGS 0.7/kWh in the survey period), Table 3 can shed light on 'across-location' comparisons of the actual quantity (kWh) of electricity consumption of households. It varies on average between the lowest expenditure (and thus quantity consumed) in Batken (KGS 2423, approximately USD 52) to the highest average consumption in Chui (KGS 3093, approximately USD 66). Bishkek once again stands out, having a different pattern than the other regions. Its average expenditure for thermal power is substantially higher than the expenditure for any other energy sources.

Total expenditure by geographical location indicates the existence of large inequalities in energy expenditure within the Kyrgyz Republic. The average household in Bishkek spends about 36% more on energy than an average household in other urban areas, 41% more than its rural counterparts, and as much as 91% more than an average household living in Issyk Kul.

Table 3. Annual household expenditures (in KGS) by type of energy, and per cent share in total household expenditure.

	Annual energy expenditure					Share of energy in total expenditure				
	Electricity	Thermal power	Piped gas	Fuels	Total energy expenditures	Electricity	Thermal power	Piped gas	Fuels	Total
Total	2,737	947	1,024	3,957	8,665	2.19	0.75	0.78	2.80	6.52
High mountain areas	2,521	49	6	4,986	7,563	2.03	0.03	0.01	3.81	5.88
Semi-mountain areas	2,960	97	15	2,564	5,636	2.43	0.08	0.01	1.88	4.41
Flat areas	2,725	1,206	1,326	4,070	9,328	2.16	0.96	1.01	2.83	6.97
Bishkek	2,819	3,915	3,430	1,072	11,236	2.14	3.18	2.50	0.74	8.55
Other urban areas	2,935	592	983	3,727	8,238	2.46	0.47	0.86	2.72	6.50
Rural areas	2,633	111	252	4,993	7,989	2.10	0.07	0.19	3.51	5.86
Issyk Kul	2,906	90	3	2,895	5,895	2.50	0.07	0.00	2.11	4.68
Jalalabad	2,707	50	471	3,119	6,347	2.14	0.03	0.37	2.24	4.78
Naryn	3,025	114	2	4,317	7,458	2.29	0.07	0.00	3.01	5.37
Batken	2,423	20	338	5,522	8,302	1.52	0.01	0.30	3.24	5.07
Osh	2,307	149	490	5,726	8,671	1.88	0.12	0.41	4.07	6.49
Talas	3,482	25	3	3,194	6,703	2.69	0.02	0.00	2.19	4.90
Chui	3,093	865	911	5,658	10,527	2.71	0.63	0.75	4.24	8.33
Bishkek	2,819	3,915	3,430	1,072	11,236	2.14	3.18	2.50	0.74	8.55
Quintile I	2,591	237	439	3,469	6,735	2.47	0.23	0.44	2.98	6.11
Quintile II	2,803	366	588	4,582	8,339	2.32	0.31	0.48	3.39	6.51
Quintile III	2,859	711	1,000	4,051	8,621	2.29	0.66	0.82	2.78	6.55
Quintile IV	2,642	1,230	1,332	3,846	9,050	1.95	0.95	0.95	2.43	6.28
Quintile V	2,792	2,189	1,764	3,838	10,583	1.90	1.61	1.22	2.43	7.15

Source: KIHS (2011). Quintiles at household level, based on total household expenditures per capita.

These differences in energy consumption are partly related to overall living standards in the various regions. Bishkek and Chui are the most affluent regions, with the lowest poverty rates; the highest poverty rates are observed in Issyk Kul, Naryn and Talas (World Bank 2011). It is true, however, that Table 3 cannot show us the actual energy well-being enjoyed by each of these groups; this could only be assessed by an estimate of the total quantity of energy consumed by households, adding up all energy sources.

The share of energy expenditure in the total household expenditure provides some insight regarding affordability. Overall, households spend about 6.5% of their total expenditure on energy consumption (Table 3, right panel). Energy consumption shows that signs of inequality in affordability are most pronounced across regions (*oblasts*). In Talas a household spends on average 4.9% of its total expenditures on energy; in Bishkek households spend a larger proportion, about 8.6% of their total expenditures. The share of energy expenditure in the household budget does not vary much across income quintiles. It is about 6.1% in the poorest quintile and about 7.2% of total expenditure in households in the highest quintile of the income distribution. This however must be interpreted with caution, since it could be the case that households in Batken have lower expenditure simply because there is less service provision and households are therefore constrained in levels of consumption.

Given the long, cold winters in the Kyrgyz Republic, space heating takes an important share of households' energy consumption. Three main space-heating technologies are found in the Kyrgyz Republic. Central (or district) heating is used by 15.8% of households, and electric heating by 37.1%; stove heating is the most common, adopted by 74.7% of households (Table 4). Households may also use a combination of different sources, for example electricity and stove heating, and therefore the columns in Table 4 do not add up to 100%.

Table 4. Percentage of households using each type of heating source.

	Central	Electric	Stove	Other
Total	15.8	37.1	74.7	7.0
High mountain areas	0.9	34.3	97.5	0.0
Semi-mountain areas	2.4	46.8	92.1	0.2
Flat areas	20.0	35.7	68.4	9.1
Bishkek	60.4	19.7	21.5	18.0
Other urban areas	15.8	53.5	64.3	8.0
Rural areas	1.2	36.3	95.6	3.1
Issyk Kul	3.9	33.5	91.9	0.0
Jalalabad	2.9	55.2	84.9	5.7
Naryn	2.0	43.1	95.2	0.0
Batken	0.2	30.6	91.4	8.8
Osh	5.7	42.4	87.3	5.0
Talas	0.9	45.9	93.7	1.2
Chui	12.1	31.4	79.9	4.7
Bishkek	60.4	19.7	21.5	18.0
Quintile I	5.5	34.9	86.6	5.7
Quintile II	6.9	41.6	85.3	5.1
Quintile III	12.2	35.9	77.4	7.6
Quintile IV	20.4	37.7	69.8	7.1
Quintile V	34.1	35.2	52.7	9.7
Hh lives in separate house	0.4	37.5	92.0	8.1

Source: KIHS (2011). Quintiles at household level, based on total household expenditures per capita. 'Other' includes gas or other sources.

Table 5. Per cent share of households by main heating source.

	Electricity only	Central heat only	Stove only	Electricity and stove	Other combo
Total	5.1	12.5	45.7	26.4	10.3
High mountain areas	1.6	0.4	65.3	32.2	0.4
Semi-mountain areas	5.3	1.1	52.0	40.2	1.5
Flat areas	5.6	16.0	42.1	23.3	13.1
Bishkek	2.6	53.2	12.5	6.6	25.0
Other urban areas	15.5	8.4	33.0	27.8	15.3
Rural areas	1.9	0.8	61.5	32.3	3.5
Issyk Kul	4.2	0.8	65.6	26.3	3.0
Jalalabad	8.2	1.4	40.1	43.3	7.1
Naryn	2.8	1.0	55.9	39.3	1.0
Batken	4.7	0.2	63.7	22.7	8.8
Osh	6.2	1.6	53.0	30.1	9.2
Talas	4.2	0.3	52.8	40.9	1.8
Chui	4.9	9.8	57.2	21.0	7.0
Bishkek	2.6	53.2	12.5	6.6	25.0
Quintile I	5.8	4.0	57.7	25.5	6.9
Quintile II	4.3	5.0	50.0	33.7	7.0
Quintile III	4.1	10.5	48.7	27.5	9.3
Quintile IV	5.6	15.8	41.4	25.5	11.7
Quintile V	5.9	27.2	30.5	19.8	16.6
Hh lives in separate house	2.2	0.2	56.7	32.6	8.3

Source: KIHS (2011). Quintiles at household level, based on total household expenditures per capita.

Classifying households according to the main heating source, the following categories are recognizable: 5.1% use only electricity as a heating source; 12.5% use only central heating (though this service is concentrated in Bishkek and parts of Chui Valley); and almost half of Kyrgyz households only use stoves (45.7%). The most frequent combination of heating sources is electricity-plus-stove, a strategy adopted by 26.4% of households. Table 5 conveys two important messages. First, a majority of households rely on a single energy source for heating. Switching to a different technology, or enlarging its energy portfolio for space heating, may imply certain costs. The second message is the importance of fuels in the livelihood of households in the Kyrgyz Republic. Table 5 shows that stoves are by far the most frequent technology adopted by households in the Kyrgyz Republic. The incidence of stove-only heating is above 50% of households in all regions except Bishkek and Jalalabad *oblast*. It is as high as 65.6% of households in Issyk Kul *oblast*.

The ability to switch to alternative energy sources

When prices of a particular energy source increase, the poorest households relying on that source are likely to be hit the hardest. This general statement may however not always be true. The ability to switch to alternative energy sources at a low investment cost may partially mitigate the monetary loss caused by the introduction of the tariff. Some alternative technologies, however, are still unaffordable for most households, as is the case with most renewable energy sources, such as solar panels, wind energy and small-scale hydropower units. In this sense, households living in dwellings which are unable to switch to alternative energy sources may be hit hard, even if they are not in the bottom percentiles of population. In the Kyrgyz Republic, households'

Table 6. Percentage of households with (operational) modern energy source.

	Total	High mountain	Semi-mountain	Flat areas	Bishkek	Other urban	Rural	Not poor	Poor	Extremely poor
Electricity	99.86	99.92	99.98	99.83	99.8	99.9	99.87	99.84	99.97	99.58
Central gas supply	24.91	0	0	32.33	73.8	32.48	5.93	29.41	12.67	11.34
Hot water	14.22	0	1.74	18.15	58.81	9.6	1.4	17.77	4.79	1.49
Central heating	16.63	0.99	3.47	20.85	60.74	16.98	2.03	20.55	5.65	7.76

Source: Authors' calculations based on KIHS (2011). Individual level weights. Except for electricity, differences across groups are statistically significant ($p < .01$).

ability to switch to alternative energy sources depends to a large extent on their location: better service provision is often concentrated in areas with easier geographical access and critical demand density, such as Bishkek and a few other urban centres.

Central gas supply, hot water and central heating are scarce or unavailable at high altitudes and in semi-mountainous or rural areas (see Table 6). For that reason, we next turn to the analysis of household space-heating choice, focusing on choices of electricity or stove/furnace, because these represent real alternative heating sources available to all households.

The household energy choice

In this section, we investigate the determinants of a household's choice of a particular energy source. Here we focus on space heating, because that represents an important final use of energy for households in the Kyrgyz Republic. Using a multinomial outcome model[8] we estimate the determinants of the household choice of heating source based on socio-demographic characteristics and environmental conditions of the household. The model also allows investigating the importance of energy prices in determining the probability of households' considering a switch to alternative energy sources.

Model specification

Households in the Kyrgyz Republic can choose between electricity, central heating, piped gas, stove/furnace, and any combination of these sources for space heating. But to perform a realistic analysis we need to restrict the sample to households that could feasibly switch to another heating source. Therefore, we do not include in this part of the analysis households using central heating, piped gas or any combination involving those. The reason is that households, as argued in the Introduction, are rather limited in their ability to disconnect from such heating sources – just as households not connected to them may also have little opportunity to start using them. For instance, once connected to central district heating the household is not able to physically disconnect from it. And a household may be able to connect to the system only if district heating is already available at its location and even at its building. As Table 5 shows, according to the 2011 KIHS, at least 72.1% of households rely on fuels (stoves) for space heating (45.7% exclusively using a stove and 26.4% using stove and electricity). Hence, the restricted sample for this analysis consists of 3788 households, of which 6.7% use electricity only, 34% use stove only, and 59% use a combination of electricity and stove (Table 7). Despite using electricity-only for heating, about 18% of households purchased or consumed firewood and 18% purchased or consumed coal throughout the survey year. Among households using stove-only, about 87.5%

Table 7. Percentage of households using electricity and/or stove, and purchase or consumption of four major solid fuels.

	All households	Solid fuel consumption			
		Wood	Coal	Dung/peat	Corn
Electricity only	6.7	17.9	18.0	4.7	1.9
Electricity and stove	34.2	84.4	83.8	33.1	16.4
Stove only	59.2	87.5	86.9	48.7	16.6

Note: restricted sample. Excludes households using central heating, other sources and other combinations. All households use electricity, because it is also used for purposes other than heating.

acquired firewood and 87% coal, showing that firewood and coal have much higher prevalence than dung/peat or corn.

The model estimates the relative probability of households' choosing alternative heating sources. The dependent variable is the three-category household space-heating energy source: (1) electricity only; (2) solid fuels only; (3) combination of electricity and solid fuels.

The particular interest of this article is in the effect of higher electricity prices on household choice of heating source. Since the price of electricity is fixed across the entire country (at KGS 0.70/kWh), we use the price of electricity per kWh, *relative to* the price of major fossil fuels used by households (firewood and coal), as key explanatory variables.[9] Solid fuel prices vary significantly across regions. Based on household-declared fuel consumption and expenditure in the 2011 KIHS, we estimated the average price of each fuel per *oblast* and area (urban or rural).[10] Fifteen different average prices were obtained for each fuel. The nominal prices were converted into price per kWh, and the ratio of the price of electricity per kWh to the price of the fuel per kWh is our variable of interest (Table 8).

Other determinants of household space-heating choice are the household economic condition (log of per capita expenditure), demographic composition (household size, number of children under 16 years old, number of members over 61 years old), individual characteristics of the household head (employment, secondary education, gender), characteristics of the dwelling (ownership by the household, area, number of rooms, whether it is a separate house or an apartment in shared building), and the geographic location (urban or rural, the terrain type – high mountain, semi-mountainous or flat – and eight dummy variables for the *oblast*s to control for regional

Table 8. Relative price-per-kWh of electricity, as compared to firewood and to coal.

	Firewood		Coal	
	Urban	Rural	Urban	Rural
Bishkek	0.89	–	1.19	–
Issyk Kul	1.25	1.83	1.03	0.93
Jalal-Abad	1.15	1.13	0.96	1.04
Naryn	1.20	1.83	1.06	1.22
Batken	1.83	0.64	0.74	0.65
Osh	1.41	0.82	0.68	0.68
Talas	1.50	1.74	0.94	0.96
Chui	1.62	1.24	1.09	1.07

Note: Estimated based on KIHS (2011). Relative prices are calculated as: (price of electricity in KGS/kWh)/(price of fuel in KGS/kWh). The relative price is unit free. A value >1 denotes that electricity is more expensive than fuel in generating 1 kWh of energy. A value <1 denotes that electricity is cheaper than fuel.

Table 9. Summary statistics of explanatory variables for choice of space-heating energy source.

Explanatory variable	All areas	Std. dev.	Urban	Std. dev.	Rural	Std. dev.
Price of electric/price of firewood	1.21	0.36	1.29	0.27	1.18	0.39
Price of electric/price of coal	0.92	0.19	0.93	0.19	0.91	0.19
Price of firewood/price of coal	1.34	0.40	1.49	0.56	1.29	0.30
Per capita expenditure (KGS)	38,437.1	19,889.5	39086.1	21,126.4	38,186.9	19,389.6
Employed members	1.77	1.12	1.61	1.02	1.83	1.15
Household size	4.17	1.77	3.98	1.75	4.24	1.77
Children under 16	1.42	1.25	1.29	1.19	1.48	1.27
Elders	0.30	0.57	0.24	0.53	0.32	0.59
Head has secondary education*	0.86	0.35	0.91	0.29	0.84	0.36
Female head*	0.33	0.47	0.35	0.48	0.33	0.47
Own dwelling*	0.95	0.21	0.91	0.28	0.97	0.17
Living space area (m^3)	57.77	26.03	49.37	22.16	61.01	26.69
Rooms	3.47	1.19	3.23	1.28	3.56	1.14
House*	0.93	0.26	0.85	0.36	0.96	0.20
Urban*	0.28	0.45	–		–	

Note: KIHS (2011), restricted sample. * dummy variables.

effects). The summary statistics are presented in Table 9. Among the information collected by the KIHS, the variables included in this model represent the most comprehensive assessment of the households' characteristics. Variables which captured similar aspects of the household, for instance household size versus the number of adult members, were selected for inclusion in the model based on the highest pairwise correlation of that variable to space-heating choice. Hence, in case of possible multicollinearity, we selected the variable which best explains the variation in the choice of heating energy source. Our model specification is similar to the models of determinants of energy choice used by Silva, Klytchnikova, and Radevic (2009) and Hertberg (2005).

The model estimates, by maximum likelihood, the set of coefficients $\beta_1, \beta_2, \beta_3$ for the probability of each outcome:

$$\Pr(y = 1) = \frac{e^{X\beta_1}}{e^{X\beta_1} + e^{X\beta_2} + e^{X\beta_3}} \tag{1a}$$

$$\Pr(y = 2) = \frac{e^{X\beta_2}}{e^{X\beta_1} + e^{X\beta_2} + e^{X\beta_3}} \tag{1b}$$

$$\Pr(y = 3) = \frac{e^{X\beta_3}}{e^{X\beta_1} + e^{X\beta_2} + e^{X\beta_3}} = 1 - \Pr(y = 1) - \Pr(y = 2) \tag{1c}$$

Given that the probabilities must sum to 1, one category is selected as the baseline to identify the model. We arbitrarily set β_3 as the baseline category ($\beta_3 = 0$). The coefficients β_1 and β_2 are then used to predict fuel choice, and the probability of a household's choosing each energy source becomes:

$$\Pr(y = 1) = \frac{e^{X\beta_1}}{e^{X\beta_1} + e^{X\beta_2} + 1} \tag{2a}$$

$$\Pr(y = 2) = \frac{e^{X\beta_2}}{e^{X\beta_1} + e^{X\beta_2} + 1} \tag{2b}$$

$$\Pr(y = 3) = \frac{1}{e^{X\beta_1} + e^{X\beta_2} + 1} = 1 - \Pr(y = 1) - \Pr(y = 2) \tag{2c}$$

These can be written as the relative probabilities:

$$\frac{\Pr(y = 1)}{\Pr(y = 3)} = e^{X\beta_1} \tag{3a}$$

$$\frac{\Pr(y = 2)}{\Pr(y = 3)} = e^{X\beta_2} \tag{3b}$$

where the individual's outcome choice $y = 1$ stands for 'electricity only' and $y = 2$ is 'stove only', setting the base category $y = 3$ as 'combination of electricity and stove'. X is the set of explanatory variables.

The results estimated from the multinomial logit model therefore refer to the coefficients β_1 and β_2 in Equations (3a) and (3b). The coefficients must therefore be interpreted relative to the probability of choosing the baseline outcome, i.e. in relation to the relative probability of choosing a given heating source (electricity-only or stove-only) rather than the base category (combination of electricity and stove), when the explanatory variable, X, changes by one unit. Note, however, that in order to interpret the magnitude of the coefficients some transformation is still required.

Discussion of results

The determinants of energy choice for space heating

Table 10 reports the estimated β coefficients in (3a) and (3b).[11] The coefficients indicate the direction of the expected effect on the relative probability of a specific outcome. A significant positive coefficient for electricity-only (the first column of the left, centre and right panels) means that a one-unit increase in the variable is associated with a greater likelihood of choosing electricity-only compared to choosing a combination of heating sources (the base outcome). In other words, a positive coefficient denotes a greater chance of moving away from using the combination electricity-and-stove towards using electricity-only. Conversely, a significant negative coefficient implies a reduced likelihood of choosing electricity-only, versus choosing the base category, when the variable is increased by one unit. A coefficient that is not statistically significant is associated with having no effect on changing the relative probability of choosing a given energy source versus the base category.[12]

Higher household per capita expenditure is associated with a reduced probability of choosing stove-only heating versus electricity-and-stove. In urban areas, wealth increase is also associated with a decrease in the relative probability of choosing electricity-only versus the combination (Table 10, central panel, *Per capita expenditure* row).

Apart from energy costs, the physical characteristics of the dwelling are also important in affecting households' choice of one source over another. First, living in urban areas is associated with a greater likelihood of choosing electricity-only over combining energy sources (Table 10, left panel, *Urban* row). This result could be anticipated, because according to the energy consumption profile in Section 3 electricity-only users are concentrated in Bishkek and other urban areas.

Table 10. Determinants of household choice of space-heating source.

	All areas				Urban				Rural			
	Elec. only		Stove only		Elec. only		Stove only		Elec. only		Stove only	
Price of electric/price of firewood	−10.70	**	8.53	***	−19.12	**	4.93		−17.26		−55.98	***
Price of electric/price of coal	9.30		−13.25	***	29.18	***	4.30		27.92		67.83	***
Price of firewood/price of coal	9.57	**	−6.95	***	22.55	***	−3.66		16.50		53.03	***
Log of per capita expenditure	−0.56	*	−0.43	***	−0.77	***	−0.36	**	−0.29		−0.43	***
Hh head is employed	−0.51	**	−0.03		−0.55	**	−0.41	***	−0.79		0.10	
Hh head has secondary education	0.18		−0.27	**	0.69		−0.47	**	−0.22		−0.24	
Hh head is femal	0.06		0.25	***	−0.32		0.07		0.59		0.32	***
Household size	−0.11		−0.02		−0.29	***	−0.10	*	0.17		0.03	
Children under 16	−0.17		0.02		−0.04		0.19	***	−0.31		−0.05	
Elders	−0.29		−0.04		−0.44	**	−0.18		−0.12		−0.02	
Own dwelling	−0.65	*	0.22		−0.66	**	−0.06		−0.42		0.40	
Space area	0.01		0.01	***	0.01		−0.01	***	−0.01		0.01	***
Number of rooms	−0.36	**	−0.08	*	−0.42	***	0.19	***	0.05		−0.15	**
Not living in house	3.84	***	−0.31		4.16	***	0.42		4.32	***	−0.63	**
Urban	1.85	***	0.06		—		—		—		—	
Semi-mountainous area	0.06		−0.83	***	13.05		3.06	**	−0.68		−1.11	***
Flat area	0.27		−0.49	***	13.12		2.75	**	−0.04		−0.63	***
Region (oblast) dummies	Y		Y		Y		Y		Y		Y	
Constant	−0.47		16.50	***	−34.39		−3.80		−22.64		−59.39	***

Note: restricted sample. Electricity-and-stove is the base category for the dependent variable. Issyk Kul is the base category for region (*oblast*). High-mountainous is the base category for terrain type (compared to semi-montainous and flat).

*** p < .01. ** p < .05. * p < .1.

Not living in a separate house (e.g. inhabiting dwellings in a shared building) is associated with a greater likelihood of choosing electricity-only versus electricity-and-stove. The effect is found in both urban and rural areas.[13] However, the probability of choosing stove-only versus the combination seems to decrease in rural areas if households do not inhabit houses (if they live in an apartment or dormitory in shared building).

The living-space area also affects the household decision of heating source in urban and rural areas. In urban areas, a one-square-metre increase in the living space of the dwelling is associated with a decrease in the chance of choosing stove-only versus the combination of energy sources (Table 10, central panel, *Area* row). In rural areas, however, the effect seems to be the opposite, increasing the probability of choosing stove-only over the combination as the space of the living area increases. Controlling for area, the variable *rooms* captures additional heterogeneity of the effect of dwelling characteristics. In urban areas an additional room decreases the chance of choosing electricity-only, while it also increases the chance of choosing stove-only rather than the combination of both sources. In rural areas, one additional room is associated with a decrease in the probability of choosing stove-only versus the combination of energy sources. In urban areas, ownership of the dwelling is associated with a reduced likelihood of choosing electricity-only versus the combination, but it plays no significant role in rural areas. This can be explained by the fact that over 97% of rural households own their dwellings.

Type of terrain is also a key determinant of the choice of stove-only heating over the combination. Moving from high-mountain to semi-mountainous terrain increases the relative probability of choosing stove-only over the combination of heating sources in urban areas. A positive effect is also found if the household is in a flat area rather than high-mountain. Yet, the effect of terrain is the opposite in rural areas: moving from high-mountain terrain is associated with a move away from stove-only, decreasing the probability of choosing this relative to the combination of electricity and solid fuels for heating.

Finally, we also control for the demographic composition of households and individual characteristics of the household head. More education of the household head is associated with a reduced chance of choosing stove-only versus the combination of electricity and stove in urban areas, although no significant effect is found in rural areas. It is interesting to note that education of the head does not affect the relative probability of choosing electricity-only over the combination. Having a female household head is associated with a higher probability of choosing stove-only versus the combination in rural areas. Despite the fact that household size is in general correlated with the amount of household energy consumption, it seems not to affect the chance of choosing a particular heating source over the combination of energy sources.

Household response to electricity price increases

We now turn to the analysis of how an increase in electricity price could affect a move from electricity-and-stove to another type of heating (Table 10, first row). An increase in the price of electricity relative to firewood is associated with reducing the chance of choosing electricity-only versus the combination electricity-and-stove in urban areas. Regarding the choice of stove-only versus the combination, an increase in the price of electricity relative to firewood is associated with increasing the chance of choosing stove-only, for households in general.

In line with demand theory, if electricity becomes more expensive, households would indeed tend to decrease consumption – 'switching off'. Table 11 shows that on average, a 1% increase in the price of electricity relative to firewood lowers by 22.9% the probability of choosing electricity-only for heating in urban areas, and lowers by 8.16% the probability of choosing stove-only. In rural areas, the change in relative prices seems not to significantly affect the probability of choosing electricity-only; however, a 1% increase in the price of electricity relative to firewood

Table 11. Elasticity of change in relative prices on change in the probability of observing a space-heating source.

	Urban only			Rural only		
	Electricity only	Electricity and stove	Stove only	Electricity only	Electricity and stove	Stove only
Price of electric/ price of firewood	−22.92***	1.79	8.16***	22.24	42.64***	−23.51***
Price of electric/ price of coal	20.44***	−6.76*	−2.76	−14.05	−39.48***	22.30***
Price of firewood/price of coal	29.34***	−4.31	−9.77**	−23.45	−44.70***	23.59***

Note: restricted sample.
*** $p < .01$. ** $p < .05$. * $p < .1$.

increases the probability of choosing the combination electricity-and-stove by 42%.[14] Moreover, Table 11 suggests that coal may not be an optional energy source in urban areas, as an increase in price of electricity relative to coal would not affect the probability of using stove-only. In rural areas, a 1% increase in price of electricity relative to coal decreases the probability of using electricity-and-stove by 39.48% and increases the probability of using stove-only by 22.30%.

Our results suggest that households in the Kyrgyz Republic would cope with higher electricity prices by switching to alternative sources. There is evidence of a substitution effect away from the use of electricity-only, and also of resilience in the use of a combination of electricity and fuels. Further investigation of changes in the composition of such an energy mix, the proportion of modern and non-modern fuels, would be a valuable addition to the literature. Kraudzun, (2014, this issue) reports widespread use of dwarf shrubs in Tajikistan following the collapse in the supply of other fuels (mainly coal). The environmental threat of unsustainable firewood extraction is particularly worrisome if model predictions foresee a massive switch towards an increasing use of such fuels. As the results suggest, households in the Kyrgyz Republic seem to prefer the combination of electricity and fuel sources, or even switching to fuel-only for heating.

An interesting issue is revealed when we split the sample between urban and rural areas. An increase in the price of electricity relative to firewood is associated with a decreasing probability of choosing electricity-only over the combination in urban areas; however, such a price shock seems not to affect the relative risks of choosing electricity-only in rural areas. This could be due to the low reliability of electricity service provision in rural areas. On the other hand, a switch from combined electric-and-stove towards stove-only heating seems unlikely in urban areas given an electricity price increase. This could be because there are physical barriers to the use of stoves in urbanized areas, like living in an apartment.[15] The results are counter-intuitive for rural areas, regarding a move to stove-only.

Firewood and coal are to some extent close substitutes; both can be used in stoves for heating purposes. Nonetheless, the analysis reveals that an increase in the price of electricity relative to coal triggers different household responses than that observed for firewood. It may be useful to note that coal is a relatively expensive energy source in some regions (see Table 8). The analysis suggests that an increase in the price of electricity relative to coal is associated with an increase in the chance of choosing electricity-only versus the combination of energy sources in urban areas. This result seems at first counter-intuitive. One explanation, however, is that in several urban areas electricity is still cheaper than coal (see energy per kWh in Table 8) and definitely cheaper than firewood (in all urban areas except Bishkek). As long as electricity is a cheaper source, households will have less of an incentive to move towards stove-only heating. In rural areas, however, an increase in the price of electricity relative to coal is associated with a move towards stove-only rather than continuing to use the combination of sources.

Conclusion

In a country like the Kyrgyz Republic, with long and cold winters, access to a reliable energy source, especially for space heating, is a basic need. While energy is relatively cheap thanks to high implicit subsidies for electricity and thermal power, the reliability of electricity provision has decreased over the last decade (World Bank 2014). Power outages are common, especially during the winter months.

Energy tariffs below cost recovery continue to hamper badly needed investments in the energy sector, resulting in depleted infrastructure and poor service provision. The government, well aware of the need for reforms, has undertaken several (unsuccessful) attempts to reform the energy sector and increase energy tariffs.

An increase in energy prices will directly affect residential consumers. Households will either decrease their energy consumption (income effect) or switch to alternative energy sources (substitution effect). This article investigated the potential impact of an electricity price increase on household energy consumption. We analysed the determinants of the choice of a particular energy source for heating and the probability that households would switch to another energy source in response to an increase in electricity prices. The findings are relevant for policy makers because a switch to alternative sources, especially if it concerns 'dirty' fuels such as firewood and coal, may carry indirect health risks due to indoor and outdoor pollution. Furthermore, the depletion of firewood in local woods may have detrimental environmental effects in the long run.

In line with the findings of Silva, Klytchnikova, and Radevic (2009) for Montenegro, we find evidence that in the Kyrgyz Republic the consumption of solid fuels, in particular firewood, would increase in response to electricity tariff increases. The analysis has shown that, overall in the country, an increase in electricity prices is associated with an increase in the relative chance of households' moving away from using combined electricity-and-stove towards stove-only heating, as well as significantly lowering the chances that households would consider electricity-only versus the combination of sources. The predicted behaviour regarding a switch towards alternative energy sources for space heating appears to depend on the type of solid fuel that is currently most important, affordable or easily accessible to the household. The prices of firewood and coal relative to electricity can differ across regions and areas.

A second message drawn from the analysis is that any energy/electricity tariff increase in the Kyrgyz Republic must carefully consider the regional disparities in energy consumption. The profile of household energy consumption showed quite significant differences across regions (*oblasts*), and rural versus urban areas, with regard to the energy consumption basket, energy expenditure, and likely energy quantity consumed by households. The consumption basket varies according to geographic terrain: households in mountainous and semi-mountainous areas are not provided with central heating, piped gas or hot water utilities and rely heavily on fuels and electricity. In spite of electricity's being cheaper than fuels in several areas in the Kyrgyz Republic, and despite the fact that electricity coverage is almost universal, only 37% of households use electric heating, while the adoption of stoves is as high as 75% (see Table 4). This confirms that coverage is not a good indicator of service quality in the Kyrgyz Republic, and that households have indeed recognized unreliable electricity service provision.

Profiling the households (learning more about their characteristics and the features of their dwellings) is essential in identifying the areas and socio-economic groups which would suffer most from an electricity price increase. Depending on dwelling characteristics, households may have rather limited strategies for coping with a price hike. Our results confirm that households not living in a house (inhabiting apartments in shared buildings), for instance, face statistically significant constraints to switching to alternative sources, probably due to physical constraints in their dwellings. Other households, however, may respond to electricity tariff increases by easily moving towards greater use of solid fuels, such as adopting stove-only heating. This strategy could decrease electricity consumption, but also could threaten their quality of life by conflicting with the achievement of other desirable development outcomes, such as good health, and create disaster risks, such as landslides. Moreover, if households collect their own firewood or prepare dung, the switch to these energy sources will increase the household workload.

One last cautious note on possible general equilibrium effects. The present study does not consider the possible effects of electricity price increase on other interacting markets. Our results predict an increase in the demand for fossil fuels following an electricity price increase. But a higher demand for fuels could, for instance, push prices up in those fuels' or other related markets. As a consequence of generalized price increases, the income effect could overpower the substitution effect and households might further reduce (switch off) energy consumption. This would certainly slow down future economic development and decrease the quality of life of the Kyrgyzstani population.

Acknowledgement

The authors gratefully acknowledge the support of the Kyrgyz National Statistics Committee in providing access to the household survey data. We also thank Jeanne Féaux de la Croix, Dave Gullette and two anonymous reviewers for their valuable comments and suggestions.

Notes

1. Authors' calculation based on KIHS (2011). These numbers compare favourably with data from 2009, when 35% of households were exposed to daily electricity interruptions (Gassmann 2011). This high share was explained by the extremely harsh winter of 2008–2009 and also confirmed by the UNDP (2011).
2. In this article 'alternative energy sources' refers to energy sources for space heating currently used by households, such as gas, firewood, coal, dung or other fuels.
3. As a reaction to higher energy prices, households could: (1) maintain their current consumption at the cost of a substantially higher energy bill; (2) reduce their energy consumption to the extent that the bill remains unchanged; (3) switch to cheaper energy sources, maintaining energy expenditure; or even (4) resort to energy theft or the incurrence of payment arrears.
4. Electricity provision is especially unreliable during the winter and affects the whole country. For example, during the cold December of 2012, Bishkek had more than 900 power outages per week (EurasiaNet. 2012). In 2011, 10.4% of households reported weekly power interruptions. Moreover, many rural residents, e.g. in Naryn, migrate in the summer to high pastures where electricity provision is either totally absent or precarious.
5. In the KIHS, 'fuels' refers to firewood, brushwood, black coal, peat, pressed dung, corn brans, kerosene, diesel, black oil and bottle gas.
6. International Energy Agency (IEA) 2014.
7. Exchange rate as of 31 December 2011: KGS 46.4847 to USD 1 (National Bank of the Kyrgyz Republic, http://www.nbkr.kg).
8. A multinomial logit model is a discrete choice model in which the outcome variable consists of a set of several possible alternatives and the outcomes carry no ordering.
9. Conversion factors: 2610 kWh per m^3 of firewood, from Silva et al. (2009); 516.72 kWh per 100 kg of coal, from http://unstats.un.org/unsd/energy/balance/conversion.htm. In the absence of a specific

estimate for the Kyrgyz Republic, we adopted the lowest factor for coal conversion, cautiously assuming that residential-use fuel is not of the highest international standard and/or that residential stoves may not be fully efficient in extracting the highest calorific value of coal.

10. When data were not available for a given region and *oblast*, we imputed the price values based on the most similar geographic region and *oblast*. Bishkek has urban areas only. Details are available upon request.

11. Caution should be used in interpreting the rural results because the sample of rural households using electricity-only is rather small.

12. To interpret the magnitude of changes as relative-risk ratios, however, one must perform some calculations. Equations (3a) and (3b) help us understand how to calculate the relative-risk ratios using the results in Table 10. For example, the relative-risk ratio for choosing electricity-only versus the combination of electricity and stove heating, for a one-unit increase in the variable *urban* (i.e. households is not in a rural but in an urban area), is 6.359 [exp(1.85), from Table 10, Urban, second column].

13. Note that within the restricted sample, households living in apartment represent only 2.3% of the rural sample.

14. Note that only a few households in rural areas use electricity-only as heating source.

15. Note that these barriers may not necessarily hold in a crisis situation. In 2008, residents in Osh suffered long blackouts following government measures to save energy. In response, some households installed stoves in their living rooms, with chimneys through the windows, despite all the associated risks, such as carbon monoxide poisoning due to improperly installed chimneys. The UN launched a Flash Appeal in 2008 for humanitarian support, acknowledging such episodes of poisoning (UN 2009).

References

Adenauer, I., and J. A. del Granado. 2011. "Burkina Faso - Policies to Protect the Poor from the Impact of Food and Energy Price Increases," *IMF Working Papers* 11/202, International Monetary Fund.

Akhmetov, A. 2013. "Coal Industry and Respiratory Health Assessment in Kazakhstan," presented at ESCAS - Biennial Conference of the European Society for Central Asian Studies. Astana, Kazakhstan, August 4-7.

Duflo, E., M. Greenstone, and R. Hanna. 2008. "Indoor Air Pollution, Health and Economic Well-Being." *Surveys and Perspectives Integrating Environment and Society,* 1 (1), 1–9. http://sapiens.revues.org/130#tocfrom1n2

Energy Poverty Action (EPA). (n.d.). Retrieved from http://www.weforum.org/pdf/ip/energy/EPA.pdf

Ersado, L. 2012. "Poverty and Distributional Impact of Gas Price Hike in Armenia," *World Bank Policy Research Working Paper*, n.6150.

Esenaliev, D., A. Kroeger, and S. Steiner. 2011. "The Kyrgyz Integrated Household Survey (KIHS) - A Primer." *German Institute for Economic Research (DIW Berlin)*.

EurasiaNet. 2012. "Kyrgyzstan: Cold Snap Sparks Energy Emergency." Accessed December 17. http://www.eurasianet.org/node/66309

Freund, C., and C. Wallich. 1997. "Public-Sector Price Reforms in Transition Economies: Who Gains? Who Loses? The Case of Household Energy Prices in Poland." *Economic Development and Cultural Change* 46 (1): 35–59.

Gassmann, F. 2011. "Energy Consumption and Tariff Increases in the Kyrgyz Republic." Background paper, The World Bank, Washington DC, mimeo.

Gassmann, F. 2013. "Switching the Lights Off: The Impact of Energy Tariff Increases on Households in the Kyrgyz Republic." *Journal of Comparative Economics*. Accessed April 25. http://dx.doi.org/10.1016/j.jce.2013.04.003

Helteberg, R. 2004. "Fuel Switching: Evidence from Eight Developing Countries." *Energy Economics* 26 (5): 869–887.

Helteberg, R. 2005. "Factors Determining Household Fuel Choice in Guatemala." *Environment and Development Economics* 10 (3): 337–361.

IEA, OPEC, OECD, and World Bank. 2010. *Analysis of the Scope of Energy Subsidies and Suggestions for the G-20 Initiative*. Joint Report prepared for submission to the G-20 Summit Meeting, Toronto, 26-27 June, 2010. http://www.oecd.org/dataoecd/55/5/45575666.pdf

International Crisis Group. 2011. "Central Asia: Decay and Decline", Asia Report No. 201. http://www.crisisgroup.org/~/media/Files/asia/central-asia/201%20Central%20Asia%20-%20Decay%20and%20Decline.pdf

International Energy Agency (IEA). 2014. "Energy Security." Accessed October 25. http://www.iea.org/topics/energysecurity/

Kraudzun, T. 2014. "Bottom-Up and Top-Down Dynamics of the Energy Transformation in the Eastern Pamirs of Tajikistan's Gorno Badakhshan Region." *Central Asian Survey*. http://dx.doi.org/10.1080/02634937.2014.987516

Kyrgyz Integrated Household Survey (KIHS) 2011. National Statistical Committee of the Kyrgyz Republic.

Lampietti, J. A., S. G. Banerjee, and A. Branczik. 2007. *People and Power. Electricity Sector Reforms and the Poor in Europe and Central Asia*. Washington, DC: The World Bank.

Price, C. W., and K. Pham. 2009. "The Impact of Electricity Market Reform on Consumers." *Utilities Policy* 17 (1): 43–48.

Silva, P., I. Klytchnikova, and D. Radevic. 2009. "Poverty and Environmental Impacts of Electricity Price Reforms in Montenegro." *Utilities Policy* 17 (1): 102–113.

Slay, B. (eds). 2011. *Energy and Communal Services in Kyrgyzstan and Tajikistan: A Poverty and Social Impact Assessment*. Bratislava: UNDP Bratislava Regional Centre.

UN. 2009. Kyrgyzstan Flash Appeal – Revision: Humanitarian Needs Beyond the Development Interventions Defined in the Country Development Strategy. http://www.unocha.org/cap/appeals/revision-flash-appeal-kyrgyzstan-2009

UNDP. 2000. *World Energy Assessment – Energy and the Challenge of Sustainability*. United Nations Development Programme.

UNDP. 2011. *Kyrgyzstan's Energy Sector: A Poverty and Social Impact Assessment*. Bratislava, Mimeo: UNDP Regional Office.

USAID. 2008. *Kyrgyzstan Household Energy Analysis and Proposed Social Protection Measures*. Mimeo: USAID Report.

USAID. 2011. *Review of the Prime Cost of Electricity*. Mimeo: USAID report prepared by Tetra Tech.

World Bank. 2011. *Kyrgyz Republic: Profile and Dynamics of Poverty and Inequality, 2009*. Washington, DC: The World Bank.

World Bank. 2014. *Power Sector Policy Note for the Kyrgyz Republic*. Washington, DC: The World Bank.

Bottom-up and top-down dynamics of the energy transformation in the Eastern Pamirs of Tajikistan's Gorno Badakhshan region

Tobias Kraudzun

Centre for Development Studies, Institute of Geographical Sciences, FreieUniversität Berlin, Germany

This paper deals with the strategies of households living in a peripheral high-mountain region in order to cope with the post-Soviet energy crisis. The Soviet modernization project failed at connecting the region to the grid, and imported coal for heating and fuel for producing electric energy at high costs over long distances. After the collapse of this alimentation system, people have substituted energy demands with wood and shrubs, and used increasingly available low-cost Chinese solar equipment to produce electrical energy. International development actors have failed to increase acceptance for energy efficiency technologies. Despite the Pamirs' high potential for solar and wind energy and decreasing installation costs, Soviet-style state planning of energy infrastructure still favours big hydropower stations, despite their high (social) costs and the limited potential on the Pamir plateau. The paper will discuss bottom-up effects of household decisions and top-down strategies as potentials and obstacles for a sustainable energy supply in the Pamirs.

Introduction

This article deals with the everyday challenges related to the supply and use of domestic energy for people living in the harsh environment of the Pamir Mountains, in the context of an ongoing energy crisis since the dissolution of the Soviet supply system. Taking the alarming accounts about the non-sustainable use of local energy resources found in current literature as a starting point, it scrutinizes the recent shifts in the energy mix as a result of changed availability and affordability of energy resources. Furthermore it enquires into the role of different actors in the transformation of supply strategies and use patterns of different thermal and electric energy sources.

Two problems related to energy can be identified in the Pamirs of post-Soviet Tajikistan. The first problem emerges out of a combination of three factors: low temperatures at this high altitude, few options for local energy resources and long distances for external fuel supplies. The settlements are located at altitudes of 3600–4000 metres above sea level, where extreme temperatures below −40°C often occur, average temperatures in January are below −18°C and remain below zero for six to seven months of the year. Much energy for heating homes and workplaces is necessary under these conditions. Due to the lack of tree vegetation at these altitudes only dwarf shrubs, mainly *teresken* (*Krascheninnikovia ceratoides*) and *shyvak* (*Artemisia* species) are available as local fuels in addition to animal manure. Imported fuels like coal have to be transported at high cost over long distances and mountain passes often blocked by snow during wintertime. The next railhead in Osh is 420 km away and only recently two mines started to produce coal at a closer but still significant distance of 250 km.

Second, electricity use has become universal for virtually all citizens of the Soviet Union, even in the remote Pamirs. However, although the Soviet modernization project is renowned for its ambitious infrastructure efforts even in the periphery of the vast empire, it was not successful in connecting the Pamirs to the main grid. It did not even install sufficient infrastructure for electricity generation from the vast regional hydropower resources and its distribution through regional grids. Therefore, the rising demand for electric energy was met by production with inefficient diesel generators.

Previous research on the topic was concerned mainly with two issues. First, it paid attention to the ecological effects of the substitution of previously imported fossil fuels by limited local resources like wood and dwarf shrubs after the dissolution of the Soviet Union. In many development project reports and scholarly works general statements about the amount of dwarf shrubs used for energy purposes were combined with rough estimates about the density of the vegetation to predict an approaching extinction of dwarf shrubs (above all *teresken*) in the eastern Pamirs. Accordingly, these publications give the impression that dwarf shrubs are a thermal energy resource without important alternatives and will possibly be used until their extinction (Aknazarov 2003; Lailibekov 2003; Droux and Hoeck 2004; BMZ 2005; Breu et al. 2005; GEF 2005; Breu 2006). In this regard Doempke (2008, 13) reports that 'already 50% of all *teresken* is believed to have been lost. It has been totally eradicated within a radius of about 100 km around Murghab town'. Bliss (2006, 331) states that 'two most important traditional sources of wood, artsha and tersgen [*teresken*], have been almost entirely destroyed in areas accessible to people'. Droux and Hoeck (2004, 149) calculate an average amount of 7.9 tonnes per year, per household, and estimate a loss of 180–800 km² of dwarf shrub vegetation (depending on density) per year. To illustrate the scope of these assessments, one may combine the estimations with Jusufbekov and Kasač's (1972, 15) calculation of dwarf shrub vegetation's prevalence. If ongoing dwarf shrub harvesting would effect in the complete eradication of this vegetation on the area of the size estimated above, the vegetation would have been rooted out completely in the eastern Pamirs in the course of 1.5–7 years.

These dramatic figures for the degradation of dwarf shrubs, which are used competitively as energy resource and as fodder for livestock, led Breckle and Wucherer (2006, 230) to term the situation drastically as '*Teresken* Syndrome', 'as it plays such a dominant role in the east Pamir'. The assumption that the actual harvesting of dwarf shrubs is not sustainable and can lead to severe ecological problems (Kassam 2009, 688) may be correct, but it has not been backed by tangible data based on extensive fieldwork and published in the academic literature.

Recent work shows differentiated views on the present situation of energy consumption in the Pamirs. Förster, Pachova, and Renaud (2011) demonstrate considerable disparities in the energy consumption patterns between five villages in the Tajik Pamirs and the Kyrgyz Alai, as well as among wealthy and poor households. Additionally, Wiedemann et al. (2012) demonstrated the potential and the reality of adapted thermal insulation technologies in Murghab.

Less attention was paid to the generation and consumption of electricity under post-Soviet conditions. Droux and Hoeck (2004) analysed in detail how the Pamirs' inhabitants are supplied with electric energy, and how the abundance of different energy sources influences their everyday patterns of energy use. Part of this study was an inventory of all hydropower systems in the Pamirs, including technical as well as some socio-economic parameters of their operation. However, the status quo of that time, with only one Soviet-built small hydropower plant producing electric energy in the eastern Pamirs, does not reflect present-day production and consumption patterns.

When the Soviet Union's supply system stopped working in Murghab district, the availability of domestic energy resources was challenged dramatically. People faced the dissolution of state organizations that had been their former employers as well as the breakdown of externally subsidized supply systems upon which they were heavily dependent. Livelihoods suffered from an economic crisis, as salaries ceased and household savings were devaluated by inflation. Households were in a desperate situation because after benefitting from three decades of subsidized and steady supplies in the Soviet Union there was not much recent experience about how to supply themselves with domestic energy. Depending on their own resources, households developed and applied different strategies to cope with the ongoing energy crisis. However, even if Soviet organizations disappeared, new supply practices did not emerge solely through the agency of households, but with repeated interference of state and external development actors in the field of energy supply. If the perspectives are widened to the general question of the development of mountain regions and especially to pastoralists mostly perceived as 'underdeveloped' by the state ideology, policies to support mountain people to become 'modern' are prevalent since many decades in the region (Kreutzmann 2012a, 2012b).[1]

The objective of this paper is to understand how everyday experiences with domestic energy resources were changed by the effects of the post-Soviet transformation processes, and to show which strategies are used by households in this peripheral high-mountain region in order to cope with the ongoing energy crisis. All activities geared at coping or adapting need to be understood in the context of the policies and programmes of the state and external development actors.

The article is based on extensive fieldwork conducted in the eastern Pamirs since 2003, including several long field stays between 2007 and 2009 (14 months), and repeated visits up to 2014.[2] Information is derived from topic-specific interviews with key and knowledgeable informants about energy strategies, energy economy and political context. Enquiries about historical contexts are based on regional archives and provided helpful insights into the current situation.

The research area and its energy resources

The high mountain area of the Pamirs in Tajikistan's east can be subdivided culturally and geographically in two parts. Traditionally, in the deep-cut valleys of the Western Pamirs farmers cultivate irrigated terraces for crop farming complemented by animal husbandry, a system which is called combined mountain agriculture. The animals are stabled during winters and driven to distant high-altitude pastures during summers.

The plateau of the eastern Pamirs is predominantly a high mountain desert and extends in parts to China and Afghanistan. Their altitude ranges from around 3500 m in the valleys to more than 7000 m in some mountain peaks, resulting in comparatively low temperatures all year round. The northern and western mountain ranges shielding the eastern plateau cause an extreme aridity with precipitation values below 100 millimetres per year. Pastures are scarce due to the climatic conditions and are mainly used by Kyrgyz pastoralists for extensive livestock herding of yaks, sheep and goats (Kreutzmann 2009; Vanselow, Kraudzun, and Samimi 2012).

The eastern Pamir region corresponds largely to Murghab district and is located within the Autonomous Province of Gorno-Badakhshan (Gorno-Badakhshanskaja Avtonomnaja Oblast' – GBAO) in Tajikistan (Figure 1). The huge district with an area of 38,300 km² is sparsely populated with 14,000 residents, around 77% of them being Kyrgyz. The Soviet development project in the region, in order to establish a modern administration and high living standards, was in need of a variety of professions. Many young specialists, mainly Pamiris originating from the Western Pamir, came to work in the administrative centre of Murghab, resulting in the district's share of 23% Pamiri people (Statkom GBAO 2002, 8). Half of the entire population lives in the district capital and economic centre Murghab, the other half in far-flung villages and hamlets. Starting in the 2000s, remittances from migrants working abroad contributed an increasing share to the household incomes. Today, one-fourth of the district's male working-age population (even

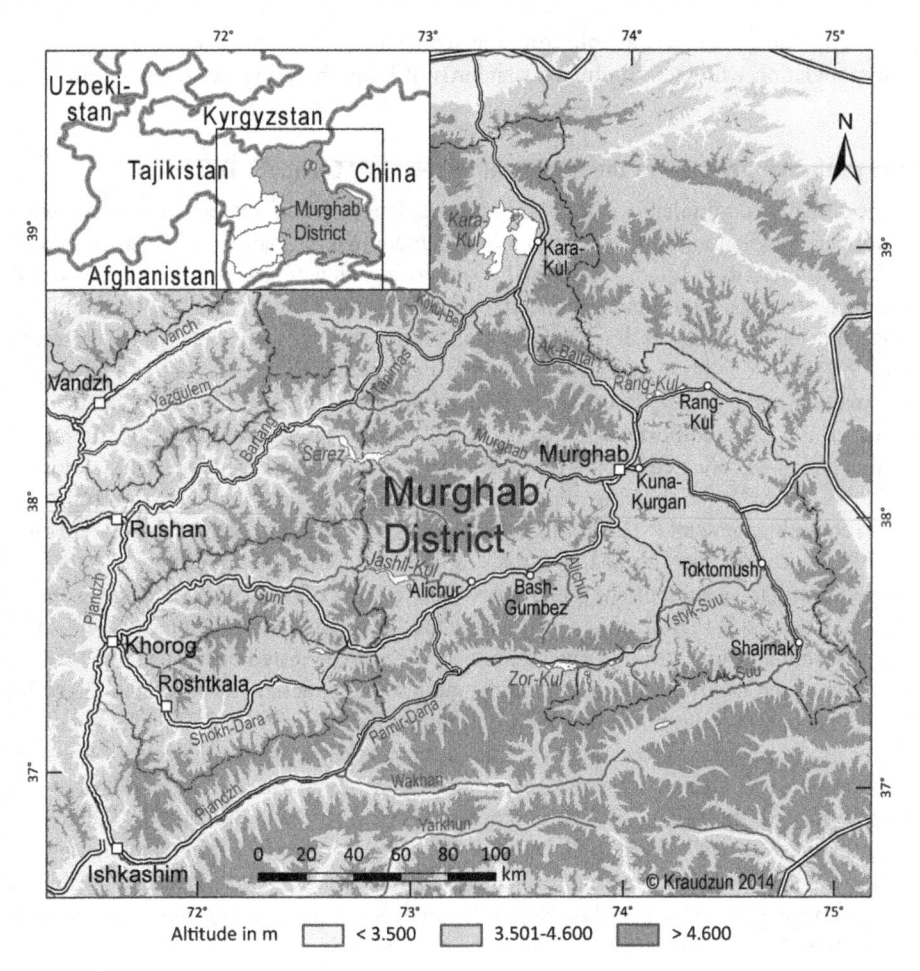

Figure 1. The Pamirs in Tajikistan.
Source: map by the author.

42% of Murghab town's working-age males) is working abroad, mainly in Russia (Statotdel Murgab 2008).

Today, most households are engaged in animal husbandry again. Livestock production is based on herd mobility. Winter camps and pastures are situated in sheltered valleys predominantly at lower altitudes; summer camps are spread to remote distances and higher altitudes of up to 4500 m. From their yurt camps herders have easy access to two sources of energy on the pastures. Varieties of animal manure (*tezek/kyk*) are collected and processed to serve as a local energy source that cannot be overused. Dwarf shrubs are the second source of energy, facing the risk of unsustainable use (Kraudzun, Vanselow, and Samimi 2014).

Although the eastern Pamirs are rich in mineral resources, all carbon-based fuels need to be transported over long distances. Other regenerative energy sources demand substantial investments in infrastructure, which can be afforded only by powerful economic structures (e.g. hydropower plants by the Soviet Union in the past). Therefore, the affordability of supplemental energy carriers – minimizing pressure on available local resources – is strongly connected with interregional systems of economic and social exchange. The Soviet Union made enormous efforts to fill the gap between the energy available from the scarce local resources and the energy needs of a growing population who were promised standards of living befitting Soviet modernity.

The use of thermal energy in the historical context of Murghab district

Given the climatic conditions, heating homes is a challenge. When Soviet coal supplies were suddenly stopped, people found the emergency replacement in dwarf shrubs. This energy transformation has a counterpart in history: imported coal was introduced only in 1961, after local Soviet development activities had already induced alarming levels of dwarf shrub extraction.

Since the 1930s buildings for the Soviet administration as well as homes were erected to improve the living conditions of pastoralists and immigrant specialists. The growing needs for heating material as a consequence of the population increase were met by dwarf shrubs. For example, in 1932 the authorities demanded 79,000 pud (approximately 1300 tonnes) dwarf shrubs that had to be collected (GosArchiv GBAO, pp. 1-1-73:64f.). In those years, state agencies seemed to be in dire need of heating material for their new office buildings. A decree of the district executive committee in winter 1932 obligated the local population to collect 18,000 pud (approximately 295 tonnes) of dwarf shrubs within a single month to heat the buildings of public administration and military headquarters (GosArchiv GBAO, pp. 1-1-73:27). Likewise, in the 1940s, dwarf shrubs were still seen as the main fuel for the local population (Baranov 1940, 7).

The unsustainable extraction of dwarf shrubs apparently persisted because in 1961 the level of deterioration of the dwarf shrub vegetation demanded urgent action. Jointly with the council of ministers, the central committee of the Communist Party of Tajik SSR, which usually got involved only in matters of top priority, issued a ban on dwarf shrub extraction. Subsidies for the substitution were introduced; mainly Siberian coal featured here. A coal fund was established within the budget of the Tajik SSR. The public funds were directed to purchase 18,000 tonnes coal per year for the Murghab district, allocating 6000 tonnes for public organizations and 12,000 tonnes for private consumption (Figure 2). Nine months per year were declared as the heating season. Fourteen kilograms per day were allocated for offices; 25 kg per day for stoves in private houses. People and organizations were eligible to buy their coal rations at subsidized prices (personal communication with TK on 15 June 2009).

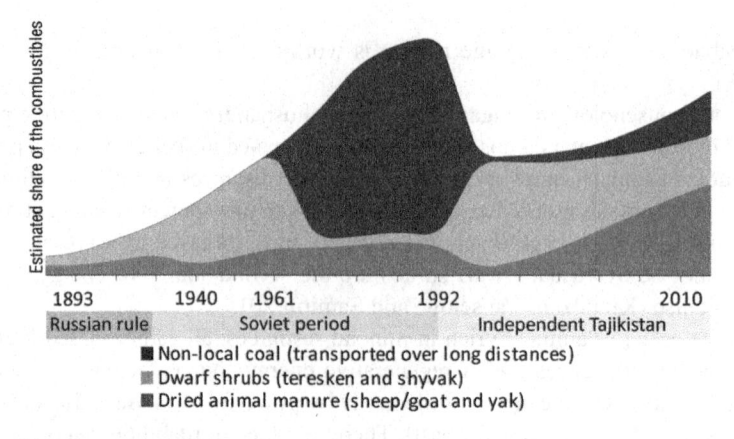

Figure 2. Approximation of variations among thermal energy sources in the eastern Pamirs.
Sources: compiled from GosArchiv GBAO, pp. 1-1-73:27, Serebrennikov (1894), 1425; Bogojavlenskogo (1905), 6; Stankevič (1910), 98; Baranov (1940), 7; personal communication with AA on 28 May 2008 and TK on 15 June 2009.

In 1992, food and fuel supplies were not delivered to Murghab and subsidies for coal were stopped. The low degree of self-sufficiency in the region caused an immediate lack of food and fuel. This situation was further aggravated after the outbreak of an intensive civil war in southwest Tajikistan, which cut off supply routes and caused enormous flows of refugees to the Pamirs.

International donors stepped in to alleviate the pending crisis. Although the Aga Khan Foundation was organizing humanitarian food supply within the framework of the 'Pamir Relief and Development Project', the severe shortage of combustibles remained. The local population revived practices of using dwarf shrubs to heat their houses (Figure 2). But the dependency on dwarf shrubs as the main source of heating energy was often mitigated by access to animal manure as a local fuel alternative. In the villages, almost every household was engaged in herding on the pastures and thus had access to animal manure. This was not the case in Murghab town, where the majority of the population was employed in the administration, welfare system or service sector. However, as the employing organizations disappeared or employees were not paid anymore during the civil war, they had to rely on dwarf shrubs as the (almost) only combustible accessible to them.[3]

Hence, the ban on dwarf shrub extraction was increasingly ignored by the people; rooting-out started around the town of Murghab and, to some degree, around the villages, leaving the vicinity of the settlements almost cleared of dwarf shrubs because of easy access (personal communications with TK on 15 June 2009 and AA on 28 May 2008).[4]

Use of dwarf shrubs for energy in the current socio-economic context

Fifteen years after the dissolution of the Soviet command economy and its exchange system of goods and services, the energy supply situation has slightly improved. An increasing share of the population owns livestock and is involved in practices of mobile herding (Kraudzun 2012). These households can often manage to transport animal manure from pastures to their homes. This applies especially to smaller villages on higher altitudes where livestock is herded on productive pastures in the proximity of the settlements and manure is used almost exclusively.

Trans-border trade conditions have improved and private coal import has emerged since the late 1990s; the coal originates from recently opened mines in the Alai valley in Kyrgyzstan and has to be brought over 250 km (Kraudzun 2011). Presently, coal counts as an affordable commodity in settlements along the Pamir Highway and is competitive when the heating value/market price ratio is calculated. On the other hand, the accessibility of dwarf shrubs deteriorated, although perceptions about complete dwarf shrub eradication within a radius of 100 km around Murghab (Doempke 2008, 13) are exaggerations that can be disproved easily in the field. Areas where dense and valuable dwarf shrubs are prevalent can still be found and are harvested – both for collection with trucks on large spots and for individual supply within a day on foot from Murghab (Kraudzun, Vanselow, and Samimi 2014).

At present, dwarf shrubs are still burned in virtually every household of the eastern Pamirs. Because of its strikingly fast heat generation this fuel is very popular for heating up the stove or instant water-boiling. For cooking meals or heating purposes, dwarf shrubs are replaced by combustibles with a more even thermal output, if available.

Seasonal fluctuation, big differences in the affordability of substitutes and the variety of heating strategies cause dramatic alternations in shrub consumption and consequently hamper reliable extrapolations. Household surveys carried out 2013 in the villages of Alichur and Shaymak as well as in the district centre Murghab show that considerable and increasing shares of domestic energy needs are satisfied by other energy sources. Animal manure is abundant in distant villages surrounded by productive pastures (Figure 3, Shaymak), whereas imported coal is available in settlements along the Pamir Highway (Figure 3, Murghab winter).

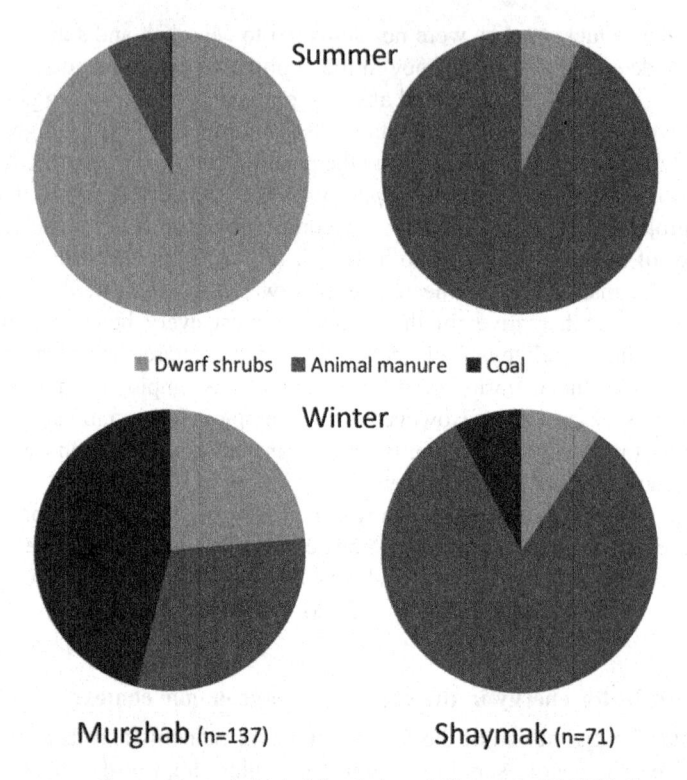

Figure 3. Energy consumption per household in Murghab and Shaymak, 2012/13 (household survey data 2013). The household surveys were conducted in March and April 2013 by a field team consisting of Fanny Kreczi, Georg Hohberg and local research assistants. The surveys were prepared and data were processed jointly by the research teams (including the author) of the ongoing interdisciplinary research project 'Transformation Processes in the Eastern Pamirs of Tajikistan. The Presence and Future of Energy Resources in the Framework of Sustainable Development' (see the Acknowledgements). These valuable survey data are interpreted here with permission granted by the above-mentioned conductors of the survey.

To highlight the social context of dwarf shrub use, it is necessary to distinguish between social groups for which typical patterns of supply and consumption were identified. Impoverished households without access to manure cannot afford coal either. In the district centre, most members of this social group organize themselves in teams of 15–25 individuals to gain access to domestic energy. They hire a lorry and give 3 litres of gasoline per participant to harvest dwarf shrubs (mainly *teresken*) on large plots within a range of about 50–80 km. During late spring and summer they manage to return to their homes the same evening, after short autumn and winter days they often have to stay overnight. Usually each member of the group collects five bundles of *teresken* and can decide to use it or to sell it for cash in Murghab. The poorest people, who cannot afford even the cost of gasoline, have to pay the lorry owner/driver with two bundles of *teresken* – an unfavourable rate, given the higher bazaar prices (Figure 4). Alternatively, some of the poorer households who own a donkey cross steep passes near Murghab to discover sufficient quantities of *teresken* to be harvested there, while others use sidecar-motorcycles to collect dwarf shrubs on smaller plots in the vicinity of roads.

Wealthier households usually make arrangements to send small teams with a lorry to distant areas, buying the complete lorry load at negotiated costs well below the retail price. In the bazaar only the instant demand for dwarf shrubs is satisfied. Therefore, the *teresken* market prices shown

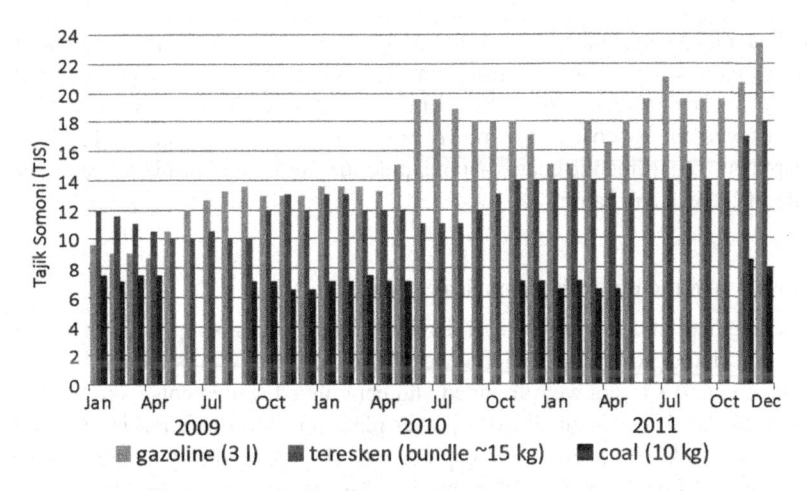

Figure 4. Fuel market prices on Murghab bazaar.
Sources: compiled by the author from field recordings made in 2009 and 2010 and by data collected by the bazaar administration (*bazarkom*) 'SaryKol' Murghab.

in Figure 4 can serve only for assessing cost trends and not for extrapolations of household expenditures.

The biggest share of dwarf shrub harvests is transported with robust but petrol-wasting off-road cars of Soviet origin, tying the selling price to the cost of petrol. A sharp increase of the dwarf shrub price could be observed, for example, after petrol rates rose considerably during the important autumn supply campaign (Figure 4, November and December 2011). Therefore, petrol prices have to be seen as a major driver of the supply costs of harvested dwarf shrubs,[5] making this energy resource increasingly unattractive in comparison with manure and coal.

Given this picture of the energy mix, the assumption of a exclusively unsustainable exploitation of dwarf shrubs, the so-called 'Teresken Syndrome', must be questioned. Depending on the harvesting teams, on some plots dwarf shrubs may have been rooted out almost completely (i.e. unsustainably).[6] However, the suggestion of a second harvest on plots having been cleared of *teresken* in the first half of the 1990s (personal communication with AA on 28 May 2008) backs the assumption of sustainable use, to some degree. The competitiveness of the dwarf shrub use as energy source and as forage needs to be seen in a differentiated way. On summer pastures, dwarf shrubs serve as forage among others, often preferred plants for sheep, goats and yaks. Especially on poor winter pastures they play a major role as a forage plant, even more when smaller plants are covered with snow (Vanselow, Kraudzun, and Samimi 2012; Kraudzun, Vanselow, and Samimi 2014). However, the interdependency of present dwarf shrub harvesting with the competitive use by livestock, as well as the impact on the degradation of vegetation, needs further investigation.[7]

Legal authorities and security forces are advocating the strict enforcement of the ban on *teresken* extraction, which has been in force since Soviet times *de jure*. But when the issue is discussed in public meetings, local people argue successfully that they do not have any other options because of the lack of state coal supplies – as an upset Murghab inhabitant put it at a public discussion on this topic with representatives of administration and security forces in September 2008: 'We have no other choice than to collect *teresken*. If you want us to stop it, you should supply us with coal – otherwise we will freeze to death!' If asked, most people are aware of the need to save the dwarf shrub vegetation. However, households' everyday decisions concerning which energy source to supply themselves with are often made regarding available workforce, financial means and individual networks. In any case, due to poor insulation standards much thermal energy is needed to heat homes. Recent development programmes initiating energy-saving house reconstruction through micro-credits, which are meant to be reimbursed soon through saved energy costs, have mostly not achieved the expected results. This confirmed existing scepticism regarding the energy-saving potential of thermal insulation technologies in the cold climate of the eastern Pamirs.

Electric energy production in its historical context

Given the remoteness and low population density of the Pamirs, supplying the inhabitants with electricity was a challenge for the Soviet power. At first electricity was brought by diesel generators, after the collective farms were founded and centralized settlements were built. Only in the district centre Murghab was a small hydropower plant put into operation in 1964 that supplied the population with electric energy. The gap between the low capacity of the hydropower plant and the electricity demand has been filled by diesel generators. This was also the case in many of the villages in the Pamirs. This was a costly endeavour as the expenses for the transportation exceeded the costs of the fuel by one and a half. However, a connection to the grid would have been economically very costly due to the long distances and low population density.

After the breakdown of the Soviet supply system, inefficient diesel generators could not be operated given the scarcity of fuel. Additionally, the output of the Murghab hydro-electric power plant (HPP) suffered from severe damage. Domestic lighting had to be covered almost exclusively by kerosene lamps. Public infrastructure such as the landline telephone system could be operated only temporarily when the Russian Border Forces helped out with fuel for generators.[8]

Today, electric energy production in Tajikistan is still organized by the state, with the exception of the private company Pamir Energy, which obtained the licence for generation and supply of electric power in the Pamirs over a period of 15 years. Founded in 2002 by the International Finance Corporation (IFC, 30% share) and the Aga Khan Fund for Economic Development (AKFED, 70% share) with financial support from the Swiss State Secretariat for Economic Affairs (SECO), the company operates 11 hydroelectric power plants built in the Soviet era, most of them in the Western Pamirs. In the regional capital Khorog and parts of the neighbouring districts the largest local grid supplies about 17,000 households with electricity that is provided by two large hydropower plants fed from the Gunt River: Khorog with 7 MW (completed 1970), and Pamir-1 with 14 MW output capacity (completed 1994). Medium-sized systems (0.3–2.5 MW) are installed in Namadgut (Ishkashim District), Shudshand (Rushan District), and Vandž, Andarbak, Tekharv (all Vandž District) (Droux and Hoeck 2004).

Similarly, the hydropower plant for supplying Murghab is operated by Pamir Energy. Today, without additional deliveries of diesel for large support generators of Soviet origin, about 1800 households connected to the local grid are supplied very unreliably with electricity, especially during the winter. The private company Pamir Energy faces challenges similar to those of the state energy sector: electricity meters could not be installed in all households. Although the tariffs are (formally) higher than those of the state sector, they barely cover the operation costs, which prevent investments in the energy infrastructure.

The appropriation of additional energy by the consumer's manipulations of Murghab grid's electric infrastructure demonstrates the effects of missing mechanisms of accountability. When the amount of produced electric energy does not correspond to its demand in the households, electricity companies usually disconnect parts of a town or whole settlements from the grid. This is the case in the local grid around Khorog. For those who are connected at the moment, this *load shedding* results in a supply of electricity corresponding to the standard voltage. In the Murghab grid *load shedding* was not applied until recently. Consumer loads higher than production levels led regularly to very low voltages even below 20 V, resulting in a power supply insufficient for the operation of any electric device. Those who could afford it pulled a wire for an additional electric phase from the junction box, doubling the voltage in the house. Many bought transformers or low-voltage light bulbs which maintain a device's output similar to the original performance at the cost of increasing the current. The more households that installed these appliances, the more the voltage decreased. Accordingly, the grid as a whole operating at ever lower voltages and ever higher currents, suffered from rising shares of line losses.

Heating water with coil cookers at these low voltages takes very long and rarely reaches boiling point. Therefore, they remain switched on for long periods of the day, even if they do not yield the desired results. However, decisions like these were economically rational. Without functioning electricity meters, Pamir Energy calculates monthly bills according to the household's equipment with electric devices multiplied with their assumed times of operation – no matter if and how long they are used.

In order to react to the decreasing performance of the grid, Pamir Energy introduced the policy of load shedding. Steered by a schedule, only parts of the town are supplied with electricity while the majority of the households remain disconnected from the grid until it is their turn. The result of this policy, voltages near the standard of 220 V, harmed many electric appliances that have been manipulated for operating with low voltages. On the other hand, devices like coil cookers were now functioning properly again, but only during the limited periods of supply.

If the production capacity of the Murghab HPP cannot be increased, the reliability of electric energy supply in the Murghab grid can only be improved by saving energy. However, without incentives it is hard to encourage people to save energy. How this could work can be observed in the Khorog grid where new electricity meters have been installed in the majority of households. Electricity cut-offs occurred often during the winters five years ago, but now they have occurred less frequently.

On the other hand, adaptation is not easy without access to alternative technologies. Although households in the Khorog grid have to use considerable shares of their income for electricity now,[9] they struggle with changing their habits of electricity consumption. Electric coil cookers and ovens are still often used in the settlements in the valley bottoms, where combustibles are rare and expensive.

Generally, the Pamir Plateau's potential for solar and wind energy seems to be easily sufficient for people and their economic activities. Cloud coverage is low on the arid plateau, solar radiation is high in altitudes above 3600 m and strong winds often occur in the open landscape of the eastern Pamirs. However, electricity infrastructure needs thorough planning that is based on differentiated estimations about the yields from solar and wind energy. In order to quantify the potential and the spatiotemporal differences of wind and solar energy, climatic measurements are being carried out at four climatic stations within an ongoing research project about the nexus of local energy resources and development in the Pamirs.[10]

Given the still falling prices for solar and wind energy technology, renewable energy would constitute a low-cost alternative to a connection to the Western Pamirs' grid. To give an example based on the 2013 solar radiation recordings, a solar system consisting of two average solar panels installed in Murghab[11] would yield about 500 kilowatt-hours (kWh) annually. This would be more than enough to supply sufficient energy for basic lighting in four rooms, a television and a refrigerator.

The reality however looks different. Most people of the Pamirs beyond the few hydropower-fed local grids of central settlements have not been supplied with electricity since the dissolution of the Soviet system. During the first 15 years the supply of basic foodstuffs and reviving the poor regional economy were determining the goals of international development programmes. Although the ongoing energy crisis was identified as a major obstacle for development, these problems were seen as secondary. Aside from some experimental house reconstructions for demonstrating the potential to improve energy efficiency and simple-technology solar-cookers nothing was done by external development actors or by state institutions in this period of time.[12] Local peoples' awareness of the potentials of alternative energy sources and energy efficiency remained limited for many years.

The availability of alternative energy technologies changed when the Kulma border crossing, being the first between China and Tajikistan, opened in 2004. Although a big investment, all-in-one solar systems with a small solar panel charging a storage battery, and a built-in car-audio system with speakers have become very popular in the yurts of wealthy livestock owners in the pasture camps and in the village households who could afford it (Figure 5). Alongside the dramatic technological development especially of solar panels the systems have become more reliable and less expensive over the last decade. Since then, the majority of the households (cf. Figure 6) invested their own funds in such a system to have basic electricity for lighting (energy-saving LEDs) and increasingly affordable low-consumption entertainment systems.

Some years later the external development actors became aware of the new opportunities and began to provide about 180 poor households with small solar systems. State programmes followed in equipping another 300 poor households. As a result, more than 90% of the households have electricity with basic lighting and often some entertainment devices (Figures 5 and 6). This development can serve as a showcase for the potential of decentralized energy systems to use local energy resources in the eastern Pamirs.

However, as the case of the hydropower plant in Murghab (and the Rogun project) shows, the Tajik Ministry of Energy still seems to favour the hydropower option. As part of bilateral agreements for development cooperation, a German-financed development initiative tried to identify sites where hydropower could contribute to a sustainable energy supply. Checking different sites on the relatively flat plateau of the eastern Pamirs revealed no site that would justify big investments in a hydropower plant for electricity supply of the district centre. Nevertheless, Tajikistan's President Rahmon laid the foundation stone for a new hydropower station near Murghab in 2010. This seems to be the reason why the donor could not withdraw from the project. Now,

Figure 5. Small-scale solar system for basic lighting with a built-in car-audio system (left) and powering a small entertainment device (right).
Source: photograph taken by the author near Murghab in September 2008 (left) and near Aličur in June 2013 (right).

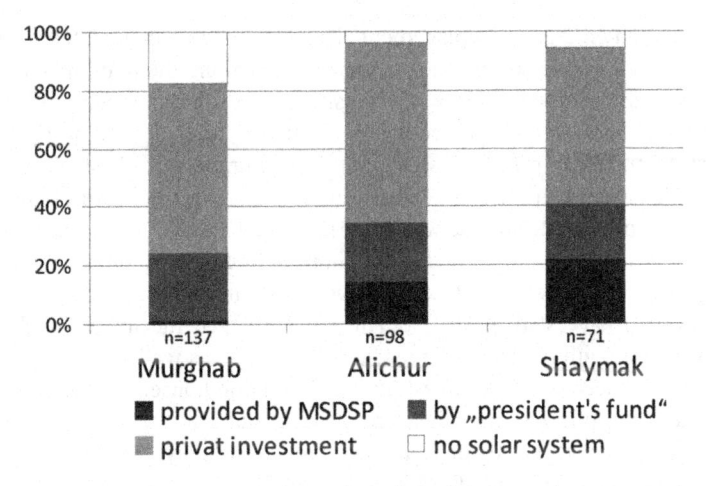

Figure 6. Equipment of households with solar energy systems funded by different sources in Murghab, Aličur and Šajmak, 2013.
Sources: compiled from data provided by the Statistics Department of Murghab district (*statotdel*), by the Murghab office of the Mountain Societies Development and Support Program (MSDSP), and from household survey data, 2013. Household surveys were conducted in March and April 2013 (see note 3).

instead of a new hydropower station, the old one built in Soviet times will be refurbished. After the costly reconstruction for approximately €5 million (but without considerable re-dimensioning of the intake canal) the output will hardly exceed that of Soviet levels, and will therefore still be insufficient for the Murghab grid. Without sound financial rationale the venture misses the sustainability standards of development projects. Therefore, it will be implemented not as an infrastructure development project, but in the humanitarian aid branch.

Small-scale solar systems seem to be an appropriate solution for electricity in mobile yurts, but the existence of isolated systems confronts every household with the challenges of proper maintenance. Solar panels, regulating electronics and especially storage batteries need to be serviced, while devices like electric cookers can quickly put small systems under stress, finally resulting in damage. In total, enormous investments were put into thousands of isolated systems, which could have been used instead for medium-scale systems supplying entire villages through the existing local grids in the settlements that were mostly modernized in 1990.

There are signs that show that the state has understood how increased affordability and performance of solar technology could contribute to an energy supply of peripheral settlements. For example, in July 2013 a commission sent out by the Ministry for Energy assessed local demand and possible options for medium-scale solar systems in some remote villages. However, although they promised local representatives to 'solve all energy problems [of the village] by autumn [2013]', nothing has happened until now. The limited capability of state organizations in the energy sector to improve energy supply in distant regions are comprehensible, given very limited public finances and the scale of ongoing projects like Rogun HPP, not to mention huge reconstruction projects aimed at the prestigious capital Dushanbe.

Conclusions

Given the harsh climatic conditions, heating homes is the major challenge for the households living on the high plateau of the eastern Pamirs. When Soviet coal supplies ceased, dwarf shrubs were used as an emergency replacement. This resulted in a degradation of this vegetation where it was easily accessible around the settlements and along the main roads.

However, recent developments show a diversification of thermal energy sources. Considerable and increasing shares of energy needs are satisfied by animal manure and imported coal. During the past decade more people possess increasing numbers of livestock, so that they have animal manure at their disposal. Moreover, coal imports from mines in Alai Valley (Kyrgyzstan) became a regular supply line during the winter period from October to May. However, given poor insulation much thermal energy is needed to heat homes. Recent development programmes trying to initiate energy-saving house reconstruction have mostly not achieved the expected results. So, dwarf shrubs are still harvested in large quantities. However, the interdependency of present dwarf shrub harvesting with the competitive use by livestock, as well as the impact on the degradation of vegetation, needs further investigation. For poor households digging dwarf shrubs remains often the only option to meet their energy demands.

For more than a decade, the region benefitted from externally funded humanitarian aid and development programmes. Although these actors identified the energy crisis as a major obstacle to development, no substantial progress was made in applying new technologies to rebuild electricity infrastructure. It was only the availability of low-cost Chinese solar products that altered individual strategies of electric power generation. Later on, non-governmental development actors and the state stepped in, equipping poor households with small-scale solar systems.

The dramatic improvements of small solar systems in output and affordability seemed to catch the responsible actors unawares. Instead of using technological advantages for a thorough planning of medium-scale systems for supplying local grids, state and external development actors somehow followed an emergency relief approach: they distributed many small systems to the households in order to mitigate the lack of electricity as fast as possible.

However, the outcome and sustainability of these re-electrification efforts remain limited. Although more than 90% of the households now have basic lighting in their houses, most devices with higher power consumption still cannot be used. Much money was spent for thousands of small-scale solar systems resulting in several disadvantages. Each has to be maintained individually by the households. In most cases, they do not have the capacity to do this; many of the systems are likely to break down soon without proper maintenance. Furthermore, the fragmented supply system lacks the advantages of electricity grids such as load balancing.

This is in contrast to community-driven electrification projects like the numerous installations of micro-hydro systems in villages of the Western Pamirs. Whereas the investment costs of micro-hydro systems require a certain degree of coordination, the affordability of small solar systems triggered the distribution of fragmented electrification schemes in the eastern Pamirs' settlements.

Although long distances between settlements and low population density require a decentralized system of power generation, the level of decentralization has to be considered carefully. Local grids that were established in Soviet times still exist in the settlements. The distribution of electricity generated by medium-scale solar power plants or wind turbines would combine the use of locally available regenerative energy resources with the properties of a grid.

Despite the Pamirs' high potential of solar and wind energy and decreasing installation costs, Soviet-style state planning of energy infrastructure still favours big hydropower stations, despite their high financial (and social) costs and a limited potential on the Pamir plateau.

All three locally available renewable energy resources like water, sun and wind need to be considered for a sustainable energy supply, given the recent technological developments. Initiatives like the costly project of rebuilding the Soviet hydropower plant in Murghab to reach an output level that will be insufficient to meet the local demands need to be compared with similar projects that draw on other energy sources. The dramatic cost decline of technology for power generation from solar and wind energy would allow the establishment of power generation systems at much lower costs.

In the post-Soviet eastern Pamirs individual investments of private households, complemented by uncoordinated development programmes have created a fragmented system of electric energy supply with an insufficient output that will hardly work sustainably. Additionally, a sustainable supply of thermal energy is far from being achieved. It remains to be seen which actors will in future provide the service of supplying electric and thermal energy – a task often associated with the state, especially in the post-Soviet context – and to what extent they will only draw from Soviet technological experiences or adopt renewable energy technologies that take advantage from the recent drop in costs.

Acknowledgements

Permission to use data from household surveys conducted by Fanny Kreczi, Georg Hohberg and local assistants, as well as from climatic recordings by Harald Zandler, is highly appreciated. Many interview partners in Tajikistan supported the author's enquiries. All support by interlocutors, bureaucrats and development practitioners living and working in the Pamirs is gratefully acknowledged. Finally, the author thanks the anonymous reviewers for their constructive and helpful comments which substantially improved earlier drafts of this paper.

Funding

The author is grateful to the Volkswagen Foundation for making possible empirical research in the Pamirs by funding the research projects 'Transformation Processes in the Eastern Pamirs of Tajikistan. Changing Land Use Practices, Possible Ecological Degradation and Sustainable Development' from 2007 to 2010; and 'Transformation Processes in the Eastern Pamirs of Tajikistan. The Presence and Future of Energy Resources in the Framework of Sustainable Development' since 2012.

Notes

1. For a contrasting description of state policies and development organizations' efforts towards electrification of certain populations or remote areas, see Chiovenda (2014) on the Hazara region in Afghanistan (in this issue).
2. Special thanks go to Kim Vanselow, who conducted field research from 2007 to 2009 jointly with the author as part of a completed interdisciplinary research project (see the Acknowledgements).
3. The troops of the Russian Federal Border Service were well supplied with coal and fuel. Local people often benefitted when soldiers sold misappropriated supplies at favourable prices (see also note 8 below).
4. Interview partners were: Adylbek Atabaev (AA), Murghab, 28 May 2008 (member of the local administration for many years, and former representative of Murghab district); and Teshebay Kolchokabev (TK), Murghab 5 April and 16 May 2009 (member of the administration for many years).
5. Transporting coal over long distances on road in large loads is comparably profitable and therefore less influenced by petrol prices.
6. Rooting out small shrubs yields no results for the harvesters: small plants have not developed considerable wooden parts, and even if they did they are too small to be bound in a bundle, which is the typical load unit. Concerning medium plants, harvesters usually ponder the physically hard work of rooting out a specific plant against the expected yield of wood.
7. This is being done within the ongoing interdisciplinary research project (see the Acknowledgements) which soon will yield results in more detail.
8. The former Soviet border troops continued to control the international borders of the Eastern Pamirs with China and Afghanistan under the command of the Russian Federal Border Service based on a agreement between Tajikistan and Russia until 2003. Their presence had a considerable impact on

the local economy. Many local people were hired as contracted border guards, as well as civilians. In this way, 20–30% of the Murghab households benefitted from the extraordinary high salary for local standards. Furthermore, many products were purchased by the affluent Russian border guards from the local market. Additionally, the troops were well supplied with coal and fuel. A considerable share of support consisted in supplies originally intended for the Russian border forces, but sold by soldiers for their own account.

9. The energy tariffs of Pamir Energy are part of the concession agreement with the government of the Republic of Tajikistan and are higher (approximately 3.0 US-ct/kWh) then those of Barqi Tojik (2.4 US-ct/kWh).

10. Climatic data are recorded by a research group of the ongoing interdisciplinary research project; first results were presented by Zandler and Samimi (2014) (see the Acknowledgements).

11. Each of them with an approximate size of 1 m², operating with an efficiency of 15% and delivering 150 W peak. The costs of the components of such a solar system would be about €600.

12. In recent years some development organizations operating in the region designed programmes to foster investments in improved insulation of houses and the efficiency of stoves (cf. Wiedemann et al. 2012).

References

Aknazarov, C. 2003. "The Present Situation of Pasture Land in Eastern Pamir." In *Natur und Landnutzung in Pamir Wie sind Erhalt der Biodiversität, Naturschutz und nachhaltige Landnutzung im Pamirgebirge in Einklang zu bringen?*, edited by S.-W. Breckle, 30–32. Bielefeld: Bielefeld University Press.

Baranov, P. A. 1940. *Pamir i ego zemledelčeskoe osvoenie.* Stalinabad: Ogiz Slechozgis.

Bliss, F. 2006. *Social and economic change in the Pamirs (Gorno-Badakhshan, Tajikistan).* London: Routledge.

BMZ. 2005. *Desertifikationsbekämpfung 2005.* Bundesministerium für wirtschaftliche Zusammenarbeit und Entwicklung.

Bogojavlenskogo, N. V. 1905. "Na ozerach Pamira." *Dnevnik Otdela Ichtologii Imperatorskogo Russkogo Obščestva Akklimatizacii Životnych i Rastenii* 2 (5–6): 5–10.

Breckle, S.-W., and W. Wucherer. 2006. "Vegetation of the Pamir (Tajikistan): Land Use and Desertification Problems." In *Land-use Change and Mountain Biodiversity,* edited by E. Speh, C. Körner, and M. Liberman, 225–237. Boca Raton: CRC Taylor & Francis.

Breu, T. 2006. *Sustainable Land Management in the Tajik Pamirs: The Role of Knowledge for Sustainable Development.* Doctoral thesis. Universitaet Bern.

Breu, T. et al. 2005. *Baseline Survey on Sustainable Land Management in the Pamir – Alai Mountains.* Berne: Centre for Development and Environment (CDE).

Chiovenda, M. K. 2014. "The Illumination of Marginality: How Ethnic Hazaras in Bamyan, Afghanistan, Perceive the Lack of Electricity as Discrimination." *Central Asian Survey.* doi:http://dx.doi.org/10.1080/02634937.2014.987967

Doempke, S. 2008. *Mission Report.* Berlin: Pamir-Alai Transboundary Conservation Area (PATCA).

Droux, R., and T. Hoeck. 2004. *Energy for Gorno Badakhshan: Hydropower and the Cultivation of Firewood. Analysis of the Energy Situation in the Tajik Pamirs and its Consequences for Land Use and Natural Resource Management.* Diploma thesis. Universität Bern.

Förster, H., N. I. Pachova, and F. G. Renaud. 2011. "Energy and Land Use in the Pamir-Alai Mountains." *Mountain Research and Development* 31 (4): 305–314.

GEF. 2005. Project Executive Summary GEF Council. Intersessional Work Program Submission. Project: Sustainable Land Management in the High Pamir and Pamir-Alai Mountains – an Integrated and Trans-boundary Initiative in Central Asia.

GosArchiv GBAO, Chorog: Gosudarstvennyj archiv Gorno-Badachšanskoj Avtonomnoj Oblasti.

Jusufbekov, C. J., and A. E. Kasač. 1972. *Teresken na Pamire.* Dušanbe: Izd. Donish.

Kassam, K.-A. 2009. "Viewing Change Through the Prism of Indigenous Human Ecology: Findings from the Afghan and Tajik Pamirs." *Human Ecology* 37 (6): 677–690.

Kraudzun, T. 2011. "From the Pamir Frontier to International Borders: Exchange Relations of the Borderland Population." In *Subverting Borders. Doing Research on Smuggling and Small-Scale Trade,* edited by B. Bruns, and J. Miggelbrink, 171–191. Wiesbaden: VS Verlag für Sozialwissenschaften.

Kraudzun, T. 2012. "Livelihoods of the 'New Livestock Breeders' in the Eastern Pamirs of Tajikistan." In *Pastoral Practices in High Asia,* edited by H. Kreutzmann, 89–107. Dordrecht: Springer Netherlands.

Kraudzun, T., K. Vanselow, and C. Samimi. 2014. "Realities and Myths of the Teresken Syndrome – An evaluation of the exploitation of dwarf shrub resources in the Eastern Pamirs of Tajikistan." *Journal of Environmental Management* 132: 49–59.

Kreutzmann, H. 2009. "Transformations of High Mountain Pastoral Strategies in the Pamirian Knot." *Nomadic Peoples* 13 (2): 102–123.

Kreutzmann, H. 2012a. "Pastoral Practices in Transition: Animal Husbandry in High Asian Contexts." In *Pastoral Practices in Pastoral Practices in High Asia. Agency of 'Development' Effected by Modernisation, Resettlement and Transformation*, edited by H. Kreutzmann, 1–29. Dordrecht: Springer Netherlands.

Kreutzmann, H. 2012b. "Pastoralism: A Way Forward or Back?" In *Pastoral Practices in Pastoral Practices in High Asia. Agency of 'Development' Effected by Modernisation, Resettlement and Transformation*, edited by H. Kreutzmann, 323–336. Dordrecht: Springer Netherlands.

Lailibekov, A. 2003. "Historisch und gegenwärtige Veränderungen, der Zustand der Verschiedenartigkeit in Badachshan und Ostpamirische Desertifikationsprobleme." In *Natur und Landnutzung in Pamir. Wie sind Erhalt der Biodiversität, Naturschutz und nachhaltige Landnutzung im Pamirgebirge in Einklang zu bringen?*, edited by S. Breckle, 37–38. Bielefeld: Bielefeld University Press.

Serebrennikov, A. G. 1894. "Pamir i Pamirskaja khanstva." *Inženernyj žurnal* 38 (11): 1395–1434, (12): 1539–1554.

Stankevič, B., Vjačeslavovič. 1910. "Po Pamiru." *Ežegodnik russkogo gornogo obščestva* 1910, 96–123.

Statkom GBAO. 2002. *Murgab 70 let. Statističeskij sbornik.* Khorog: Statističeskoe upravlenie Gorno-Badachšanskoj Avtonomnoj Oblasti.

Statotdel Murgab. 2008. *Svodnoe o polovom i poluvozrostnom sostave naselenie v džamoatah Murgabskogvo rajona na 01 janvarja 2008 goda.* Murgab: Otdel statistiki Murgabskogo rajona.

Vanselow, K., T. Kraudzun, and C. Samimi. 2012. "Grazing Practices and Pasture Tenure in the Eastern Pamirs: The Nexus of Pasture Use, Pasture Potential and Property Rights." *Mountain Research and Development* 32 (3): 324–336.

Wiedemann, C. et al. 2012. "Thermal Insulation in High Mountainous Regions." *Mountain Research and Development* 32 (3): 294–303.

Zandler, H., and C. Samimi. 2014. "Potential erneuerbarer Energieressourcen im Ostpamir." *Jahrestagung der Arbeitsgemeinschaft für Vergleichende Hochgebirgsforschung und Arbeitskreis Hochgebirge. 19.–22. Juni 2014.* Bern.

Index

Entries in **bold** denote tables; entries in *italics* denote figures.